CHHAVA

THE BRAVE SAGA OF CHHATRAPATI SAMBHAJI MAHARAJ

ADITYA NIGHHOT

BOLD

An Imprint of
Srishti Publishers & Distributors

Srishti Publishers & Distributors
A unit of AJR Publishing LLP
212A, Peacock Lane
Shahpur Jat, New Delhi – 110 049

editorial@srishtipublishers.com

First published by Bold,
an imprint of Srishti Publishers & Distributors in 2026

10 9 8 7 6 5 4 3 2 1

This is a work of non-fiction, based on the author's thorough research of Indian history. Some events have been fictionalised for dramatic effect. While due care has been taken to verify all information at press time, any inadvertent miss brought to notice shall be updated in the subsequent editions. The views expressed in the book are the author's own and are not intended to hurt the sentiments of any individual, community, sect, group, or religion. The author asserts the moral right to be identified as the author of this work.

Dedicated to Chhatrapati Sambhaji Maharaj, the lion-hearted Maratha, whose indomitable will and sacrifice remind us that true warriors never bow.

In the heart of battle, fierce and bold,
A warrior's tale in valour told.
With fire in his eyes and steel in hand,
He stood unbroken for his land.
Against the tides, he dared to fight,
A beacon in the darkest night.
With chains unbound and spirit high,
He resides within us, never to die.
This tale I pen, this homage I pay,
To the warrior king who led the way.
For in his veins, the Maratha pride,
Lives on in hearts where heroes abide.

मंत्री
सार्वजनिक बांधकाम
(सार्वजनिक उपक्रम वगळून)
महाराष्ट्र राज्य

मंत्रालय, मुंबई ४०० ०३२
www.maharashtra.gov.in

दिनांक : 22/02/2025

Heartfelt congratulations to Aditya Nighhot for his commendable effort in writing "**Chhatrapati Sambhaji Maharaj: The Chhava!**"

The life of Chhatrapati Sambhaji Maharaj is a shining example of courage, unwavering loyalty to Swarajya, and indomitable bravery. His relentless struggle and supreme sacrifice for Swarajya continue to inspire us even today.

His fearlessness, strong leadership, and deep patriotism are as relevant in today's world as they were in his time. This book offers an opportunity to embrace his values and draw motivation to achieve their own goals with determination and resilience.

Through deep research and a compelling narrative, Aditya Nighhot has brought this glorious legacy to life.

My best wishes to Aditya Nighhot for this remarkable endeavor! I hope this story reaches every home and serves as a source of inspiration and pride.

(Chh. UdayanRaje Bhonsle)

(Shivendrasingh Bhosale)

3
RLPC

ACKNOWLEDGEMENTS

Writing this novel has been a deeply rewarding journey, one that would not have been possible without the support, guidance, and encouragement of many remarkable individuals.

First and foremost, I express my deepest gratitude to the historians, scholars, and custodians of Maratha history, whose meticulous research and dedication have preserved the legacy of Chhatrapati Sambhaji Maharaj. Their invaluable insights helped shape this narrative and bring his extraordinary story to life.

An author without readers is as incomplete as a story without an ending. I would like to thank each and every reader who has constantly supported me and helped me become a national bestselling author. Without your love, this successful journey as an author would have been incomplete. I hope you continue to shower your love on this book and many other books to come.

I am grateful to God for blessing me with the art of writing and for guiding me through every chapter of this journey.

My heartfelt thanks go to my wife, Saisha, and my parents, the strongest pillars of my life, who have stood by me through thick and thin. Your unwavering support, love, and belief in me are the foundation of everything I do.

I would like to extend my sincere appreciation to Arup Bose and the entire team at Srishti Publishers & Distributors for backing my instincts and decisions with this book. Your constant support made this project a fulfilling experience.

I am also deeply thankful to Team Dreamboat—your relentless efforts in marketing have been invaluable. I am proud to lead this incredible company and grateful for the dedication of each team member.

Special thanks to Rajaram Rawool, who is always just a phone call away. Your friendship and unwavering support mean the world to me.

Meena Shetye for being the right guiding light for the fact checks and helping me with the updates.

Each of my family members who has supported me through thick and thin.

I would also like to acknowledge every bookstore, retailer, and supplier for their efforts in connecting my books with readers.

A heartfelt thanks to my editor, whose keen eye and thoughtful suggestions brought clarity and depth to the story, ensuring that every word honours the spirit of our legendary warrior. To my literary team, your unwavering support and belief in this project have been my anchor throughout this journey, and I am grateful to each of you for standing by me.

To my family and friends, thank you for your patience, encouragement, and unwavering belief in my vision. Your love and support have been my greatest source of strength. A special note of gratitude goes to my readers—your passion for history and storytelling inspires me to bring tales of the past to life. This book is for you, a tribute to bravery, resilience, and the undying spirit of a true Maratha warrior.

To each and every person whom I may have unintentionally missed mentioning here, please know that your support has been invaluable, and I am truly grateful.

Lastly, I bow in respect and admiration to the legacy of Chhatrapati Sambhaji Maharaj, whose courage and sacrifice continue to inspire generations. This work is a humble attempt to keep his story alive, reminding us that the fight for freedom is eternal.

Stay Connected and Never Miss Out!

Join my exclusive personal WhatsApp community to get updates on events, exciting gifts, exclusive merchandise, and more!

Just send a 'Hi' with your name and city to +91-9623068037 and be the first to know when I come to your city. Let's stay connected!

AUTHOR'S NOTE

Are you ready to embark on a journey through the life of one of the greatest kings India has ever known? This book is the result of years of meticulous research, countless hours of writing and rewriting, and the unwavering commitment to honour the legacy of a remarkable warrior. I humbly bow my head in respect to this extraordinary Maratha King.

Drawing on hundreds of reference books, articles, and conversations with historians, I have sought to capture the true essence of Chhatrapati Sambhaji Maharaj and his Maratha empire. This narrative is my heartfelt attempt to capture his spirit and bring his story to life with authenticity and reverence. While every effort has been made to ensure historical accuracy, any mistakes or discrepancies are purely unintentional, and I sincerely apologize for them in advance.

I hope you have a captivating and enriching experience reading this book. Your thoughts, reviews, and feedback are invaluable, so please do share them once you've turned the final page.

Thank you for joining me on this historical ride.

Maratha History

Shivaji Maharaj Family Tree

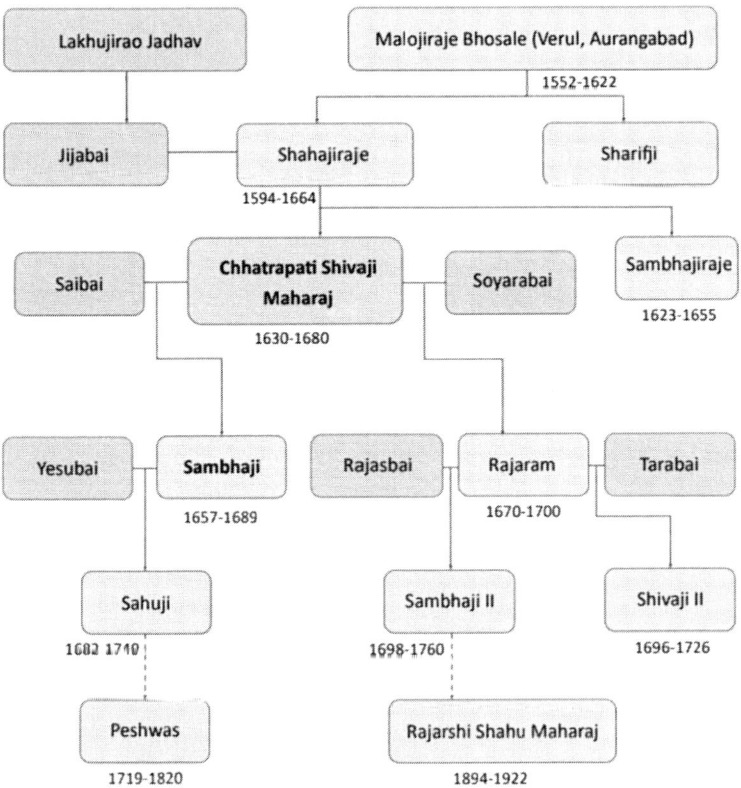

Empires before Shivrai

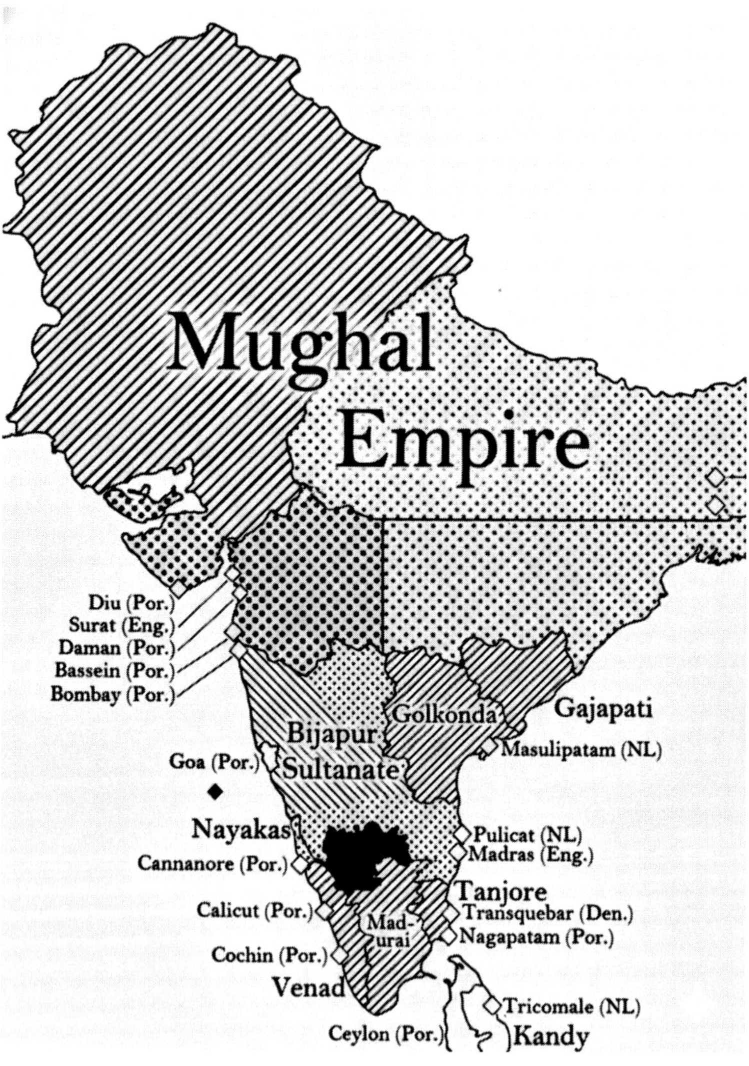

Maratha Empire during Chhatrapati Shivaji Maharaj's rule

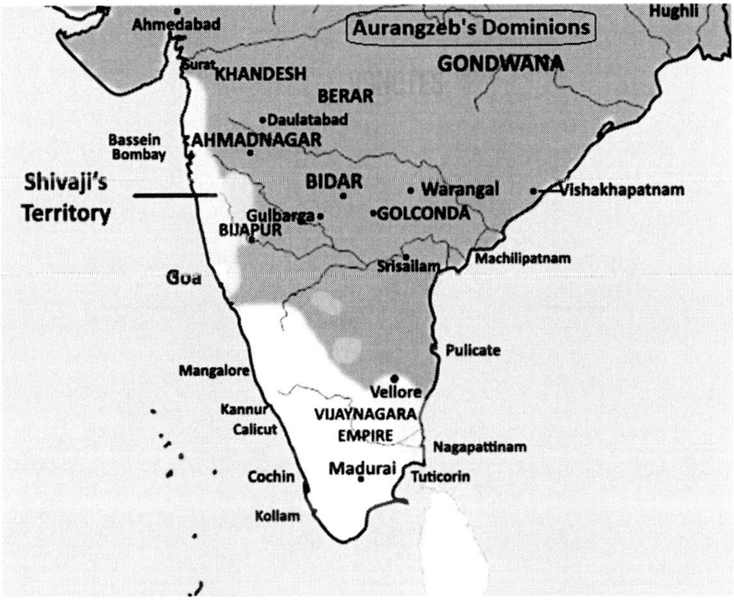

Maratha Empire during Chhatrapati Sambhaji Maharaj's rule and afterwards

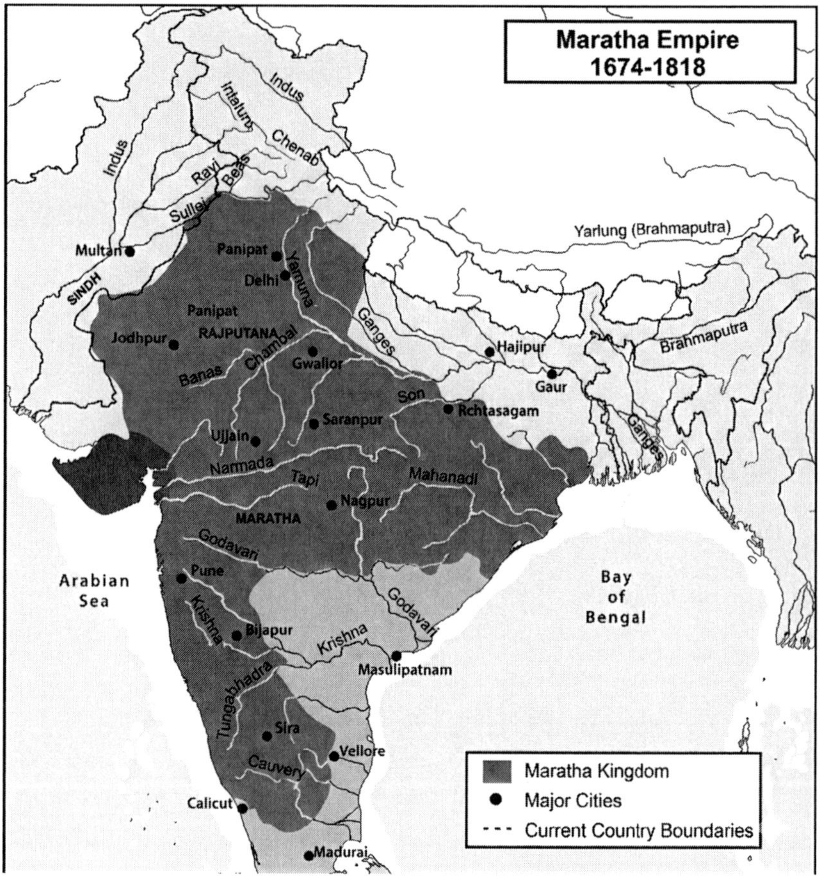

PROLOGUE

In the dark, breezy night, beneath a sky speckled with twinkling stars and a luminous moon, the only sounds that accompanied the incessant chorus of crickets and the hooting of owls were the constant neighs of horses at Sangameshwar. It was the early winter of 1689. The Chhatrapati had been longing to depart from Sangameshwar. He had discussed the plan at length with his subordinates. A plan that could shackle the Mughals forever!

Sambhaji Maharaj's childhood companion and adviser, Kavi Kalash, who shadowed the king wherever he went, was also gearing up for a battle. It had been a long time since Sambhaji had been away from Rajgad, his capital. Going back was perilous. The Mughals were everywhere, but Sambhaji planned a retaliatory attack.

Adjusting his imperial crown and sword, Sambhaji commanded the Sarnobat, "Malhoji, ready the palanquin and troops for departure."

"Ji Raje," responded Malhoji Ghorpade, leaving the chambers.

"I admire what transpires in your mind, Sambhaji," remarked Kavi Kalash.

With a smile, Sambhaji placed a reassuring hand on Kavi's shoulder. He looked directly into his eyes, "It won't be long before Aurangzeb and his Mughal Empire will crumble before the Marathas. The day will come when the foundations of Swaraj laid by my father shall be fulfilled. Once we finish Aurangzeb and his tyrannical rule in the Deccan, we shall march onto Delhi."

The brutality brought by the Mughal Empire had incited every Maratha to rise against it. The goal set by the great Shivrai, Sambhaji's father, was yet to be achieved. Having fought countless battles against the Mughals, the Adilshahi, and the Nizams, Chhatrapati Shivaji Maharaj liberated Maharashtra from the oppressive Mughal regime. Renowned for his wisdom and valour, Shivaji Maharaj established the Maratha empire with the support of his loyal followers. The heroism of martyrs like Tanaji Malusare and Bajiprabhu Deshpande had shaken Aurangzeb to his core. Shivaji Maharaj fought the Mughals, the Portuguese, and the British for nearly a decade. His mission was to secure India's freedom from the Mughals. The final blow was still pending. His son, Sambhaji, yearned for it.

"Are we ready?" asked Sambhaji, eagerly. He had been thinking of his wife, Yesubai, who was at Rajgad, where the Mughals had been laying their siege. He hoped she was safe.

"Raje!" Malhoji burst into the chamber, panic evident in his eyes. "There is an ambush. Muqarrab Khan and the Mughals are here. Our hideout has been tracked!"

Sambhaji was stunned, struggling to comprehend how their secret refuge had been discovered. The hideout was known to only a select few; the betrayal was a bitter pill to swallow. Without hesitation, he grabbed his sword, his face set with determination. "Then let's fight them! We have no other choice," Sambhaji declared.

But Malhoji, recognizing the sheer magnitude of the Mughal forces, pleaded with his king, "No, Raje. They outnumber us greatly. We cannot fight them. Your safety is of utmost importance for the future of our nation. You must leave, now!"

Sambhaji shook his head defiantly, "I cannot abandon you, Malhoji. We fight together, win together, and if fate allows, we die together."

Malhoji's eyes filled with tears. Sensing the gravity of the situation, he said, "Raje, you are our hope. Your survival means there is still a chance to defeat the Mughals. If we all perish here, who will save our people? Please, do not worry about me. Kaviji and you must escape to the south now. I will hold them off as long as I can."

Sambhaji was torn. He could feel the weight of his Sarnobat's words and the painful truth behind them. His thoughts flashed back to his father, who had once escaped from Panhala to Vishalgad under similar dire circumstances, protected by the valiant Baji Prabhu Deshpande. Today, Sambhaji found himself in the same predicament, with Malhoji standing as his shield.

Applying the sacred angara of Goddess Jagdamba, Sambhaji said, "Take care of yourself, Malhoji kaka. We need you. I want to see you on the other side."

"Of course, Maharaj! Let me teach these Mughals a lesson and savour a dawat with you by my side."

"My eyes will be searching for you, Malhoji," Sambhaji said, his eyes welling with tears.

Malhoji called for his son, "Santaji, you will accompany Raje."

With a heavy heart, Sambhaji, Kavi Kalash, Santaji Ghorpade, and 25 of his loyal men began their escape. As they made their way through the dense forest, Malhoji and his troops stood as the last line of defence, shielding their king from the advancing Mughals. Malhoji glanced at Muqarrab Khan, who was seated on his mighty elephant, exuding arrogance and rage. Raising his dandpatta, Malhoji shouted defiantly, "Let's see what you're made of!"

He knew their chances of survival were slim, but the Marathas were prepared to embrace death rather than surrender. To them, protecting Sambhaji was a cause worth dying for.

Mashals in hand, the small unit led by Sambhaji darted through the dense jungles of Sangameshwar. Refusing the palanquin, which would have slowed their escape, Sambhaji decided to sprint through the wilderness. As he ran, the sounds of his men, led by Malhoji Ghorpade, chanting 'Har Har Mahadev' echoed in his ears. Swords clashed, heads rolled, bones shattered, and blood stained the earth as Malhoji and his men fought fiercely.

"Hand over Sambhaji, and we will spare your lives!" Muqarrab Khan bellowed from atop his elephant, offering them a chance at survival.

"Muqarrab Khan," Malhoji roared in response, "We are not traitorous serpents like you, who abandon their king for personal gain. Sambhaji Maharaj is our God, and for our God, we shall happily lay down our lives a thousand times!"

The Mughal cockiness faltered as Malhoji's words echoed through the battlefield. Muqarrab Khan, angered and unyielding, shouted, "Attack!"

"Har Har Mahadev!" Malhoji and his men charged at the Mughal forces with unrestrained ferocity. The Marathas fought relentlessly, disregarding their injuries and the overwhelming odds against them. From a distance, Sambhaji watched the battle rage, the clash of steel, and the cries of the wounded filling the air. Malhoji, bloodied but unyielding, pressed forward, each strike fuelled by sheer determination. He knew his life was the price of his king's escape, and he embraced it without hesitation.

Killing hundreds of Mughals, Malhoji was suddenly struck by an arrow that pierced his chest. Ignoring the pain, Malhoji continued his onslaught. With one hand, he yanked the arrow from his chest, even as another struck him from behind. Wielding his dandpatta, Malhoji slashed through his enemies. Despite countless wounds, the warrior remained unstoppable.

Meanwhile, Sambhaji pressed on through the forest. Muqarrab Khan, perched atop his war elephant, spotted Sambhaji and his men slipping away.

"I want that man!" he roared, seated on his huge elephant.

The horsemen galloped in the direction of Sambhaji, the distance between them narrowing rapidly. Realizing the Mughals could reach him at any moment, Sambhaji decided to confront them. Turning towards the approaching troops, his sword rang out as he drew it from its scabbard. With Kavi Kalash by his side, Sambhaji and his men charged the horsemen.

'Jai Parvati Pateh!' The battle cries were relentless as Sambhaji and his men struck down the first wave of attackers. Soon, reinforcements arrived, but Sambhaji and his men fought them off with equal valour. The second wave met the same fate as the first.

Swiftly advancing, Sambhaji and his men continued to fight. At the other end, a gravely wounded Malhoji did his best to hold the Mughals at bay with his remaining men.

Sensing Sambhaji and his men escaping, Muqarrab dismounted from the elephant, mounted a horse, and spurred more soldiers into pursuit. Malhoji, reading his intent in an instant, charged forward to intercept, his battered body moving with unwavering resolve.

The Mughals swarmed around him, swords flashing, spears thrusting. Blows rained down from all sides, yet Malhoji fought like a tempest, his dandpatta slicing through flesh and steel alike.

"Malhoji, I admire your loyalty," Muqarrab said, "You are now the lone warrior left. I am giving you the last chance to drop your weapon and surrender to save your life."

"Muqarrab," Malhoji spoke with effort, breathless and bloodied, "Even if you chop me to pieces, my soul shall still fight for my Raje."

With his last defiant swing, a relentless tide overwhelmed him. As he fell, his sacrifice was written in blood; a testament to his courage, his loyalty, and his unshakeable duty to his king.

Charging at Malhoji, Muqarrab took Malhoji by surprise. His sword pierced through Malhoji multiple times as the Maratha Sarnobat retaliated in defence.

Lying on the ground, breathing his last, he could see Sambhaji at a distance. He muttered, "*Raje, akhri mujra swikarava* (King, accept my last bow)."

At a distance, Sambhaji's heart skipped a beat as if Malhoji's voice had reached him. He knew his Sarnobat had fallen, his instincts had told him.

"Jagdamb!" Sambhaji exclaimed, closing his eyes. The pain of losing his trusted Sarnobat hit him like a tidal wave, but there was no time to mourn.

With the Sarnobat out of the way, Muqarrab Khan embarked on a horse again. He and his cavalry started gaining on Sambhaji.

The air was thick with smoke and dust, the deafening roars of warriors drowning out the cries of the wounded at a distance. The battlefield was no longer just earth and stone. It was a graveyard of the fallen, their blood seeping into the soil. Sambhaji now knew escaping was no longer an option. Turning around, he raised his sword and decided to face the enemy. Amidst the chaos, he stood tall, his presence alone a beacon of unyielding defiance.

The Mughals attacked in multiple waves, hoping to overpower the Marathas through sheer numbers. Positioning themselves in crescent formation, Sambhaji and Kavi Kalash defended themselves.

"Har Har Mahadev," they growled, turning them to dust.

The Mughal horses galloped wildly, kicking up clouds of dust. At the centre of it all was Muqarrab Khan, his eyes locked onto Sambhaji with ruthless determination.

"Muqarrab!" Sambhaji growled, a lone warrior, his eyes red-hot with rage. Muqarrab hesitated. He let his cavalrymen charge as he stopped at a distance.

Sambhaji dropped his shield and grabbed another sword, tightening his grip.

"Kavi!" Sambhaji shouted as he saw the cavalrymen charge towards him.

Kavi Kalash knew precisely what he had to do. He bent down with his shield held up high as Sambhaji sprang towards the shield, stepped over it, and jumped towards the cavalrymen. Giving him a higher altitude and better position for the attack, his sword slashed through the cavalrymen as he fell to the other side of the battlefield. Getting up, he swiftly dodged a cavalryman's attack and turned towards the other, pulling him down. He jumped onto the horse and galloped towards the other side.

"Do whatever it takes, I want that man captured," Muqarrab ordered, still in disbelief over the swiftness of Sambhaji's attack.

The Mughals crashed into them like a wave against a rock, swords clashing, spears piercing, shields shattering. Sambhaji, like a storm, rode into the thick of battle, his blade a blur of death. Seeing Kavi Kalash surrounded by Mughal soldiers, Sambhaji rode towards him, his sword kissing the Mughal necks to rescue his old friend.

A Mughal soldier lunged at him. With a swift flick of his wrist, Sambhaji parried the attack and countered, his sword slicing through flesh and bone. Another came at him; this time, he raised his shield, bashing the attacker with such force that he collapsed to the ground, lifeless. But the real test was yet to come.

"Ya Allah!" Muqarrab said, astounded by Sambhahji's fighting skills. He had no choice but to dominate the attack himself now.

Across the battlefield, Muqarrab Khan and Sambhaji finally locked eyes. There was no hesitation, no turning back. Muqarrab Khan spurred his horse forward, his blade gleaming under the sun. He swung it downward, aiming straight for Sambhaji's head.

Sambhaji reacted instantly, raising his sword to meet the strike. The clash of metal rang out like thunder, reverberating across the battlefield. Blow after blow, Muqarrab Khan attacked with brute force, but Sambhaji was swift, dodging, blocking, and countering with an attack.

Sambhaji single-handedly stopped a dozen Mughal soldiers. Sambhaji covered Santaji as the latter disappeared into the dense forests. The next minute, he was sprinting toward Rajgad.

Sambhaji knew what lay ahead, but he was not ready to surrender. As the Mughal soldiers perished, Muqarrab aimed at Sambhaji. Sambhaji continued fighting with an arrow pierced through his back. Fuelled by rage, he and his 25 men fought with unparalleled ferocity, proving themselves nearly invincible.

Muqarrab's attacks had been in vain. The Chhatrapati of the Marathas was beyond control.

Agitated, Muqarrab Khan ordered his men, "Throw the barbed wires."

The Mughals followed their master's orders. The wires pierced through Sambhaji. The Mughals tightened their grip as Sambhaji bled. He held the wires and pulled them out of his body, roaring, fiercer than ever.

"Muqarrab!" he roared, rechallenging him, "Your barbed wires cannot stop me and my Swaraj."

"Chain him down!" shouted Muqarrab.

Muqarrab threw a chain at Sambhaji, binding him. Another Mughal soldier threw another chain from behind. Sambhaji held the chains and pulled, making the Mughals topple. With the other hand, he used his sword to turn them into lifeless bodies.

By then, Muqarrab Khan had managed to chain Kavi Kalash and the others. But Sambhaji was still unstoppable. Although deeply injured, another attempt at chaining Sambhaji was in vain. In the third attempt, the Mughals managed to chain Sambhaji but couldn't bring him to his knees. The soldiers pulled at the chains, but Sambhaji, with his immense strength, dragged them down instead.

What Muqarrab had been witnessing was no less than one of the greatest battles. Sambhaji's roaring reverberated in his ears. He thought how aptly Diler Khan had named Sambhaji as Sher ka bacha – a Chhava!

"Muqarrab!" shouted Sambhaji, "Neither your men nor your techniques can stop me. Bring all that you have, and I will still chop your men to pieces."

Muqarrab was left astonished. He ordered his mahouts to pull the chains with the help of elephants. As the elephants advanced, Sambhaji could feel the pull. He roared. Holding the chains, Sambhaji overturned the elephants upside down, crushing the Mughal soldiers under them.

Bleeding and exhausted, Sambhaji shouted, "What more have you got, Muqarrab?"

Exasperated, Muqarrab dismounted his horse and approached Sambhaji. "Surrender, Sambhaji. You're captured. You have no other option," Muqarrab shouted.

"You may capture me, but you cannot stop the thousands of Marathas who will now rise with twice the strength to shake your empire," Sambhaji's voice echoed in the jungles.

Muqarrab was taken aback, but he laughed derisively, "We will find a way to capture and crush anyone who dares to oppose us. Just like we did this time."

Fixing his gaze on Sambhaji, Muqarrab said, "Your own man helped us, Sambhaji!"

Sambhaji stared intently at Muqarrab, desperate to uncover the traitor's identity. Moments later, a figure emerged from the ranks of the Mughal troops. As Sambhaji saw the figure, a profound sense of defeat washed over him. The hundreds of chains, the multitude of soldiers, and even the mighty elephants that had earlier failed to subdue the warrior now seemed to tighten their hold on him.

A tumult of emotions surged within Sambhaji—betrayal, anger, and deep sorrow. He closed his eyes in agony, memories flooding his mind: his wife, Yesubai, son Shahu, and daughter Bhavani at Rajgad, and the visage of his late father, Chhatrapati Shivaji Maharaj. It wasn't the myriad of wounds inflicted upon his body that caused him the greatest pain; it was the treachery of a trusted ally.

"Why, what made you do this?" he yearned to ask the traitor standing before him. His spirit was shattered, and as the Mughals threw the final rope, it not only ensnared Sambhaji but also threatened the very hopes of Swaraj.

1.

THE MOONLIGHT softly illuminated Sambhaji's face, and the cool breeze gently caressed his wheatish skin as his hair fluttered in the wind. Bound from head to toe in chains and suspended upside down on an elephant, the one thought that incessantly tormented Sambhaji was why he had been betrayed. Not only had his trust been shattered, but also the hope of Swaraj was withering away, almost slipping through his fingers.

'Who shall be my successor? Who will lead the Maratha troops? How will we fortify the foundations of Swaraj? Is this the bitter end of the Marathas?' Sambhaji's mind was inundated with countless thoughts, each more troubling than the last.

With Sambhaji's capture, the entire Maratha empire now faced a grave threat. The Mughals had grown stronger, and their newfound confidence was evident in their demeanour as the Mughal army marched triumphantly through the dense jungles, chaining Sambhaji, Kavi Kalash, and 25 Maratha advisers, showcasing their victories.

As blood trickled down Sambhaji's bruised face, he glanced at his dear friend Kavi, who was bound and hanging on an elephant just ahead of him. Kavi, too, appeared utterly dejected and defeated. When their eyes met, Sambhaji felt a lump forming in his throat, a choking sensation of helplessness. He was unable to save his friend from the ruthless clutches of the merciless Mughals.

Chained, Chhatrapati Sambhaji and his loyal advisers were dragged through villages and royal provinces, their captors flaunting their triumph. The Mughals paraded them like trophies, a ruthless display of power meant to humiliate the fallen and terrify the defiant. This was no mere victory march—it was a warning, a chilling proclamation to all who dared resist the might of the Mughal Empire. The Marathas had been broken, or so the Mughals wished to prove.

The villagers lined the streets, their faces etched with despair. Some watched in silent grief, others with helpless resignation. Fear flickered in a few eyes, while some burned with quiet rage, swallowing the cries they dared not utter. Sambhaji met their gazes, reading their pain, their anguish, their shame. He saw no surrender in them—only the heavy weight of the moment, the silent storm brewing beneath their sorrow.

Amidst the night filled with despair, he could still hear the faint but fervent chants of 'Har Har Mahadev' and 'Shambhu Maharaj ki jai' from the crowd. These were young men who still believed in Sambhaji's valour and hailed him with reverence. The chanting rekindled the nearly extinguished spirit within Sambhaji. He had a burning desire for revenge against those who had captured him. Shaking off his despondency, he became even more determined to confront Aurangzeb. There was still enough mettle in the Marathas, and a second Shivaji Maharaj or Sambhaji Maharaj was bound to rise from these very villages.

Sambhaji looked at Kavi Kalash once more, this time with renewed resolve and determination. As their eyes met, memories of their first encounter surged through his mind—the moment they had defied death together and emerged victorious years ago. The past felt both distant and close, weaving itself into the present as Sambhaji found strength in the bond they had forged through countless trials.

Years Ago…

"Shh, Shambhu Bala, don't make noise," whispered his Abasaheb, and the Watandar of the Maratha province—Shivaji Maharaj.

It had been months since Shivrai and Sambhaji were placed under house arrest in Agra Fort by Aurangzeb. It had all begun with the Purandar Treaty, signed with Mirza Raje Jai Singh, the Mughal mansabdar.

Shivrai's war against the Mughals had not begun here. It had been a long and bloody struggle—one that had defined his life.

For years, he had been a thorn in the empire's side, striking where the Mughals least expected. His guerrilla warfare had unsettled them; his swift cavalry raids had shaken their foundations. He had captured forts like Torna, Kondhana, and even Purandar itself, proving that the Marathas were not mere rebels but a rising power.

Aurangzeb had taken notice. In 1660, the emperor had sent his uncle, Shaista Khan, to crush Shivrai's growing influence. With overwhelming numbers, the Mughals had stormed Pune and seized control. But Shivrai had not cowered. Instead, in 1663, he had led a daring night raid into Shaista Khan's heavily guarded palace, slashing through his ranks and wounding the commander himself. The Mughals had been humiliated, Shaista Khan fleeing Pune in disgrace with chopped fingers that haunted him day and night.

Then, in 1664, Shivrai had struck again. To replenish his treasury and weaken the empire's hold, he had raided Surat, one of the richest Mughal ports. He had taken what he needed, crippling the empire's finances, further enraging Aurangzeb.

But Aurangzeb had now learned from his failures. This time, he had sent not just a general, but a tactician—Mirza Raje Jai Singh, a Rajput warrior who understood both war and diplomacy. Jai Singh had come prepared, launching a full-scale invasion of Shivrai's lands. One by one, his forts had fallen, his men forced into desperate battles. And now, Purandar stood on the edge of defeat.

The walls of Purandar had trembled under the relentless Mughal assault. Smoke curled into the sky, the acrid scent of gunpowder and blood hanging heavy in the air. The deafening roar of cannons shattered stone, and the cries of the wounded echoed across the battlefield. Murar Baji Deshpande, Shivrai's fiercest commander, had led his men with unwavering bravery, but the Mughal forces had been too strong. Surrounded and outnumbered, he had fought to his last breath before falling to Diler Khan's blade.

Inside the war chamber, Shivrai stood silent, his gaze fixed on the map of his dwindling territory. The Maratha strongholds that had once been symbols of defiance were now under siege. His men, exhausted and outmatched, had given their all, but the enemy's numbers were overwhelming. Twenty-three forts stood vulnerable. If Purandar fell, the path to Swarajya would crumble with it.

Shivrai clenched his fists. The warrior in him wanted to fight to the last man, to defy the Mughals no matter the cost. But the king in him, the leader responsible for thousands of lives, knew the bitter truth. If he chose war, it would not be a glorious battle. It would be a massacre. His men would perish, his forts would be lost, and his dream of Swarajya would die with them.

Jai Singh had made his offer. The treaty demanded the surrender of 23 forts, a severe blow to Maratha pride. But in return, Shivrai would still retain some lands. It was also an opportunity—one that Shivrai, ever the strategist, could turn to his advantage.

He turned to his men. Their faces were grim, their silence heavy. He could see the anguish in their eyes, the same battle raging within them.

Finally, he spoke, "We sign the treaty."

The words felt like iron on his tongue, but his voice did not waver. He was not surrendering; he was surviving. The Mughals could take his forts, but they would never break his spirit. He would wait, he would learn, and when the time came, he would rise again.

As the ink dried on the Purandar Treaty, Shivrai knew one thing for sure: this was not the end. It was only the beginning.

The treaty also demanded that Shivrai be a Mughal mansabdar. Still, he had convinced Jay Singh to appoint Sambhaji as a Mughal mansabdar instead, thus forging a bond of friendship between the Mughals and the Marathas. This was a calculated political decision taken by Shivrai not only to end the animosity but also to strengthen his own provinces. The Treaty of Purandar was meant to bring peace. After the treaty was signed, Mirza Raje Jai Singh persuaded Shivrai to meet Aurangzeb at Agra Fort. Shivrai had been sceptical for days. Shivrai doubted Jai Singh's motive. Although Rajputs were known to keep their words, Jai Singh's closeness with Aurangzeb and Aurangzeb easily opening his arms and welcoming Shivrai to the Agra Fort was something Shivrai hadn't really expected. It was only after Jai Singh assured Shivrai of his safety that he relented. The sole purpose of meeting Aurangzeb was to extend a hand of friendship and protect the Maratha empire from the treacherous Mughals and their inevitable mayhem. Travelling through numerous mountains, jungles, and rivers, Shivrai, along with a nine-year-old Shambhu, reached Agra from the Maratha provinces, a journey that was as perilous as it was necessary.

As Shivrai reached Agra, he had expected Aurangzeb to welcome the Maratha ruler, but it had been otherwise.

"Maharaj, the Alamgir could not be here to welcome you, so I…" uttered Ramnath Gopa, a Mughal officer who had arrived on Aurangzeb's orders and was stopped mid-sentence by Shivrai.

"I appreciate your presence, Ramnath ji," Shivrai said, calm despite the fact that it was very inappropriate of Aurangzeb not to send gifts or garlands to welcome Shivrai and his men, as per the customs that should have been followed.

After resting in the camps, on the 12th of May 1666, Ramnath Gopa arrived to escort Shivrai to the court. This was the first time Shivrai and Shambhu would face Aurangzeb, eye to eye. Shivrai had asked his subordinates to ensure they would carry sweets, pearls, gold, and ornaments to gift to Aurangzeb when they met his gaze.

"Abasaheb, why the gifts? Isn't Aurangzeb your enemy?" young Shambhu questioned on their way to the court.

"Shambhu Bala," Shivrai responded, placing his hand over his shoulder, "Because Aurangzeb could steep low by not welcoming us with gifts, it doesn't necessarily mean that we should steep low too. We are not him. Moreover, Aurangzeb believes that only he controls all the wealth. Let him see our wealth as well."

"How does it help us, Abasaheb?" Shambhu questioned.

"Aurangzeb does not acknowledge us as mighty rulers, so be it! Let him sink in his own delusion, while he witnesses our rituals as he lacks his hospitality himself."

Moments later, Shivrai and determined Shambhu marched towards the court. Head held high, a spark in his eyes, and chest up, Shivrai entered, followed by young Shambhu, who witnessed his father's aura and learned from him. As Shivrai entered the court, all eyes turned towards him.

Gifts were sent to Aurangzeb, and, as a ritual, he placed his hands over the sweets and signalled that they be distributed to the public.

"Shivaji!" Aurangzeb acknowledged, "The Marathe!"

"Aurang!" Shivrai remarked back.

"Maharaj," Ramnath Gopa whispered, "Acknowledge him as the Badshah or Alamgir, and bow before him"

Shivrai glanced at Ramnath Gopa with fiery eyes.

"Maharaj, it is the court ritual. He is the Alamgir," whispered Ramnath.

"For you, not for me," replied Shivrai, his voice loud enough that Aurangzeb could hear what Shivrai said.

"I have come here as the Maratha ruler, and I don't intend to bow before him. I consider myself equal and not inferior," Shivrai was loud.

Aurangzeb, who wanted to humiliate Shivrai, himself felt humiliated by Shivrai's act. He signalled Ramnath to take Shivrai away and make him stand in the third row of the panchhajari mansabdars.

"That's your place," Aurangzeb muttered.

The Diwan-E-Khas, designated for such gatherings, had its own set of norms and protocols. Subhedars, watandars, mansabdars, and kings from every province of India were required to bow before the Alamgir, i.e., the emperor who ruled over the entire nation. Every attendee was made to stand by their rank. Despite being aware of Shivrai's countless achievements and capabilities – how Shivrai had looted Surat, won the Mughal forts, challenged the Adilshahi, killed Afzhal Khan, attacked his uncle Shaista Khan and chopped his fingers... Aurangzeb insulted him by relegating him to the third row among the panchhajari mansabdars. It meant that he considered Shivrai inferior to a mansabdar.

He was asked to bow before Aurangzeb once again and yet again refused, defying the unspoken rule of submission. Aurangzeb desperately wanted him to submit.

"Aurang!" he shouted in the court, "I have been quiet till now, accepted your poor hospitality, but forcing me to bow before you is unacceptable."

"Maharaj, lower your voice," Ramnath ran towards Shivrai, "It is not allowed in the court."

Aurangzeb chose to remain quiet. He decided to ignore Shivrai, another way of humiliating him.

Without waiting for the meeting to conclude, furious Shivrai turned and walked out of the court. Such an audacious act was unprecedented in the history of Mughal court proceedings, a bold affront to Aurangzeb, one that cut deep into his pride.

"Why did you do that, Abasaheb?" a young Shambhu had asked his father, his innocent eyes wide with confusion.

"Why should anyone bow before another? He claims to be the Alamgir but does not consider me a king or an independent ruler, calling me a self-proclaimed king. Isn't he a self-proclaimed Alamgir? He cannot be my ruler. I do not recognize him as one," Shivrai had replied with a calm yet firm conviction that resonated with his deep sense of pride.

Sambhaji could scarcely grasp the intricate political strategy unfolding in his father's mind, but what he witnessed that day left an indelible mark. It was an act of unparalleled valour and courage; one that no one in history had dared to display before Aurangzeb.

This act enraged Aurangzeb, and in a fit of pique, he ordered his soldiers to capture Shivrai and the young Shambhu. Even as he was overpowered, Shivrai held his head high.

"That's all you have, Aurangzeb, betrayal," Shivrai had said, maintaining his composure. The tender eyes of Shambhu looked up to his father, who stood confident and determined in Mughal territory. Any boy of his age might have been terrified, but seeing his Abasaheb, he imbibed the courage to confront the Mughals, a lesson that would stay with him for the rest of his life. Young Shambhu had now witnessed what Aurangzeb was. He had heard stories of how Aurangzeb had betrayed his own brother and killed him to win the throne, how Aurangzeb had imprisoned his own father, how he had invaded the Adilshahi and killed thousands of Hindus and allowed his men to rape women in the name of jihad openly.

The Purandar Treaty meant peace, and according to its terms, Aurangzeb had no authority to arrest Shivrai or Shambhu. But the Mughals were notorious for their treachery. With deception, Aurangzeb had house-arrested Shivrai and Shambhu. He aimed to keep the Maratha warrior and the future of the Maratha empire captive, allowing his troops to descend upon the Deccan. The news of Shivrai and Shambhu being confined within the walls of Agra Fort spread like wildfire, reaching Rajgad, the capital of the Maratha province.

Seated against the mashals, adjusting her saree, Jijau, Shivrai's mother, felt her heart ache for her son and grandson, but she concealed her worries.

"Jagdamba," she whispered, remembering the Goddess she worshipped, "Give strength to my son and my grandson. You cannot be cruel to them."

"Aausaheb," Putalabai, who had accompanied the subordinate with the news, looked up to Jijau worriedly, "What do we do?"

Putalabai was in tears, her heart pounding for her husband's safety.

Hiding her worry, Jijau turned towards her, her voice strong, she commanded, "Putala, this isn't the time to worry, but prepare ourselves for the worst. The Mughals may invade us, and we should be prepared. Bring out the swords and sharpen them, let the Mughals know that the Marathas are not done yet."

In Shivrai's absence, she knew she had to manage the Maratha empire. If she faltered, it would demoralize hundreds of Maratha soldiers who looked up to her as their deity. In an assembly filled with Tanaji, Netaji Palkar, Bahirji Naik, and a few of her close subhedars, she resolved to uplift the morale. The plan to rescue Shivrai and Shambhu was being crafted from scratch, a task as monumental as the threat they faced.

On the other hand, Shivrai harboured deep resentment toward Mirza Raze Jai Singh and Ram Singh, son of Mirza Raje Jai Singh, for betraying him. Ram Singh, on behalf of Mirza Raje Saysingh, boldly confronted Aurangzeb, urging him to release Shivrai and Sambhaji, reminding the emperor of the promise his father, Mirza Raje Jai Singh, had made to Shivrai regarding their safety. For a Rajput, a word of honour was far more precious than life itself. Yet, his heartfelt plea met with cold indifference.

"It's better that you and your father not meddle in court proceedings. *Taklia* (Dismissed)!" shouted Aurangzeb, a ruler who placed little value on honour or promises, dismissing Ram Singh's words without a second thought.

Ram Singh then met Shivrai and once again promised that no harm would come to him or his son in Agra Fort.

"Does your promise mean anything now, Ram Singh? The Purandar Treaty has no meaning in Aurangzeb's fort. You will remain a puppet with Aurangzeb pulling your strings," Shivrai retorted, his voice tinged with both sadness and anger.

Ram Singh and his father were men of words, but the situation left them powerless against Aurangzeb's will. Despite his father being the architect of the Purandar Treaty, Ram Singh knew he couldn't confront Aurangzeb's decision. Unable to endure Shivrai's righteous indignation, he quietly turned and left the room.

Meanwhile, Shivrai plotted an escape. Though separated by the boundaries of Rajgad and Agra, Shivrai and Jijau remained united in their resolve, bonded by an unbreakable trust. Though the fort had few Marathas, Shivrai knew that they could overpower the Mughals with their wits and sheer willpower.

Shivrai was always one step ahead. He had foreseen the possibility of treachery when signing the Purandar Treaty and had positioned his most trusted men in strategic places. One such man was Hiroji Farzand, who had been with Shivrai since childhood and was among his most trusted people. Hiroji had infiltrated the ranks of Aurangzeb's men while Bahirji Naik, the chief of the Maratha spies, coordinated the plan from Rajgad. Jijau's words to Bahirji were clear: "I want my son and grandson back in Rajgad, unharmed."

For weeks, Shivrai meticulously laid out the plan for their escape. It had to be flawless; one mistake could cost them their lives. Shivrai was well aware of the tight security around the fort and the meticulous checks on everything that entered or left the fort's premises. The room Shivrai and his men were house arrested in was surrounded by a heavily guarded force. Faulad Khan, a merciless Mughal mansabdar, led the security. Soldiers then guarded this security from watch towers. Neither Shivrai nor his men were allowed to leave the premises at any time.

"Ram Singh," called out Shivrai, one day, "I know that Aurangzeb will not let us roam out of the premises, but I request that Shambhu be allowed to do so, as he is a child and arresting a child doesn't suit Aurangzeb and his sultanate. Moreover, as per the treaty, he is a Mughal mansabdar, and Aurangzeb is arresting his own mansabdar. Please pass my message to Aurangzeb."

"Ji Raje," Ram Singh assured him of support.

Confronting Aurangzeb, yet again, Ram Singh requested that Shambhu be allowed to roam around in the city. Aurangzeb pondered upon it for a while before he caved in. Shambhu was allowed to roam around the city freely for a certain period of time each day, while a few eyes kept a check on him. Shivrai had just succeeded in his first plan.

Although captured, Shivrai could now witness what was going on outside through Shambhu's eyes. Shambhu would roam around the city, memorize the lanes, houses, and watchtowers of Agra until they led to the riverbanks, then return to the residence, remove a coal piece he had once stolen from the market, and draw a map on the floor. Every day, Shambhu would come up with new information, leading the escape plan for Shivrai and his men.

"Abasaheb, a few kos south of the grocery market, lies the slave market, out of which leads a small walkway to the river. If we reach the river somehow, we can swim across to the other side of the river and join Bahirji on our way back to Rajgad," Shambhu led the discussions. Shivrai was awestruck by the young Shambhu, who was now leading his men.

As the days passed, Shivrai began to feign illness, his condition seemingly worsening with each passing moment. His health visibly declined, and the Mughal soldiers grew convinced that he was succumbing to his fate, believing he had abandoned all hope. To them, he appeared a broken man; too frail to stand, let alone contemplate an escape.

What they didn't realize was that this frailty was an illusion, meticulously crafted as part of Shivrai's grand plan. Weeks slipped by, and the guards gradually grew complacent. With his apparent decline, their vigilance waned, confident that their prisoner posed no threat. But Shivrai was merely biding his time, patiently waiting for the perfect moment to strike.

During this time, Shivrai began sending gifts of sweets and fruit to well-wishers, priests, and ordinary people, a gesture initially met with suspicion but later accepted as a sign of submission. However, the shrewd Aurangzeb had his doubts. He had his soldiers inspect the baskets meticulously before allowing them to be sent out.

When the day of escape finally arrived, Shivrai turned to Shambhu and said, "Shambhu bala, this will be a long journey. We must remain silent. Our survival is our victory. If we succeed today, our escape will be remembered for generations."

The plan was perilous. Shivrai and Shambhu would hide inside the six-foot baskets that contained fruits and sweets, and escape from the residence, as their men would lift the baskets in the broad daylight, least suspicious to the complacent security. With Shambhu's help, Shivrai and his men now knew the routes to escape to the river banks. They would then swim across the river, join Bahijri, who would be waiting for them, and, through various routes, all of them, individually, would head back to Rajgad, except...

The exception was told to no one, not even Shambhu, till the right moment came.

With his father's encouraging words and unshakeable faith, Shambhu lay perfectly still inside a fruit basket, not daring to make a sound. Shivrai and Shambhu, hidden among the fruit baskets, kept a low profile. Over time, the guards had become accustomed to the routine of allowing the fruit baskets to leave the Agra Fort without thorough checks. Hiroji Farzand, a loyal follower of Shivrai who bore a striking resemblance to him, lay on Shivrai's bed, feigning illness. Once the baskets had safely passed beyond the fort's walls, Shivrai and Shambhu emerged from their hiding places. Swimming across the river, awaiting them at a safe distance stood Bahirji Naik, the Maratha spy, with two horses, ready to aid in their escape. Jijau from Rajgad had managed to send him at the right time.

As Bahirji approached Shivrai, tears welled up in his eyes, overwhelmed by the sight of the Maratha leader he revered as a deity. Shambhu, too, was deeply moved by the way people venerated his father. And then came the exception to the plan, which even Shambhu was unaware of.

"Shambu bala, I must leave now. Bahirji will take you with him," Shivrai said, embracing his young son tightly.

"Where Abasaheb?" Shambhu questioned, his eyes looking for an answer, unsure of what lay in front of him.

"Shambhu bala, you shall now head to Mathura," responded Shivrai, looking into Shambhu's eyes and caressing him with affection before he could bid him away.

Back in the Agra Fort, when Aurangzeb learned of Shivrai's escape, his face flushed with anger. Furious, he ordered severe punishment for the guards and dispatched his troops in every direction to hunt down Shivrai and Shambhu.

Striding angrily to the room where Shivrai had been held, Aurangzeb searched for him personally. To his astonishment and disbelief, the doppelganger had also managed to escape before Aurangzeb could capture and torture him. The exact details of how Hiroji Farzand escaped remain a mystery to this day.

"I want every town, every village, every house searched from top to bottom. I want Shiva and that nine-year-old boy captured immediately!" Aurangzeb shouted, his voice thick with frustration. The reality that two Marathas had outwitted his heavily guarded Fort and an army of over a hundred thousand soldiers was a bitter pill for him to swallow.

"What a disgrace!" he roared, pounding his fist against his throne in rage.

"Whoever captures Shiva and Sambha, dead or alive, will be rewarded with the rank of *Das-hajari Mansabdari* and a thousand Ashrafis," he declared, hoping to incentivize his soldiers to intensify their efforts.

The scouts spread out to search for the fugitives, apprehending anyone accompanied by a nine-year-old boy and bringing them before Aurangzeb. Yet, each time the emperor eagerly examined their faces, he was only met with disappointment and the sting of defeat.

Unbeknownst to him, Shivrai had outmanoeuvred Aurangzeb and his carefully laid plans again. Instead of travelling together, which would have increased the risk of capture, Shivrai headed back to Rajgad, while Shambhu took a different route under Bahirji's guidance. Shambhu was en route to Mathura, far from Agra, where he was destined to meet Kavi Kalash. In the sacred land of Lord Krishna, Kavi Kalash assisted Shambhu in adopting the guise of a Brijwasi local. Shambhu's mother tongue, Marathi, was replaced by Brij, the language of Mathura. Kavi not only taught him the Brij language but also immersed him in the local culture. To truly become a Brijwasi, Shambhu had to adopt not just the dress and speech but the very spirit of the people.

Over the six months of his disguise, Shambhu's transformation into Sambhaji began as he learned more about the teachings of Lord Krishna, the *Mahabharata*, and Hindu mythology, often accompanying Kalash to temples.

Kavi Kalash, significantly older than Sambhaji, became a guiding force in his spiritual journey. An accomplished scholar, Kalash would narrate stories from ancient scriptures, weaving lessons into each tale. Well-versed in astronomy, geology, and multiple languages, including Sanskrit and Brij, Kalash served as an invaluable mentor, imparting a vast reservoir of knowledge that broadened Sambhaji's understanding of the world.

The bond between them deepened over time, evolving into a close friendship. Together, they would rise before dawn and visit the sacred banks of the Yamuna River. There, they performed ritual baths, offered prayers at Krishna temples, and spent hours in meditation. This disciplined routine became transformative for Sambhaji, drawing him ever closer to spirituality and instilling in him a sense of purpose.

With time, Sambhaji grew to be a knowledgeable young man. However, despite the peace and wisdom he was gaining in Mathura, certain questions continued to haunt him: *Why had his Abasaheb not taken him along? Why had he been left behind? What was his purpose here? When would he be able to return to Rajgad?*

These questions weighed heavily on Sambhaji's mind, leaving him to ponder his future and the role he was destined to play in the grand narrative of the Maratha empire.

2.

IT HAD been almost a year since Shivrai had returned to Rajgad. On the day of his arrival, Rajgad was filled with both joy and sorrow.

The air in Rajgad was heavy with conflicting emotions. Jijau, Soyrabai, and Putalabai rejoiced at his safe return, but their joy was soon drowned in a wave of heartbreak. Shivrai's words hung like a dark cloud: Shambhu had fallen ill and perished during their perilous escape from Agra.

Putalabai, Shivrai's devoted wife, was inconsolable. She locked herself in her room for days, unable to face the world. Childless herself, she had poured all her love into Shambhu, treating him as her own after Saibai, Sambhaji's mother, had passed away. Saibai's death had been a devastating blow, its cause long uncertain, until it was believed to be typhoid.

"How could you not bring Shambhu Bala's body with you?" Jijau had been furious when she saw the pandits offering the last rites for Shambhu. She wept inconsolably.

Deep down, Shivrai felt guilty for faking his son's death. He wished he could reveal the truth to his family, but he was compelled to keep it a secret because, to ensure that Shambhu lives, he had to die for his family.

The news of Shivrai's return to Rajgad and young Shambhu's death spread like wildfire, reaching Aurangzeb's ears. Shivrai's plan worked perfectly, just as he had envisioned.

The search for Sambhaji ceased, ensuring his safety just a few kilometres away from Agra, in Mathura.

Sambhaji's stay in Mathura, a town under Aurangzeb's rule, ironically ensured his safety; Aurangzeb searched everywhere but his own territory. Meanwhile, Shivrai's triumphant return to Rajgad and Aurangzeb's inability to capture him stung the emperor with humiliation. Determined to restore his authority and reassert control, Aurangzeb knew he had to act swiftly and decisively. He needed to set an example.

As Mirza Raje Jai Singh was seated in residence in the Deccan, he felt himself growing breathless as soon as he chewed the food that was served. His body turned heavy, sweaty as his throat dried up and his tongue began to fall back on his windpipe, causing him to choke. The man who served the food watched him from a distance. Mirza Raje Jay Singh wanted to call for help, but couldn't. He looked at the man in front of him, who smiled devilishly, before escaping. Panting heavily, Mirza Raje Jai Singh breathed his last.

The man escaped the cantonment and reached Daulat Khan, a Mughal mansabdar.

He bowed before Daulat Khan and said, "Huzur, the work is done." Daulat Khan's eyes shone in greed for a reward as he wrote to Aurangzeb about the execution of Mirza Raje Jai Singh. The poisoning with arsenic had worked. This did not go well with the Rajputs, but they dared not rebel against the Mughals, as the death of Mirza Raje Jai Singh had been a mystery. A few accused Aurangzeb of being the culprit, while a few others called it a natural death, as Aurangzeb never admitted to the execution of Mirza Raje Jai Singh.

Next, Faulad Khan, the in-charge of security, went missing until Aurangzeb himself paid a visit to him in the dungeons.

"Rehem Hujur," Faulad Khan pleaded for his life.

"You have sinned. The kafirs have escaped because of your negligence." Aurangzeb was furious as he grabbed Faulad Khan's hair. Aurangzeb removed a dagger and pierced it inside Faulad Khan, making him cry in pain.

"Because of you, I am being mocked everywhere," Aurangzeb twisted the dagger inside to make Faulad Khan bleed. Every soldier who was in-charge of security, imprisoned in the same dungeons, watched their master being tortured.

"You should die a thousand deaths now," Aurangzeb was wild and equally cruel.

He clapped his hands, calling his subordinate and ordering, "I want this rat to be chopped to pieces."

As Aurangzeb walked out through the dungeons, he could hear swords slashing, bones being broken, and Faulad Khan and his men being slaughtered to pieces as the dungeons were filled with rivers of blood.

Back in Rajgad, Shivrai was more furious than ever. His and Sambhaji's house arrest had violated the terms of the Purandar Treaty. For Shivrai, the Purandar Treaty no longer held any validity. Filled with rage, he discussed the situation with his subhedars. It was time to reclaim the 23 forts from the Mughals. These forts, once ruled by the Marathas, now flew green flags, a sight Shivrai could no longer tolerate. He longed to see the saffron flags of his sultanate once more wavering high. This reclamation had to begin with a victory. Subhedar Tanaji Malusare and his men resolved to take down Kondhana at the sad demise of the subhedar himself. Shivrai, who was close to Tanaji, renamed the Fort Kondhana after him, now known as Sinhagad.

"The fort was won, but the lion (Sinha in Marathi) had gone," Shivrai had expressed his feelings, embracing the wounded subhedar before he could breathe his last.

The quest for *Swaraj*, which he had sworn to pursue with his companions, including Baji Pasalkar, Dadaji Naras Prabhu, Sarjerao Jedhe, Yesaji Kank, Tanaji Malusare, Suryaji Kakade, Chinmaji, and Balaji Narhekar at a tender age in the Raireshwar Temple, was still unfinished. The Mughal tyranny had to end, and this was just the beginning.

'IS ABASAHEB even worried about me? Is he looking for me? Why haven't I heard from him? When will I get to go back to Rajgad?' Sambhaji was plagued with countless thoughts. Slowly but surely, an unsettling sense of disconnection began to creep over him in Mathura. Life around him seemed to have returned to normal, and the relentless Mughal hunt appeared to have ceased. Sambhaji convinced himself that the Mughals had grown weary and abandoned their search.

What he didn't realize was that it wasn't exhaustion that had halted the pursuit—it was his Abasaheb's masterful deception.

One evening, as Sambhaji sat on a charpoy, eating his dinner, his mind drifted once again.

"What is it, Yuvraj?" Kavi Kalash asked, "You look lost today."

Sambhaji was called by many names—Shambhu and Yuvraj were just a couple of them.

"Nothing, Kalash. Just battling my thoughts," Sambhaji exhaled, still pondering why his father had left him behind. Although he was a prince, he was also just a child who needed his father. He was too naïve to understand the state's politics and war strategies.

"It's just the test of your life, Yuvraj," Kalash said, "Whenever you feel surrounded by darkness, just remember that it's not the end. The night might be long, making things unclear for a while, but with time, the dawn always comes. The struggles you face now are not without purpose—they're preparing you for what lies ahead. The weight you bear is not only your own; it is the future of the Maratha empire that rests with you. Be patient, stay strong, and in time, things will make sense."

Kalash's words reverberated in Sambhaji's mind for a while. He wanted answers, and he wanted them now.

Sambhaji was known to be impulsive. Although Kavi Kalash's words meant a lot of wisdom to him, he couldn't stop being himself. Throughout his childhood, he was known to have taken impulsive decisions that many times didn't go well with his Abasaheb, but he still hadn't succeeded in getting over the habit, despite wanting to. He was restless for an answer. The impulsive child within him made him take a quick decision.

"I should get going, Kalash," he said, "At sunrise, I should leave for Rajgad."

As soon as the sun rose and Sambhaji was about to leave Mathura, a rare coincidence occurred. One of the persons from the Ahstapradhan Mandals of the Marathas appeared before Sambhaji. Sambhaji instantly recognized the person. One of the Maratha Pradhans, standing before Sambhaji, had something important to say.

"What's the message?" Sambhaji asked, getting straight to the point.

"Yuvraj, we need to leave for Rajgad. Shivrai wants to see you."

The words echoed in Sambhaji's ears for a moment. A broad smile spread across his face. Just when his impulsive and restless mind had been battling against himself, Shivrai's man had arrived out of nowhere as if his father had read his son's mind. For the first time in a year, his heart finally found peace. The long-awaited message he desperately wanted had finally arrived.

Sambhaji hugged Kavi Kalash in excitement.

"Finally, you are going back home, Sambhaji," said Kavi Kalash, seeing Sambhaji's face light up.

"Yes, Kaviji," replied Sambhaji and embracing his friend, "I would want you to come along with me."

"I wish I could," replied Kavi Kalash, took a pause and added, "My people need me here. Aurangzeb might put an end to the Hindus here, and I need to stay here to offer some resistance to him, but I assure you that we are destined to meet again."

"How can you be so sure that we are destined to meet again?" questioned Sambhaji.

"I have had dreams of us leading battles against the ruthless Aurangzeb, and I trust my spiritual power. Mark my words, we shall meet again."

As Sambhaji mounted his horse to leave, he looked at Kavi Kalash one last time. The bond of friendship he had built with Kavi Kalash over the past year was special. He was definitely going to miss Kavi Kalash and the streets of Mathura. Sambhaji could feel the pain of leaving his friend behind. He wondered how capricious minds are. Moments earlier, he was tormented by the thought that his father hadn't reached out to him and was determined to leave for Rajgad on his own. Now, the same man was reluctant to leave his friend behind. Controlling his emotions, Sambhaji bid Kavi Kalash goodbye as he waved back at him. As Sambhaji rode his horse through the open terrains, he wondered if he would ever see Kavi Kalash again.

'We will meet again, how, when, why, I don't know, but we shall definitely meet again,' he reassured himself, just like Kavi Kalash had assured him.

3.

THE MUGHAL empire was crumbling like a house of cards. Every strategy Aurangzeb tried to implement failed. In the Deccan, under Shivrai's leadership, the Marathas inflicted significant losses on the Mughals. If the humiliation of two prisoners escaping from the capital fort wasn't enough, the Marathas had now openly disregarded the Purandar Treaty, winning the battles for Swaraj and reclaiming their forts one by one.

It all began with the martyrs Tanaji and Suryaji, who captured Kondhana Fort. The fort, later renamed Sinhagad in honour of Tanaji, meaning 'the fort of the lion' in Marathi, marked the beginning of a string of victories. In the aftermath, the Rajput commander Udai Bhan, who had defended Kondhana, was killed. In retaliation, Diler Khan from Daulatagad and Daud Khan from Khandesh were swiftly sent to the Deccan to halt Shivrai's advances. Yet, neither could stop the Marathas. Despite lacking advanced arms, ammunition, and military might, they were driven by an unyielding valour that enabled them to overcome any formidable force that stood in their way.

The cry of 'Har Har Mahadev' reverberated across the Deccan. For the Marathas, this was no longer just a battle; it was a fight to reclaim their pride. One by one, they recaptured the forts that had been lost. The turning point came when Razi-ud-Din Khan, the killedar of Fort Purandar, was imprisoned by Nilo Pant. With his capture, Aurangzeb's last hope of holding onto the forts was extinguished. The fall of Mahuli Fort soon followed, marking the end of the bitter legacy of the Purandar Treaty.

Aurangzeb was shattered. He never anticipated Shivrai's return with such strength. As whispers of his own failing rule spread, Aurangzeb feared even his men might challenge him. History showed that Mughal emperors often fought for succession, but Aurangzeb's actions were unprecedented. He had seized the throne by imprisoning his father, Shah Jahan. To solidify his power, he executed his brother Dara Shikoh and kept his father in brutal captivity, starving him with only half a glass of water a day. The message was clear: follow me, or face a cruel end.

Aurangzeb needed to act quickly to restore his men's faith. Determined, he ordered the mansabdars and watandars across the empire to collect the jizya tax from Hindus. Those who paid the jizya on time were spared, but those who failed to do so faced brutal public torture and execution. The tax functioned as a form of protection money, where compliance ensured safety. The only way to avoid it was to convert to Islam and join the Mughal army.

"If you are Muslim, you will be spared. Islam is the only religion to supremacy." Aurangzeb started brainwashing people. Men were beheaded on the streets, their wealth snatched, the cows they worshipped slaughtered for meat, women raped for days and nights together, and children captured to be made slaves or eunuchs who could later serve the Mughal dynasties for ages. Aurangzeb gave his mansabdars and soldiers unrestricted power to capture Hindu women, subject them to forced marriages, abuse, and ultimately kill them.

"Convert them forcibly or marry their women, have kids, and make them join Islam," he declared. He intended to break the spirit of the Marathas and make them feel the full extent of his cruelty. Temples were destroyed, and idols shattered under the banner of Islam.

The Mughal cantonment quickly became a place where the soldiers felt a deep sense of loyalty to their Badshah. They were richly rewarded with money and allowed to indulge their every desire, which only hardened their cruelty. In the name of religion, Aurangzeb had manipulated them into believing their actions would lead them to spiritual reward, further fuelling their brutality.

Then, he began to hatch more sinister plans. With the Deccan slipping from his grasp, he was keen to expand his territories. Marwar in Rajasthan, a long-time ally of the Mughals, became his next target. Despite Jaswant Singh Rathod, the ruler of Marwar, being of advanced age, his son and heir, Prithvi, dared to defy Aurangzeb. However, the emperor was about to do something far more devious than anything he had done before.

4.

"PRINCE SAMBHAJI will meet you shortly. Please take a seat," Hiroji Farzand said to Henry, who had arrived at Rajgad Fort with his entourage.

It had been nearly a month since Sambhaji had returned to Rajgad. The fort, a symbol of strength and resistance, was buzzing with renewed energy. Yuvraj's return stunned and delighted everyone, from Jijau Mata to Putalabai and Soyrabai. His arrival brought relief and excitement throughout the Maratha kingdom. Shivrai apologized to all, including the people, for the deception of Sambhaji's death.

Jijau Mata, Shivrai's mother, had been particularly furious with him for some time. Her displeasure was palpable. "How could you fabricate such a story and keep us all in the dark? You even performed the last rites for Shambhu. It is highly inauspicious!"

Shivrai knelt at her feet and offered a sincere apology, "Ausaheb, this decision was made for his safety. It was part of a strategic manoeuvre, a war tactic strategized to protect him. Had I not done it, Aurangzeb would have captured him. Also, bringing Shambhu along with me meant the Mughals could easily look out for a man with a nine-year-old kid. They never in their dreams could think of Shambhu hiding in Mathura, a place owned by Aurangzeb himself."

"I'm just a grandmother who wants her grandchild to be safe," she said, her voice trembling. "I don't understand these war tactics, especially at the cost of Shambhu Bala. He's young and innocent. This was wrong, and nothing you say can justify it. Even the Gods would disapprove," she sulked.

"I understand your feelings, Ausaheb, but I have my own compulsions. I am his father, but more than just being a father, I am also the ruler of the Maratha Province," Shivrai responded, his voice steady but filled with empathy. He looked at Jijau Mata and questioned, "Didn't you, yourself, teach me that freedom comes at a cost, and as the protectors of our men, we have to place ourselves last when it comes to personal gains and do whatever it takes for our men's freedom. I ensured that we both remained apart for a while, each capable of building our own kingdoms. If anything had happened to me, Shambhu would have led the army, and if anything had happened to him, my returning to Rajgad and teaming up with my men would have been equally important for me to fight back. I placed the kingdom ahead of personal gains."

"Shambu is everything to me. With his mother gone at a young age and you battling the Mughals, I was his sole caretaker. He holds my heart. We should not involve Shambhu in the complexities of politics and wars."

It took Shivrai several days to console Jijau Mata. Her raw emotions for her grandchild rendered her inconsolable. Shivrai had never seen his mother so openly emotional and distressed. Perhaps her advancing age made her more susceptible to such feelings. He could sense that his Ausaheb was no longer the unyielding and resilient mother he had always known. Jijau Mata had always been a figure of strength and vigilance. From enduring separation from her husband, who was serving the Adilshahi, to raising a young Shivrai amidst adversity, she had faced numerous trials. Her guidance had been instrumental in shaping Shivrai's path. She had urged Shivrai to rise against the tyrant Mughals, irrespective of the personal costs. Years later, when Afzal Khan had arrived at Pratapgad, a fort near Wai province, with a vast army and had treacherously planned to assassinate Shivrai, Jijau Mata had been a beacon of courage. She had encouraged Shivrai to confront Afzal Khan with bravery and decisively end his tyranny.

Afzal Khan, all the way to Pratapgad, had looted houses, burnt a few, killed thousands of men, crushed Godly idols, destroyed temples, raped women, and been a demon just like Aurangzeb. Lying a siege around Pratapgad, he had challenged Shivrai to a battle with his tremendous force. Shivrai had devised a brilliant plan to lure Afzal Khan into a private meeting rather than going all out against him on an open battlefield. He feigned fear of facing Afzal Khan on the battlefield. A tent was erected at the base of Pratapgad for their meeting, adorned with the finest jewels and pearls to distract Afzal Khan. Shivrai had asked his men to leave no stone unturned in welcoming Afzal Khan with the most precious stones, so that he would lose focus in the meeting. Shivrai's men had also conveyed to Afzal Khan that Shivrai was terrified and feared meeting him. For days, the discussions went on, and Shivrai demanded that Afzal Khan meet him in private without his army. Eager to confront Shivrai and kill him by deceit, Afzal Khan accepted the conditions. A day was set when the two rulers, each with a bodyguard, would meet in private, armless. Afzal Khan, accompanied by his loyal bodyguard Sayyad Banda, waited inside the tent as Shivrai, accompanied by Jiva Mahal, made his entry. Upon seeing Shivrai, Afzal Khan, with a wicked smile and treacherous intent, invited Shivrai to embrace him.

"Aao, gale lag jao, Shiva!" the wicked Afzal Khan opened his arm with a devilish laugh. As they embraced each other, Afzal Khan seized Shivrai's arms and attempted to crush his neck. With a hidden dagger, Afzal Khan struck at Shivrai's back, but the attack failed. Shivrai had worn a metal jacket inside to protect against the sharp weapon. In a swift act of rebellion, Shivrai drew his concealed Wagh Nakh (Tiger's Claws) and pierced it inside Afzal Khan's stomach. Shocked and in agony, Afzal Khan tried to resist as Shivrai tore out his intestines, crushing them in his hands. Afzal Khan's bodyguard charged at armless Shivrai with his sword, but his attack went in vain as Jiva Mahal, Shivrai's bodyguard, came blazing at Sayyad Banda with his dandpatta and killed him. The news of Afzal Khan's demise spread rapidly, and in the following 15 days, the Marathas captured over 23 forts, attacking every Mughal fort in their path. The success was attributed to Jijau Mata's inspiration from the story of Lord Vishnu's Narsimha avatar, who tore the demon apart with his hands.

Back in Rajgad, Jijau Mata's health was rapidly declining, and her only wish was to see Shivrai crowned as the Chhatrapati of the Maratha Kingdom. Honouring her wishes and the people's desires, Shivrai made the bold decision to crown himself king. This move was not just a fulfilment of his mother's desire but also a direct challenge to Aurangzeb, who refused to acknowledge anyone else as emperor. The humiliation in Agra still burned in Shivrai's memory By becoming the first King of the Marathas, Shivrai sought to protect his people and gain recognition from other Hindu kingdoms, with the hope of forming crucial alliances.

On the 6th of June 1674, following the auspicious time set by the pandits, the grand coronation ceremony commenced in the presence of Gaga Bhatt, a renowned Brahmin from Varanasi, to affirm his Kshatriya lineage. Shivrai was bathed in holy waters from the seven sacred rivers: Ganga, Yamuna, Godavari, Krishna, Narmada, Sindhu, and Kaveri. Rajgad was now renamed to Raigad. The event was a spectacle, attracting attention from far and wide, including distant lands. It became a major topic of discussion from north to south and even abroad, as Shivrai sent emissaries to Persia, Arabia, and Europe to declare the establishment of an independent Maratha kingdom. Aurangzeb, in particular, was deeply displeased. The ceremony reminded him of his blunder and negligence that allowed Shivrai to escape.

The news of Shivrai's coronation and Sambhaji's return reached Britain, prompting the East India Company in West Bengal to instruct Henry Oxenden, an English officer and his men to visit Raigad and meet the soon-to-be king, and convey their regards in person. Henry's visit was intended to build friendly relations with the Marathas, recognizing their growing significance. The Portuguese, too, planned a visit to Raigad, aiming to solidify their influence. At that time, the Portuguese held a dominant position in the Arabian sea and the Indian Ocean through trade routes from Europe to Malay (now Malaysia), while the English had a more limited presence in Bombay and were establishing the East India Company in West Bengal.

At the coronation, hundreds of pandits, Hindu and Muslim mansabdars, watandars, Kings from various provinces, and thousands of spectators gathered to witness one of the grandest coronation ceremonies of a Hindu king. Henry and his men bowed to the newly crowned king and presented him with gifts and a letter from the East India Company. After the ceremony, Henry observed the ritual of distributing gold and diamonds equivalent to the weight of the king to the common people. This display of grandeur left him in awe. He attempted to engage with Chhatrapati Shivaji

Maharaj to discuss political matters, but found it challenging due to Shivrai's focus on the ceremony. Henry was also struck by Shivrai's commanding presence, which left him feeling nervous for the first time in his life. On a few occasions, Henry broached topics such as allowing Britain to trade freely with the Marathas and other provinces, using Bombay as a shipyard, and treating Maratha territories as allies. The Portuguese had similar objectives, seeking to expand their trade across India, with Goa as their capital. However, Shivrai had limited opportunities to engage in these discussions. He expressed his openness to free trade as a means of fostering good relations but entrusted the detailed negotiations to young Sambhaji and his ministers – Peshwa, the chief minister of eight ministers in Shivrai's council; Dabir, the minister of external affairs; and Surnees, the minister of land revenue.

"With your permission, we would like to trade across India and use your territories as routes for trading," Henry said to the council.

"What is that you wish to trade?" asked the Dabir.

"We wish to trade spices, cotton, and foodgrains across the globe and strengthen our presence in Bombay. Your farmers can cultivate while we shall purchase the raw materials and foodgrains from them, pay you the taxes and export the goods to Europe and other provinces," replied Henry.

"Aren't you in an alliance with the Mughals for the same?" questioned the Surnees.

"We wish to have a separate alliance with the Marathas through the company we establish in Bombay. This company shall have no connection with the East India Company and shall function independently."

Sambhaji, who had been a spectator for all the while, had remained silent throughout the discussions and let the guests speak through the translators before he granted permission for trading. Henry and the Portuguese had come to believe, throughout the discussions, that Sambhaji was naïve and spoke little. They felt they had the loudest voice in the discussions before their delusions were put to an end. Sambhaji, through his silence, had studied his opponents' motives and made them believe he understood nothing of what they said before he could conclude the discussion. The British and Portuguese then experienced the Maratha hospitality. After a sumptuous lunch, as they prepared to take their leave, Sambhaji addressed Henry for the first time in English, "You may trade freely in our lands, but we strictly prohibit human trafficking, slavery, drugs, alcohol, and prostitution. You can be our allies forever, but you must adhere to our ethics and morality. Should you or your government violate these terms, we will not hesitate to do whatever is required to protect our own."

Turning to the Portuguese leader, Sambhaji repeated the same thing in Portuguese, "*Você pode negociar livremente em nossas terras, mas rejeitamos o tráfico humano, a escravidão, as drogas, o álcool e a prostituição. Vocês podem ser nossos aliados por toda a vida, mas é melhor não lidar com nada que não se adapte à nossa ética ou moralidade. Caso você ou seu governo ultrapassem o limite que estabelecemos, não demoraria muito para levantarmos os braços.*"

Both leaders, struck by the prince's eloquence and commanding presence, could only nod in agreement. Their astonishment and respect were palpable, as they recognized not only the strength and decisiveness of the Maratha king but also how the prince embodied these same qualities. The Marathas had firmly established their stance on trade and alliances, ensuring that any engagement would have to align with their values and ethics.

As Henry and the Portuguese leader departed Raigad, the impression left by the ceremony and the interaction with Sambhaji was profound. The strategic implications of their visit would resonate across their respective empires. For the Marathas, it was a moment of triumph and assertion, starting a new chapter in their history. The coronation had not only solidified Shivrai's position as Chhatrapati but had also set a precedent for future diplomatic engagements.

Henry could not help but marvel at how a region once considered marginal had risen to become a significant player in global politics. The Marathas, under Shivrai's leadership, were not a mere regional force anymore; they were now a formidable empire with the potential to shake the throne of Agra.

5.

UPON RETURNING to his residence from Raigad, Henry Oxenden immediately penned a letter to the East India Company, dated 6th of June, 1674:

The Deccan has the most able rulers of all time, which makes the Marathas invincible. While the Sahyadris in the west and the plateau in the east are aptly controlled by Maratha valour, it is Shivrai's able administration that sets them apart from other rulers in India. There is prosperity, happiness, and everything that one could ask for. People worship the king like God, and why shouldn't they? They feel protected under their king's rule. It's not just the people of the Maratha kingdom who feel protected, but also the families of the enemies. Shivrai and his men do not attack families. They do not attack women and children. They respect every religion. Although their fight is against the Mughals, they are open to Muslim subhedars working under them. Shivrai is blessed by the Gods. He has the aura within him that can make any successful ruler feel ordinary in front of him. And if that's not enough, his son Sambhaji is no less. He has the best knowledge of literature, geography, history, economics, and politics. Their administration is way ahead of its time. At this point, if we have to strengthen our roots in Bombay and build relations with Portugal, it is the Marathas whose support we need. Unlike us in Kolkata with the East India Company, which is behind Aurangzeb's support, we need the Marathas by our side, here in Bombay. The trade is not going to be easy here, and we need to keep them pleased.

Henry read the letter again, recalling his brief meeting with Shivrai and his son, Sambhaji. How larger-than life an impact the Marathas had had on him!

ELEVEN DAYS after the coronation, the joyous atmosphere that had enveloped Raigad was suddenly overshadowed by profound grief as Jijau, the matriarch of the Maratha empire, breathed her last. The exuberance and pride that had surged through the people upon witnessing their first Maratha Chhatrapati now seemed distant, replaced by a deep sense of loss. The kingdom, which had only recently celebrated with such fervour, now found itself plunged into mourning. Most were unsure how to navigate the sudden shift from triumph to tragedy. Shambhu, now tasked with the weighty responsibilities of his princely duties, also had to console his younger brother Rajaram, who was just a child, 13 years his junior, and equally devastated by the loss.

Yesubai, Sambhaji's young wife, who had only recently joined the royal family, was deeply affected as well. She had grown to admire and adore Jijau and often wished she had more time to spend with the woman who had been the backbone of the Maratha kingdom. Jijau had not just been a mother-in-law but a guiding force, a source of wisdom and strength. As the last rites were performed, an overwhelming sense of sorrow and unease hung heavily in the air. Soyarabai, Sambhaji's stepmother, was inconsolable. Through her tears, she lamented, "These rites only remind me of the inauspicious ones we performed for Shambhu. If we hadn't done that, perhaps the Gods would have been more merciful."

Sambhaji, who had faint memories of his own mother, Saibai, had always held his stepmothers, Soyarabai and Putalabai, in high regard, cherishing them as if they were his own. Walking close to Soyrabai, he gently took her hands, trying to soothe her. "It was only a ruse to deceive the Mughals," he said softly, trying to comfort her. "Please, Ma Sahib, don't let superstitions cloud your mind."

With Jijau gone and his father, Shivrai, preparing for a southern expedition following a visit to Konkan, Sambhaji felt the full weight of responsibility settle on his shoulders as the Yuvraj of the Maratha Kingdom. For the first time, he truly understood the magnitude of his role. He had to comfort young Rajaram, who remained inconsolable, support two grieving mothers, and guide his wife, Yesu, as she navigated the complexities of royal life.

With Shivrai away in Konkan to strengthen the Maratha navy, Sambhaji's duties doubled. Not only was he tasked with ensuring his family's well-being, but he also had to oversee Raigad's administration and safeguard its people. Throughout his life, the walls of Raigad had stood firm under Jijau's impeccable governance, allowing Shivrai to focus on expanding the kingdom without concern for his family or his people. Now, that mantle of responsibility had passed to Sambhaji, who had to quickly adapt and manage the kingdom with the same skill, precision, and vigilance his grandmother had exemplified.

A year passed, with Shivrai engrossed in building his navy along the Konkan coast and Sambhaji taking on the responsibilities at Raigad. Throughout that year, Sambhaji grappled with an intense internal struggle. In a household filled with ministers who revered Chhatrapati Shivaji but harboured reservations about the young prince's involvement, Sambhaji found it difficult to determine whom he could trust. His vigilance sharpened as he grew increasingly aware that all was not well within the kingdom.

One night, while poring over a stack of documents detailing the kingdom's revenue, Sambhaji could feel a sense of unease creeping over him. The numbers didn't add up. Something was clearly wrong.

"What's troubling you, Yuvraj?" Yesu asked gently as she entered the room, lighting the lamps that illuminated their quarters.

Sambhaji, deeply disturbed, looked up from the papers. "This isn't right, Yesu," he said, his voice tinged with frustration. "There's a mole in our system. While we dream of establishing Swaraj, some of our own men have treacherous intentions. I can't believe this."

Yesu had never seen her husband so troubled. She approached him and sat beside him, her concern growing. "What do you mean? What have you found in these documents?" she asked, trying to understand the situation.

"The taxes we collect from our people don't match the taxes accumulated in the treasury. The amount mentioned in the papers does not coincide with the actual revenue," Sambhaji explained, his eyes scanning the numbers once more. "Someone is siphoning off the money that should be returning to the government; money meant for the people, for developing the kingdom, for strengthening our army, and for maintaining our forts. Where is it all going? For instance, the documents mentioning the total taxes coming from Dabhol district do not match the Raigad income report. Either the people involved in the entire chain are corrupt, or the revenue master in Raigad is. This is treachery of the highest order. It's nothing short of betrayal. The funds that should be benefiting the entire nation are being hoarded by a few individuals for their gain."

"Who do you suspect?" Yesu asked softly, her heart aching at the sight of her husband's distress.

"I don't know, Yesu," Sambhaji replied, his voice heavy with determination. "But I must find out and put an end to this treachery before it's too late."

WHILE A great deal was transpiring in the Deccan, Aurangzeb had become a mere spectator. The Mughal emperor was steeped in regret, consumed by thoughts of his past misjudgments and negligence, which had allowed both Shivrai and Sambhaji to slip through his fingers.

Years earlier, a similar scenario had unfolded when Shivrai, aiming to foster peaceful relations with the Mughals while quietly strengthening his own forces, sent Sambhaji to Aurangabad as a Mughal mansabdar. During his time there, Sambhaji worked closely with Muazzam, Aurangzeb's son. However, Aurangzeb, ever mistrustful, ordered Muazzam to betray and capture Sambhaji, imprisoning him in the dungeons of Gwalior. But Muazzam, moved by a growing camaraderie with Sambhaji, defied his father's orders and secretly aided his escape. Aurangzeb remained unaware of his son's defiance. Had he discovered Muazzam's role, the emperor would have shown no mercy, imprisoning his own son and condemning him to languish in the dungeons of Aurangabad for life.

Years later, Aurangzeb found himself in a similar predicament during the encounter at Agra. Once again, he had failed to seize his opportunity.

Seated on his majestic throne in the Diwan-E-Khas, Aurangzeb was deep in thought, plotting his revenge and his strategies to curb the expanding influence of the Maratha empire. As his thoughts churned, Asad Khan interrupted his brooding, announcing,

"Prithvi Singh Rathod from Marwar is here, Your Majesty."

Aurangzeb paused, a sly smile spreading across his face as he inhaled the sweet scent of a rose that he had been toying with. "Bring him in," he commanded, cunningly smiling at Asad Khan.

As Prithvi Singh Rathod approached the throne, Aurangzeb's eyes narrowed, and for a fleeting moment, he saw not the young prince before him, but the towering figure of Jaswant Singh Rathod, his father. The same regal stride, the same fire in his eyes, the same unwavering confidence. It was as if the spirit of the mighty king had been reborn in his son, and for a brief instant, Aurangzeb was transported back in time, facing the very warrior who had once stood defiant against the Mughal Empire. A chill ran down his spine as he realized that the Rathod bloodline, unbroken and fierce, still had the power to challenge him.

Jaswant had been a complex figure, loyal yet unpredictable. He allied with Aurangzeb's brother, Dara Shikoh, during the bitter battle for succession. Despite this, Aurangzeb, after emerging victorious, chose to forgive Jaswant, appointing him as a general in his army. Yet, Jaswant's loyalty wavered. During a later battle against Suja Bhai of Bengal, Jaswant betrayed Aurangzeb by killing the emperor's men and fleeing the battlefield once Aurangzeb had secured victory.

"Prithvi, the renowned prince of Marwar," Aurangzeb greeted him, his voice dripping with insincerity, and eyes glinting with calculated intent.

After a brief exchange of pleasantries, Aurangzeb wasted no time in revealing his true purpose. "Your father, Jaswant Singh Rathod, served us loyally throughout his life," Aurangzeb began, his words laced with a thin veneer of respect. Yet, a fleeting pause betrayed the irony of his words; the man he now praised had, in his eyes, walked the fine line between loyalty and defiance. Suppressing the bitterness that threatened to surface, Aurangzeb pressed on, a faint smile curling his lips, "Marwar has always been like family to us. The affection and allegiance I receive from your people are treasures I hold dear, beyond measure."

Prithvi, sensing the underlying tension, decided to cut through the facade. "What is it that you want from us, Your Majesty?" he asked, his tone firm, eyes unwavering.

"Nothing that is not rightfully mine already. Marwar," Aurangzeb declared bluntly, his voice sharp and unyielding.

Prithvi's breath hitched, his mind reeling at the emperor's audacious demand. Marwar had bled for the Mughal Empire, its warriors sacrificing their lives and its people bearing the weight of imperial decrees. What more could Aurangzeb possibly demand? What new cruelty lay hidden behind his measured words?

"I want Marwar to be directly under my control. You must dissolve it as an independent entity and integrate it fully into my empire," Aurangzeb stated, his tone leaving no room for negotiation.

A murmur of shock rippled through the court as the enormity of Aurangzeb's demand sank in. Realizing the gravity of the situation, Prithvi clenched his fists in anger, yet he remained silent, his mind racing as he contemplated the consequences of refusing the emperor's command. Finally, unable to contain his defiance any longer, Prithvi spoke, his voice steady, even as fury burned in his chest, "This will not happen."

"Oh, really? I am the Alamgir, the ruler of all kings. It is I who decides what happens," he said with a cruel laugh, the sound echoing ominously in the hall.

But Prithvi remained undeterred, his resolve unshaken by the emperor's threats. "If you say so," Aurangzeb continued, his voice now tinged with menace, "My ten thousand cavalrymen, eight thousand horses, and five thousand archers are already on their way to Marwar." The emperor rose from his throne, his eyes narrowing as he glared at Prithvi, intent on breaking the young prince's spirit. "Your father and his men will be crushed beneath the hooves of my army, while your women will be forced to commit Jauhar as my forces march upon your lands."

Prithvi's jaw tightened as he fought to keep his temper in check. But he refused to show weakness in the face of such provocation. "We are not a mere handful," Prithvi retorted, a fierce pride in his voice. "The day your men set foot on our soil, every man, woman, and child in Marwar will take up arms to defend our land. We will not bow to your tyranny."

There was a spark in Prithvi's eyes, a defiance that reminded Aurangzeb of Shivrai and the many others who had stood against him. The prince's boldness momentarily took the emperor aback. The court buzzed with murmurs of astonishment; none except Shivrai and now Prithvi had ever dared to speak to the Badshah in such a manner. Prithvi, though young, carried the spirit of a warrior who would rather die than submit.

Aurangzeb, however, managed to keep his composure. "I respect your valour," he said, though his tone was laced with sarcasm.

"And I respect your hospitality," Prithvi responded with equal sharpness. With that, he turned on his heel and began to walk out of the court. But before leaving, he stopped and turned back to face Aurangzeb one last time. "See you on the battlefield," he declared, his voice echoing through the grand hall.

Aurangzeb watched as the young Rajput strode out of the court, his heart filled with both admiration and fury. The emperor gestured to Asad Khan and his eunuch, Mutamad, instructing them to follow the prince. Once Prithvi was out of sight, Aurangzeb clenched his fists, his mind already scheming. He would not let Marwar slip through his grasp. It was a vital territory, connecting Agra to Ahmedabad and Surat, and Aurangzeb was determined to claim it. He needed Marwar to expand his trade routes, just as the Marathas had done with the British and the Portuguese. He could not afford to lose it, even if it meant waging war. But was he truly prepared for war? Aurangzeb knew all too well the valour of the Rajputs, who held their land and religion above all else. Still, he had a plan, one that did not require him to march to Marwar personally.

Meanwhile, Prithvi rode his horse across the scorching desert, his mind focused on returning to Marwar and rallying his people for the impending battle. He was determined to defend his homeland at all costs, but fate had other plans. Midway through his journey, Prithvi's hands and feet began to stiffen, and, drenched in sweat, he struggled to breathe. He gasped for air, his vision blurring as he fell from his horse. His throat felt as if it were closing, his voice choked as he tried in vain to call out to the few people nearby. Lying on the burning sand, Prithvi fought for every breath until finally, the life drained from his body.

Back at the Mughal court, Aurangzeb received news of Prithvi's death with a satisfied smile. Just as Mirza Raja Jai Singh had met a mysterious end, so too had Prithvi Singh Rathod breathed his last. Although shrouded in secrecy, it was believed that Mutamad had poisoned the robe gifted to Prithvi by the Mughals, the fabric laced with arsenic-tipped needles that sealed his fate.

In Marwar, Jaswant Singh Rathod sat in his tent, having just finished his meal, when Durgadas Rathod rushed in with the tragic news of Prithvi's demise. "I wish this were not true," Durgadas lamented, tears welling in his eyes.

Jaswant Singh Rathod felt a deep pain in his heart, a sense of loss so profound it nearly brought him to his knees. "Prithvi," he cried out, his voice trembling as Durgadas hurried to support him.

"I will not spare the Mughals," Jaswant Singh Rathod vowed, his eyes burning with the fire of vengeance.

"Prepare our men," he ordered, his voice filled with determination. But as the words left his lips, his body began to tremble, beads of sweat forming on his brow. Durgadas, thinking it was the result of the Maharaja's emotional turmoil, soon realized something far more sinister was at play. Seconds later, Jaswant Singh Rathod collapsed, gasping for breath before falling silent.

Panicked, Durgadas called for a medic, but it was too late. Jaswant Singh Rathod had drawn his last breath. As Durgadas surveyed the scene, his eyes fell upon the huge plate of food that Jaswant had eaten moments before. Anger flared within him as he shouted, "I want all the cooks here immediately!"

6.

WALKING THROUGH the expansive verandah, Annaji Datto, the revenue minister at Raigad, took cautious steps, wiping off the beads of sweat trickling down his face. He was anxious, almost petrified, as Sambhaji had summoned him to the courtroom. As he approached the courtroom, his mind scrambled to find any explanation for the summons. Adjusting his Peshwa turban with trembling hands, Annaji entered but was abruptly halted in his tracks.

"Datto Ji," Sambhaji remarked coolly, seated in the centre of the room, his voice cutting through the thick silence. He glanced pointedly at Annaji's feet, signalling the breach of etiquette.

"Ji," Annaji stammered, hastily removing his footwear before taking a few tentative steps forward. He stopped in front of Sambhaji, aware of the court officials' penetrating stares: Kondaji Farzand, the cavalry chief, Peshwa Moroji Pinglay, and Rahuji Somnath, among others.

"Ji Yuvraj," Annaji finally spoke, his voice barely above a whisper. He was trying to mask his anxiety, but the quiver in his tone betrayed him. He couldn't fathom why Yuvraj had called him here, especially in the absence of the Chhatrapati, who was away in Konkan. The empty throne served as a stark reminder of the power dynamics at play. Even Moroji Pinglay, who believed that only the Chhatrapati or his appointed officials had the authority to summon someone, was silently questioning the legitimacy of this meeting.

Sambhaji leaned forward slightly, his gaze unwavering. "Annaji, do you know why I have called you here? A man of your intellect and experience, a great mathematician, surely must have guessed."

Annaji offered a weak smile, unsure whether to take the statement as a compliment or a veiled threat, "I do not, Yuvraj. Perhaps you seek my counsel on some matter of importance?"

"Counsel?" Sambhaji's laugh echoed coldly, devoid of any humour. "Not exactly. What I seek is the truth, a harsh truth that can no longer be ignored."

With a wave of his hand, Sambhaji signalled a subordinate to bring forth the account books. Ledgers and diaries were placed in front of the Yuvraj, one after the other, creating a small mountain of records. Annaji felt his stomach drop as the realization dawned on him. The ground beneath him seemed to shift, and his knees threatened to give way.

"Annaji," Sambhaji began again, his voice steely, "With all the years of experience and your esteemed position as the Surnees, the one responsible for keeping meticulous records of the taxes payable to the government, I ask you, "Why is it that the revenues collected at various provinces do not coincide with the revenues received at Raigad? I have thoroughly examined the population, cultivation, and terrain of each of our territories. I exactly know how much foodgrain is cultivated and the equivalent revenues that should reach the central government. I also know how closely you are associated with the Shirke family, who play a dominant role in Dabhol. Where is it all going?"

Annaji's mouth went dry, his throat tightening as he struggled to find his voice, "Yuvraj… everything in the books… is properly documented. I have ensured that all accounts are accurate."

"Is that so?" Sambhaji's voice dripped with sarcasm as he stood up, the movement sudden and sharp. "If that's true, then I don't need to look any further. The traitor in our system stands right before me."

Annaji's heart pounded in his chest as Sambhaji's words hit him like a physical blow. He had never seen the Yuvraj so enraged, and the sight of it was terrifying. "Annaji," Sambhaji's voice echoed in the hall, "You have betrayed the very kingdom you swore to serve. I once believed the corruption was confined to those beneath you, but now I see the decay starts at the top. A man who betrays his own people has no place but in chains."

Annaji was stunned, reeling from the accusation. "How dare you speak to me like this?" he blurted out, his pride wounded. No one had ever addressed him with such disrespect, not even the Chhatrapati, to whom he was directly accountable. "I am answerable only to the Chhatrapati, not to you, Yuvraj," he added, his voice laced with indignation.

Sambhaji's temper flared even more, "And how dare you speak to a prince like this? Haven't you heard that when the Chhatrapati is away, it is either the queen consort or the prince who leads? When the Chhatrapati returns, I will make sure you pay for your sins," he thundered.

The tension in the room was palpable, with everyone holding their breath. Hiroji Farzand, sensing the escalating situation, decided to intervene. He approached Sambhaji cautiously, placing a hand on the Yuvraj's shoulder. "Yuvraj, please calm down. We do not yet know the full extent of what is happening. Someone else may be involved, perhaps someone lower in the ranks. Annaji has been instrumental in reviving our nation's finances after significant losses. We must consider the possibility of a larger conspiracy. Let the Chhatrapati return and decide how to proceed."

Despite Farzand's attempts to soothe him, Sambhaji's fury was difficult to contain. His temper, always quick to ignite, refused to be doused. He continued to hurl accusations at Annaji, narrating every suspicious transaction recorded in the ledgers. His relentless questioning lasted over an hour, with the tension mounting. Something like this had never happened in this courtroom before. Annaji, feeling increasingly cornered, decided not to further indulge Sambhaji.

Seeing no solution in sight, Sambhaji stormed out of the courtroom, leaving everyone behind in a state of uneasy silence. Hiroji Farzand and the others exhaled in relief, but the damage had been done. Yuvraj's accusations had left a lasting mark on the court and on Annaji.

As the sun dipped below the horizon, Annaji made his way alone to a secluded spot near the fort's wall. The encroaching darkness swallowed him, leaving only the faint glow of the lamp he carried to light his path. The grass, thick and overgrown, crunched beneath his feet, amplifying his unease. He couldn't shake the nagging fear of both encountering a snake and being spotted.

"Don't worry, there's no one around," a voice said from the shadows. Annaji recognized the voice instantly and relaxed slightly, knowing it belonged to the man he had come to meet. In the dim light, he could barely make out the man's figure.

"The Yuvraj is a sharp man," the man continued, stepping closer. "He nearly exposed us."

"I fear what will happen when the Chhatrapati returns," Annaji whispered, his voice trembling. "If he learns of this, not only we, but everyone involved in this scheme will be dead."

The man in the shadows remained calm, almost dismissive, "Nothing will happen. The Chhatrapati will be preoccupied with his southern expedition. He won't have time to dig into these matters."

"What about the Yuvraj? He's not a boy anymore. We have to be wary of him," Annaji said, his fear evident.

"Yes, he is a problem," the man acknowledged. "Although I'm certain he won't be joining his father on the expedition."

"How do you know that?" Annaji said doubtfully.

"The Chhatrapati won't risk taking both himself and the prince on the same expedition. It's too dangerous," the man explained. Then, with a sly grin, he added, "But if the Yuvraj remains here, he will indeed become a nuisance."

Annaji's fear shifted into a calculating resolve. "I can make sure he doesn't stay here," he muttered to himself. "I know someone who loathes him even more than we do."

The man's eyes gleamed with a dark understanding, a silent recognition of the game Annaji was playing. Slowly, he stepped forward, his smile stretching into something far more sinister. As the dim light of the lamp flickered, casting an eerie glow on the face of Hiroji Farzand.

In that moment, an unspoken agreement passed between them, a pact of treachery bound by their shared hatred and fear of Sambhaji. The seeds of conspiracy were sown, and the shadows of Raigad Fort held their dark secrets close.

SEATED INSIDE her opulent quarters, the queen consort gazed into the mirror, her thoughts a whirlwind of emotions. A housemaid carefully brushed her long, lustrous hair, while another gently washed her feet with a mixture of milk and saffron, the aroma filling the room with a calming scent. The queen's heart was brimming with joy. Clad in a resplendent red saree, she had instructed her maids to adorn her like a new bride. This day held a special significance, for her husband was returning from the Konkan after several months. The longing in her heart to see him had grown unbearable, and now, the moment of reunion was just a breath away.

In a nearby room, something similar was unfolding. Putalabai, another wife of the Chhatrapati, was also preparing herself, her heart fluttering with the anticipation of seeing her husband after such a long absence. Her eyes sparkled with the same longing that had filled her soul for months. Meanwhile, several miles away, Sambhaji's mind a storm of thoughts. As he awaited his father's return, his resolve grew stronger. His mission was clear: to unearth the traitors who hid in the shadows of the court, plotting to bring down the very kingdom his father had so tirelessly built.

Seated next to Sambhaji was his wife, Yesubai, her gentle presence offering him silent support. She, too, awaited the return of her father-in-law, the Chhatrapati, with hope in her heart. The Chhatrapati had always been distant, his duties as the ruler of a vast empire consuming most of his time. Yesu longed for a chance to spend some quality time with her Abasaheb, to connect with him in a way she had never been able to before.

As the palace hummed with activity, an unusual scene was unfolding outside the queen consort's residence. Annaji Datto stood waiting, a rare sight that did not go unnoticed. The housemaid who delivered news of his arrival could feel the weight of the moment, an unspoken tension hanging in the air. Intrigued by the unexpected visit, Soyrabai stepped out without hesitation. It wasn't usual for Annaji to come to the queen's quarters. This surely meant it had to be discussed away from the prying eyes of the courtroom.

With a gracious nod, Soyrabai invited Annaji to sit on an *asan* in her lavishly adorned living room. "What brings you here, Annaji Datto?" Soyrabai asked, her voice gentle but laced with concern.

"Queen, it's a matter of sheer insult, one that you might already be aware of. The Yuvraj humiliated me in front of my subordinates, in a room filled with the men who have served under me for years.

How could he do this to me? I have always been loyal to you and worked for the betterment of the kingdom as much as possible. And what do I get in return?" Annaji's voice trembled with a mix of anger and despair.

Soyrabai could feel the pain of humiliation in his words. Annaji had always been her go-to person, a pillar of strength and wisdom in her life. He had served her with unwavering loyalty, always treating her with the utmost respect, even when Saibai, the Chhatrapati's first wife, was alive. He had made her feel like the first queen, the most important woman in the empire.

"Annaji, there is nothing to worry about. The topic shall fade with time. You know how Shambhu is; volatile by nature, impulsive in his actions," Soyrabai said, trying to console him.

"Of course, I will worry, Rani saheb. There is no way that Chhatrapati will side with me over his own son. If I am caught, not only will I be sentenced to life imprisonment, but the entire chain of people involved will be exposed," Annaji's voice lowered to a whisper, the fear in his eyes unmistakable, "including *you*."

"All the princely luxuries we enjoy come at a price, Queen. Although most of the time I have cared for the kingdom, not everything can go towards the development of the people. I have a family to look after, too. If we devote everything to them, then what about our own well-being? Are we here only to serve others, with no regard for our own lives, our own futures?" Annaji spoke his heart out, his voice growing more passionate with each word. "The Chhatrapati shall return soon, and when he does, that will be the end of all this."

The joy that had lit up Soyrabai's face at the thought of her husband's return now faded, replaced by a cold dread. She had been longing to see the Chhatrapati, but now, the very idea of him around filled her with fear. The consequences of his return, if Annaji's fears were valid, would be catastrophic.

Annaji watched his queen closely, his eyes imploring her to understand the trouble they were in.

"What can be done, Annaji?" Soyrabai finally asked, her voice barely above a whisper.

Annaji's face betrayed a subtle transformation, his furrowed brows smoothed, and the flicker of despair in his eyes dimmed, replaced by a glint of quiet determination.

"With all due respect, Queen, if I may suggest," Annaji began, pausing to gauge Soyrabai's reaction. Seeing her nod, he continued, "The Yuvraj must be kept away from the Chhatrapati."

"How on earth would that happen, Annaji? Shambhu is his son! How can you keep them apart under one roof? Be realistic," Soyrabai's frustration was evident in her voice.

"Keeping them apart does not necessarily mean a physical separation," Annaji was desperate to convince the queen "When the Chhatrapati returns, he will visit you first, as he always does. If you manage to plant doubts in his mind about the Yuvraj… then the Chhatrapati will believe you. He is often away from Raigad and trusts you to keep an eye on the family. If you can convince him that Yuvraj is not fit to be the prince yet, the Chhatrapati will distance himself from his son. And if you add testimonies from others whom the Chhatrapati trusts, it will only strengthen your case."

Annaji paused to let his words sink in. Soyrabai was listening intently, her mind racing with possibilities.

"The rift between father and son will spread like wildfire among the people. Overnight, Yuvraj will become the rogue prince, the one who is not trusted by his own father. The people love the Chhatrapati; they trust him implicitly. If the Chhatrapati distances himself from the Yuvraj, people will follow suit," Annaji's eyes gleamed with the vision of his plan unfolding.

"But why would the Chhatrapati believe me?" Soyrabai asked doubtfully.

"After Jijau Mata and Saibai, you are now the queen consort. He has already entrusted the duties of the fort to you after their demise. There is nobody apart from you who has been given the right to govern the fort. Also, Yuvraj has been away from the Chhatrapati most of his life, and the two haven't interacted much of late. You can easily frame Yuvraj, the way you want," Annaji replied, his voice firm.

"Isn't it too wicked, Annaji? To create a rift between a father and his son?" Soyrabai's conscience pricked at her.

"It might seem wicked, but it is for the greater good," Annaji's voice was calm, almost persuasive. "Distancing the Yuvraj from his father will pave the way for your son, Rajaram, to step into the light. He will become the favoured prince, the one the Chhatrapati and the people will rally behind as the future king. Surely, that is a sacrifice worth making, isn't it?"

For a fleeting moment, the vision of Rajaram as the next Chhatrapati ignited a spark of pride in Soyrabai's heart. She could almost see the crown resting on her son's head, the glory of the Maratha throne within his grasp. But the weight of reality quickly pulled her back. "The Yuvraj will never allow it," she said, her voice laced with resignation. "He reveres his father, worships him like a deity. You and I both know he would never take a step that might drive a wedge between them."

"Not if he is sent away. The Chhatrapati is planning a southern expedition, but Farzandji believes he will not take Yuvraj along. If he stays back at Raigad, he will interfere in everything, undermining your authority as queen and destroying Rajaram's future as a king. The best course of action would be to have Yuvraj sent away to a distant place."

"And why would the Chhatrapati do that?" Soyrabai asked, her brow furrowed in confusion.

"Because you will convince him that Yuvraj's arrogance and disrespect stem from the power he holds. You will suggest that he needs to learn humility by spending time with the common people, away from the luxuries of the palace," Annaji explained, as he watched his plan take root in Soyrabai's mind.

The entire scheme that Annaji had just laid out now seemed both feasible and desirable to Soyrabai. She could see the cunning and ruthlessness in Annaji, but she was willing to accept it if it meant securing her own power and ensuring that her son, Rajaram, would one day ascend to the throne. She looked at Annaji, whose eyes were now filled with a fierce determination, a burning desire to see Sambhaji ousted from the kingdom. Soyrabai knew that only she could make this happen.

7.

THE BLAZING sun hung high over Marwar as Durgadas Rathod, a man fuelled by vengeance, stood before a gathering of soldiers. The last rites for their fallen leaders, Jaswant Singh Rathod and Prithvi Singh, had been completed. The air was thick with the smoke of funeral pyres and the palpable rage of betrayed people. The men before him were no longer just soldiers; they were avengers, driven by a searing desire to make the Mughals pay for their sins.

"The Mughals must perish and pay for their treachery!" Durgadas roared, his voice cutting through the heavy silence. His eyes, burning with determination, scanned the crowd.

Durgadas had wasted no time in hunting down the cook who had poisoned Jaswant Singh. The traitor was swiftly brought to justice, hanged in public as a warning to all who might think to betray Marwar. The youngest prince was then crowned King of Marwar, though still a child. Durgadas was appointed as the leader to oversee all military decisions, while the queen assumed control over political matters until the young prince came of age.

"Aurangzeb thinks we are finished, that we are powerless," Durgadas declared, his voice filled with conviction as he addressed the soldiers. "But are we defeated?"

"No!" the crowd bellowed, their voices merging into a single, thunderous roar.

Durgadas could feel the raw energy, the unyielding anger that coursed through the people of Marwar. They were ready for battle, prepared to fight to the last man.

"Aurangzeb has dispatched his son Akbar with 10,000 cavalrymen and infantrymen to crush us. But can they defeat us?" Durgadas continued, his words a rallying cry.

"No!" the soldiers shouted back, their voices rising with fervour.

"They believe they can tear us apart, that they can abuse our women, enslave our children, desecrate our religion, and shatter our sacred idols. Will we let this happen?"

"No!" the crowd cried out again, their defiance echoing across the plains.

"We are few in number compared to them, but they cannot break our spirit. Our Gods are with us! Every single one of us can fight through hundreds of them. We are not alone; we are blessed by the Gods!" Durgadas's voice rose to a crescendo as he drew his dagger from its scabbard. Holding it high, he proclaimed, "We may die in this war, but we shall never retreat from the battlefield. *Jai Karnimata*!"

"*Jai Karnimata*!" the soldiers responded in unison, their voices reverberating with unwavering resolve. Durgadas then slashed his finger with the dagger, letting the blood drip into the holy fire as an offering to the Goddess, seeking her divine blessings for the battle ahead.

Durgadas had achieved his immediate goal. He had reignited the fierce valour of the Rajputs, a flame that had momentarily dimmed after the devastating losses of their prince and king. But he knew that valour alone would not win them this war. The Mughals were a formidable enemy, and mere courage, however indomitable, was not enough to ensure victory. Durgadas understood that he needed to outmanoeuvre the enemy before they could set foot in Marwar and unleash their destruction.

He reached out to the Sisodia and Kacchavah clans, traditional foes of the Mughal Empire, seeking their support. He explained the impending threat, how the Mughals were about to descend upon them with the full might of their forces. The Sisodias and Kacchavah, with their own long-standing enmity towards the Mughals, readily agreed to join forces with Durgadas. This alliance bolstered Marwar's strength, uniting the Rajput clans in a common cause against a formidable adversary.

Meanwhile, in Agra, Aurangzeb was consumed with his grand ambitions of territorial expansion. His army, driven by the doctrine of jihad, had been unleashed upon Mathura, leaving a trail of devastation in its wake. Temples were destroyed, homes set ablaze, innocent men slaughtered, women raped, and children enslaved. The Mughal emperor's call for jihad echoed through the streets as his men chanted 'Allah-u-Akbar!' with fervour.

Aurangzeb's campaign of terror reached a boiling point when a group of Hindus dared to rebel. It was a Friday, and as Aurangzeb made his way to the mosque, surrounded by his close security, a mob of Hindus blocked his path. Perched atop a towering elephant, Aurangzeb demanded that the crowd make way for him. But the mob had had enough. They refused to bow down, raising their voices in defiance, hailing Lord Krishna and denouncing the emperor's jihad.

"You are all kafirs! A disgrace to humanity!" Aurangzeb shouted from his elephant; his voice laced with contempt. "You all must die!"

The Mughal soldiers, enraged by the crowd's audacity, charged forward. The mob was ruthlessly crushed under the feet of elephants, their cries drowned out by the sounds of slaughter. Men, women, and children alike were trampled as Aurangzeb's forces showed no mercy.

In Mathura, the destruction continued unabated. The Mughal soldiers stormed temples, smashing idols, looting treasures, and converting the sacred spaces into mosques. The land, once vibrant with the worship of deities, was now a scene of desecration and despair.

But amidst this carnage was a man who refused to stand by and watch the annihilation of his people. His heart burned with the injustice and cruelty inflicted upon his kin. He knew he could not remain in Mathura any longer. It was no longer safe. The only person he could trust in this dire situation was a friend who might offer the help he desperately needed. Mounting his horse, Kavi Kalash set out on a journey to the Deccan, determined to reach Sambhaji, the one ally who might stand with him against the tyranny of Aurangzeb.

RAIGAD WAS bustling with activity as a new war strategy was meticulously crafted. Chhatrapati Shivaji Maharaj, the revered Maratha leader, had returned to his fort, preparing for what would be his next bold move. The impregnable Golconda Fort, under the rule of the Qutubshahi, was about to face one of the most devastating assaults in history, led by none other than Shivrai himself. Aiding him in this monumental endeavour was his Sarnobat, Hambirrao

Mohite, the head of the Maratha defence forces. Mohite, with his team of seasoned men, had orchestrated the movement of thousands of infantrymen, cavalrymen, goldsmiths, blacksmiths, labourers, cooks, and tonnes of cannons, arms, ammunition, and food supplies that could sustain them for years. Every logistical detail was attended to with precision, ensuring that nothing would hinder their advance.

Amidst the relentless preparations for the upcoming battle, Shivrai found his mind preoccupied with a different, weightier concern. His son, Sambhaji, had been determined to unmask the traitors within their ranks who sought to sabotage the Maratha cause. Yet, despite his resolve, Sambhaji chose to remain silent. He refused to burden his father, freshly returned from a gruelling year-long campaign in Konkan, believing that Shivrai needed time to recover both physically and mentally.

But the truth was far more intricate than Sambhaji realized. Shivrai's silence was not born of exhaustion. It was the result of a more insidious influence. Soyrabai's and Annaji's plan had worked to some extent. Poisonous seeds of doubt had been carefully and skillfully planted in his mind.

Soyrabai had waited patiently for the right moment to act. After his return, when Shivrai visited her quarters, she played her role flawlessly, cloaking her manipulation beneath a veil of concern. She shed crocodile tears, lamenting Sambhaji's supposed waywardness, and performed the part of a worried stepmother with chilling precision, gradually eroding the trust between father and son.

"I worry constantly for Sambhaji," she would say, her voice heavy with feigned emotion. "All my life, I've tried to be a mother to him, loving him as my own, but I've failed. He has no respect for elders, tries to step into your shoes prematurely, and believes he has the authority to govern and even speaks ill of those who are most loyal to you. He was never like this. I'm certain he's been corrupted by the bad influences he encountered either in Mathura or during his time with the Mughals. Even women do not feel safe around him. I have seen him drink to excess and lose all control, behaving recklessly with everyone around him. He is volatile, always consumed by fury, his temper flaring at the slightest provocation."

Shivrai, hearing these words from Soyrabai, felt a pang of sorrow for her. Having spent years apart from his son, Shivrai found himself increasingly uncertain about the man Sambhaji was becoming. Doubts gnawed at his heart. Could his beloved boy truly be turning into a spoiled prince? Adding to his unease were memories of his mother, Jijabai, whose wise counsel still echoed in his mind. She had often cautioned him about Sambhaji's fiery temper, warning that a prince, and especially a future king, required a calm and measured mind to govern wisely and make sound decisions.

"A prince and would-be king should have a calm mind so that he can make the best decisions," she had advised, genuinely concerned for her grandson.

Shivrai's mind drifted to a memory that still sent a chill down his spine. Sambhaji, barely a boy at the time, had faced a tiger in life-threatening combat, unarmed and alone. He had wrestled the beast with nothing but his bare hands, gripping its powerful jaws and dislocating them, ultimately killing it. The ferocity of the act had stunned everyone who witnessed it. Later, when Shivrai questioned him, Sambhaji had replied with unsettling calmness, "Abasaheb, I did it to save the young girl and her cattle. Had I not intervened, the tiger would have torn them apart."

"How could you be so careless? Who asked you to intervene? Couldn't you have called for help?"

"Don't you say, Abasaheb, that it is our duty to protect our people from every threat? The tiger was a threat to the girl and her cattle. I only did what I felt was right at that moment. Had I waited for help, the girl would have died."

"Son, I'm concerned about you," he had said. "I'm sure it was your anger that drove you to do what you did, wasn't it?"

"Yes," Sambhaji had admitted, his head held high. "I couldn't stand the tiger challenging me. And perhaps, my only strength is my anger."

The memory had filled Shivrai with both pride and unease. Pride in his son's courage and strength, but also concern for the fearlessness that bordered on recklessness. It was a glimpse into the fire that burned within Sambhaji; a fire that could either illuminate the Maratha kingdom or consume it.

Now, Shivrai reflected on Sambhaji's current behaviour; he felt a deep sense of helplessness and concern. Sambhaji was no longer a child who could be easily reprimanded. He was a grown man, and if there was any truth to Soyrabai's accusations, Shivrai feared for the empire.

Despite the damage Soyrabai had attempted to inflict, Shivrai was not one to be easily deceived. He was a wise man, seasoned by years of leadership and battle. He harboured his own doubts about the veracity of her claims. To seek clarity, Shivrai had also consulted with Putalabai, his other wife, who loved Sambhaji dearly. Putalabai had no complaints about Sambhaji, but there were whispers of his misbehaviour among the men. These rumours had been strategically spread by Soyrabai's ally, Surnees Annaji Datto.

One evening, as Shivrai sat alone in his chamber, he found himself thinking of Saibai, Sambhaji's late mother. "I wish you were here, Sai, to guide our son Shambu. While I've been away, I don't know how he's been coping with everything. I don't know who to believe or trust. My heart aches for Shambu, who has faced so many challenges from a young age… sent to Mathura, then to Aurangabad as a Mughal mansabdar when he was just 12, and now possibly being entangled in family politics. While others live comfortably within the safety of the fort, he bears the brunt of life's harshest realities. How I wish I could shield him from all of this, change his fate, give him the peace and ease he deserves."

The day before Shivrai was to leave on his southern expedition, Sambhaji finally broached the topic with his father. He shared his concerns, hoping for guidance. Shivrai, however, advised his son not to get involved in the financial matters for the time being. He did not want to burden Sambhaji mentally or physically, and he also believed it wasn't the right time to take action against Annaji Datto and his associates. Shivrai needed Annaji's support for the southern campaign, which required substantial funding. Changing the financial leadership at this crucial time could destabilize the entire operation. Shivrai's priority was the success of the expedition, and for that, he needed all the resources and stability he could muster.

Shivrai turning down Sambhaji's concerns had not gone well with him. Sambhaji could sense a sudden change in Shivrai's behaviour and was equally hurt because his concerns had mattered least to Shivrai.

'Why is Abasaheb not believing me?' he wondered, 'Is somebody else brainwashing him against me?'

Sambhaji sulked in his residence, pondering the consequences. He could see Annaji Datto turn even more rigid whenever he crossed paths with him. Although Annaji could not meet Sambhaji's eyes, deep down, Sambhaji could sense Annaji and his men mocking him for his failed attempt. Their laughter behind his back made him feel miserable.

Before leaving, Shivrai decided to take some tough calls. If there was even a shred of truth in Soyrabai's words, he had to ensure that Sambhaji was correctly guided. Conversely, if it was all a lie, he had to safeguard Sambhaji's well-being during his absence.

In the courtroom with mansabdars and subhedars, Shivrai addressed his men. He declared, "Peshwa Moropant Pinglay will oversee the region north of Raigad Fort, while Annaji Datto will command the areas south of Panhala Fort up to Karwar. Rahuji Somnath will protect Raigad Fort." Pausing for a moment, Shivrai looked directly at his son before continuing, "Sambhaji will go to Shringarpur to oversee the Ratnagiri province in Konkan."

The announcement hit Sambhaji like a blow. Not only had his father bothered to take any action against Annaji Datto and his accomplices, but he had also assigned him to a distant, insignificant region. Sambhaji had hoped to be part of the southern expedition, or at least given a significant role in the central Maratha kingdom Instead, he was being sent far away from the heart of the empire.

Sambhaji expressed his anguish to his wife, Yesubai, in private, too pained to question his father directly.

"Yesu," he said, sitting next to her, his eyes moist and his heart paining, "Why am I being kept away from my people? Why am I not a part of the Maratha's biggest ever battle?"

Sambhaji looked at Yesu for his answers. Yesu hoped she could console her husband and wished she had an answer to his questions. All she could say was, "Yuvraj, probably Shringarpur is more important for Abasaheb at the moment. I think he wants you to build your own empire there."

"No, Yesu," Sambhaji was distressed, "It is a very insignificant place. I cannot make it big, even if I strive hard there."

The entire night, Sambhaji was distressed. He tossed and turned on his bed, making conjectures of what really made his Abasaheb take such a call.

The next morning, as the golden rays of dawn bathed the fortress in a soft glow, the aarti ceremony concluded with reverence. Chhatrapati Shivaji Maharaj, flanked by Sarnobat Mohite and his trusted soldiers, mounted and steered toward the southern frontier. The rhythmic pounding of hooves echoed through the vast courtyard as Shivrai passed through the Mahadarwaza, his eyes fixed ahead, yet his heart heavy with an unspoken burden. He longed to explain to his son the rationale behind sending him to Shringarpur, why, despite the weight of his own affection, he had chosen this path for the future of the kingdom.

Sambhaji stood at a distance, watching his father ride away. As Shivrai's figure faded into the horizon, a quiet ache gripped his chest. *What had he done to earn such distance from his own blood? What was his father hiding behind that stoic mask?*

LIFE IN Shringarpur was far from what Sambhaji had expected. The quiet, simple town felt worlds apart from the grandeur of Raigad. Here, Yesu and he lived in a modest house with a small front verandah, much like the homes of the local people. The houses were made of brick, with floors smeared in cow dung, a common practice believed to keep them cool and clean. The towering fort walls and the constant bustle of the royal court were replaced by a slower, humbler way of life… one that Sambhaji was still learning to embrace.

Accustomed to a life of physical vigour and mental stimulation,

Sambhaji adapted to his new environment by incorporating elements of his previous routine into his daily life. He set up a pole in his premises for Mallakhamb, a traditional sport that involves gymnastics. His days were filled with weightlifting, horseback riding, wrestling at the akhada, and swimming in the river. He would often spend time by the riverbank, finding solace in writing poetry that celebrated Lord Krishna and the Hindu Goddesses.

Despite his attempts to find contentment in his new surroundings, Sambhaji frequently pondered his absence from the southern expedition. He was kept in the dark about the happenings around the Golconda Fort and Raigad. Even though he was stationed far from the centre of power, the people of Shringarpur treated him with remarkable affection. The local peasants would often present him with baskets full of vegetables, grains, and fruits, demonstrating their love and respect. This genuine display of warmth made Sambhaji feel a deep connection with the people.

One day, deeply engrossed in thoughts, Sambhaji, seated in the open ground outside his small house, wondered what lay in front of him. He was missing Raigad and his people. He missed his Abasaheb, his stepmother, Putalabai, and his cousin, Rajaram.

His chain of thoughts was interrupted when a peasant who had been watching him said, "Raje, would you allow me to say something?"

Sambhaji signalled him to continue.

"Yuvraj…I really admire that our prince is living with us. We are all blessed to have you around. Goddess Jagdamba has been kind to us."

Another peasant who followed the first one came with a basket of fruits and foodgrains and placed them beside Sambhaji.

"*Hai kai?*" Sambhaji reacted in Marathi.

"Yuvraj…," the man stammered, "The day you set your feet into our lands, we felt assured of a good future. You are a blessing to us. We want you to taste the fruits and foodgrains that we have cultivated."

"There is no need for all of this, kaka," replied Sambhaji, placing his shoulder on the poor man's shoulders.

"What else can we poor offer you, Yuvraj!" the man remarked,

"We feel blessed to have you among us, the very own blood of Shivrai, making us believe we are in safe hands. Years ago, when the Siddhis looted us, Shivrai protected us."

Sambhaji embraced them both and thanked them for their gifts.

The outpouring of love from the people around him was overwhelming. Slowly and steadily, people started opening up their hearts. Sambhaji grew more friendly towards them. As he engaged with the local issues, Sambhaji began to learn the nuances of governance. He wondered whether his father wanted him to understand the challenges faced by ordinary people and to acquire the skills necessary for effective governance.

A few months passed, and a peasant approached Sambhaji with a pressing complaint. "Yuvraj," he said, "We are struggling immensely. The watandars and revenue collectors are exploiting us with exorbitant taxes. When the gods do not favour us with rain, our crops fail, yet we are forced to pay taxes and supply produce. We are left with nothing to feed our families on most occasions. Are we only born to serve? Will no one listen to our plight? Shivrai used to visit us regularly, but now even he has gotten too busy with other work. We feel abandoned."

Sambhaji listened intently to the peasants' grievances. The revenue collectors were assigned by the Maratha Empire to collect taxes only during times of profit, not to exploit the farmers. On some occasions, when conditions were unfavourable, they were expected to carry out social work by helping the peasants with foodgrains, adequate water, and even agricultural tools and assistance, as and when needed. He was troubled by the notion that the very people who were supposed to protect and serve the common folk were exploiting them instead. He knew he lacked the political influence to make significant changes, and his previous experience with rebellion had not ended well. This time, he resolved to make a decision that would truly benefit the people. He spent days and nights contemplating possible solutions, with Yesu offering valuable advice along the way.

Yesu, a member of the Shirke family, had her own insights into the matter. The Shirke family had once been influential Watandars of Dabhol, a nearby seaport under Adilshahi control until Shivrai captured it. The Shirke family had lost their prestigious status with the end of the Watandari system, and Yesu's brother, Ganoji, was eager to restore their lost honour. The current collectors, who had replaced the old watandars, were now exploiting the farmers just as their predecessors had. Yesu's perspective resonated with Sambhaji.

"Yuvraj," said Yesu, as Sambhaji was all ears to her. "These people are poor. The rains don't support them, the enemies invade them, the wild animals kill their cattle, and if not them, the Mughals kill their cattle for meat. Raigad, and we are far from these people. The appointed watandars don't listen to them and exploit them in the name of taxes. How are these people to survive?"

"I feel sorry for them too, Yesu. I want to do something for them."

"You can, Yuvraj."

"How? Shivrai is on the southern expedition, and people at Raigad won't listen to me. How am I supposed to do anything?"

Yesu walked close to Sambhaji and sat next to him and said, "Yuvraj, you are the prince of the Marathas. Please do not forget that. The court is known by its prince; the prince is not known by his court. You still are the prince and capable enough to make a decision."

Yesu's words made him realize that he had the authority to make a difference in Shringarpur. As the appointed in-charge of the region, Sambhaji decided to waive the taxes until the drought conditions improved. He issued a decree instructing the collectors to cease tax collection and sent an official letter to Raigad, signed by him, to inform Annaji Datto of his decision. This move, although intended to alleviate the burden on the peasants, soon became a source of anxiety for Annaji Datto, who found Sambhaji's actions a persistent challenge even from afar.

Sambhaji's decision to prioritize the welfare of the people in Shringarpur over political expediency marked a significant step in his growth as a leader. His time in Shringarpur gave him insights into the real struggles of common people, and he began to understand the importance of empathy and effective governance.

As days passed, Sambhaji found solace in knowing that his actions were making a tangible difference in the lives of the peasants. His commitment to their well-being earned him their unwavering loyalty and respect.

The people of Shringarpur, who had once been burdened by the harsh realities of taxation and exploitation, now saw a glimmer of hope in their prince's leadership. Sambhaji's efforts to alleviate their suffering and his dedication to understanding their plight marked the beginning of a new chapter in his journey, one that would ultimately define his future as a leader of the Maratha empire.

"WHERE ARE the people? Why has this land turned barren and desolate?" questioned Akbar to his men.

Akbar, the son of Aurangzeb, ventured into the Marwar province with a grand entourage, but his arrival was met with barren and desolate lands that were far from what he had anticipated. The once-thriving region now lay in emptiness—abandoned villages, deserted houses, and silent temples. The fear of imminent violence had driven the villagers away from their homes. They had fled to the safety of the hilly terrains, leaving behind only ghostly remnants of their lives. The dread of looting, the threat of rape and murder, and the enslavement of their children had propelled them to seek refuge in the hills. The temples, once bustling with worshippers, now stood silent, their deities untouched by invaders' hands.

Akbar was a stark contrast to his father. Unlike Aurangzeb, who pursued his jihad with fervour, Akbar was known for his respect towards all religions. He had no desire to perpetuate the religious intolerance that marked his father's rule. Akbar wanted to prove to the people of Marwar that he was different, that he could bring a new era of tolerance and peace.

Upon arriving in the deserted plateau, surrounded by rugged hills, Akbar's men set up their camps. They established their presence with tents and made themselves at home. Akbar had come well-prepared, ensuring his army had enough supplies to endure the unforgiving desert for months. Yet, despite his careful planning, he found himself struggling against the relentless heat, which often left him drained and unwell. To escape the scorching sun, he took refuge in the shade of his tent, where he surrounded himself with indulgences—fine liquor, fragrant hookah, and the company of concubines who attended to his every whim. The freedom from his father's oversight in Agra allowed him to enjoy the independence that he relished.

Aurangzeb had sent Akbar to Marwar to find Durgadas Rathod and either kill or imprison him to put an end to the rule of Marwar. It would also expand the Mughal territories in Rajasthan to ease trade in Surat and secure a strategically dominant position to attack the Deccan. But days turned into weeks, and Akbar continued to immerse himself in his own pursuits, enjoying the pleasures of Marwar's cuisine, particularly the *lal maas*—a spicy, red meat curry that was a local speciality.

Meanwhile, Aurangzeb, back in Agra, awaited updates from his son, while his advisers puzzled over Akbar's unorthodox behaviour. Akbar's deep indulgence in luxury stood in stark contrast to the relentless pursuit of conquest that had defined the Mughal rulers before him. Though his ambition to ascend the throne burned bright, it often seemed at odds with the discipline and hardship expected of a future Badshah.

Durgadas Rathod, a prominent figure in the Marwar resistance, was stationed in the hills with his loyal followers. He was acutely aware of the strategic advantage the hilly terrain provided. The people of Marwar's best chance of countering the Mughal forces lay in the mountains, where the terrain neutralized the effectiveness of the Mughal elephants and exhausted their infantrymen. Durgadas knew that a confrontation on open ground would spell disaster for his smaller force. Thus, he relied on guerrilla tactics, launching surprise attacks on Akbar's scouts with relentless precision. Day after day, his men disrupted Mughal operations, eroding their confidence and morale.

Despite the ongoing skirmishes, Durgadas noticed that Akbar was not fully committing to the conflict.

"Why isn't Akbar coming out in full force?" he asked one of his ministers one day.

To uncover the reasons behind Akbar's reluctance, Durgadas dispatched spies to infiltrate the Mughal camps and returned with the intelligence.

"Akbar does not wholeheartedly support Aurangzeb's campaign," said the head spy.

"Why is it so?" questioned Durgadas.

"Akbar is a complete contrast to what Aurangzeb is. He hates his father converting Hindus into Muslims forcibly and wishes to put an end to the tyrannical rule. He also dreams of becoming the next Badshah and is waiting for the right time to turn the tables around. He is unwilling to engage in a confrontation, partly out of fear of the consequences and partly because he lacks the resources to mount a serious challenge. He is happy playing a diplomatic game, neither fully supporting Aurangzeb's conquest nor actively opposing it."

Durgadas, armed with this crucial information, realized that Akbar's ambivalence presented an opportunity. He knew that the key to turning the tide in Marwar's favour lay in leveraging Akbar's discontent for their benefit. With determination and urgency, Durgadas set out for the Mughal camps. The sun beat down mercilessly, and the dust of the desert clung to him, but he pressed on, driven by the prospect of a pivotal moment that could alter the course of events.

"Durgadas Rathod is here to meet you, Shehzada Akbar," the aide reported.

Akbar's mind raced with questions. "Why does the enemy want to see me? Could this be part of a plot against me?"

He decided to proceed with caution, arming himself and ensuring his bodyguards accompanied him as he made his way to the tent where Durgadas awaited.

"Rajputs only attack an armed person in battlefields, Shehzada Akbar," Durgadas began, acknowledging the heavily guarded Akbar with a respectful nod.

Akbar, though still sceptical, was intrigued. "You never know! That might be the only strategy you have to ensure that you are kept away from the Mughal invasion," he responded with a hint of sarcasm.

"I have something even better," Durgadas said, unfazed, meeting Akbar's gaze.

"What is it?" he asked.

"If I may speak," Durgadas said, pausing for effect, "in private," he added, glancing at the bodyguards surrounding them.

Akbar hesitated, torn between his distrust and the potential opportunity. However, Durgadas's bold statement about the Rajput's honour pushed him to take the risk. Reluctantly, Akbar signalled his bodyguards to step outside, positioning them at a distance where they could still observe but not overhear the conversation.

As the guards retreated, Durgadas leaned closer and spoke with conviction. "I can make you the Badshah."

The gravity of Durgadas's words resonated deeply with Akbar.

"How is that possible?" Akbar asked, his voice tinged with excitement.

Durgadas explained, "You and your men can join forces with us. We have the backing of the Sisodia and Kacchavah clans, who are eager to support our cause. Aurangzeb is our common adversary. If you align with us, our combined strength will be formidable. We, the Rathods, are driven by vengeance for the deaths of Jaswant Singh Rathod and Prithvi, who were betrayed by Aurangzeb. His treachery has fuelled our resolve to overthrow him. Together, we can dismantle his empire and elevate you to the position of Badshah."

The notion of becoming the Badshah resonated powerfully with Akbar. He envisioned himself fulfilling his long-held dream of ruling without the constraints of caste discrimination. The idea of dethroning his father, who had orchestrated the imprisonment of his grandfather Shahjahan and the execution of his uncle, Dara Shikoh, the rightful heir, seemed justifiable. The moral ambiguity of his father's actions only solidified Akbar's resolve.

"I am ready," Akbar declared, his voice brimming with anticipation.

This meeting marked the beginning of a transformative chapter for both Akbar and the men of Marwar. For Durgadas and his allies, it was a chance for survival and revenge. For Akbar, it was a glimmer of hope that his aspirations could finally be realized.

In a gesture of gratitude and newfound camaraderie, Akbar extended his arms towards Durgadas, and the two embraced, sealing their pact with a promise of mutual support.

THE LANDS turned saffron as the flags waved, horses galloped, and the soldiers marched on the outskirts of the Golconda Fort. The Maratha army, under the leadership of Chhatrapati Shivaji Maharaj, continued its southern expedition, taking intermittent rests along the way, Shivrai turned to his infantry chief, Yesaji.

"Yesaji, arrange a meeting with Hassan at Golconda Fort," Shivrai instructed.

Yesaji Kank, perceptive and familiar with Shivrai's strategic mind, understood the significance of the request. Golconda Fort, located in Hyderabad, was under the control of the Qutubshahi dynasty, ruled by Sultan Abdullah Qutub Shah Hassan. The Qutubshahi rulers had long been caught in a perilous struggle between the Mughals and the Adilshahi sultanate. Despite their resilience against Mughal invasions, they had seen their domain shrink to just 66 forts.

"What's the plan, Raje?" Yesaji inquired, seeking clarification on Shivrai's intentions.

Shivrai, with a determined gleam in his eyes, outlined his strategy. "Yesaji, our primary objective is to forge an alliance with the Qutubshahi to bolster our campaign against the Adilshahi. Their support will be crucial in our bid to consolidate power in the Deccan."

"I hope this materializes as planned," Yesaji admitted, a hint of nervousness in his voice.

Shivrai responded with a reassuring smile, "What do we have Madan for, if not for this?" His confidence in Madan, the Hindu wazir and adviser to Hassan, was well-founded. Madan's deep understanding of both Maratha and Hindu customs made him a key asset in this diplomatic venture.

Strategies were meticulously devised, and letters were dispatched to the Qutubshahi court, formally requesting a meeting between Shivrai and Hassan. On the appointed day, Shivrai, accompanied by Yesaji and a contingent of a hundred men, set out for Golconda Fort. Meanwhile, Sarnobat Mohite and thousands of Maratha cavalrymen were stationed at the foothills of the fort, ready to assist, if needed.

Hassan went to great lengths to prepare for Shivrai's arrival. The city of Hyderabad, including the Fateh Darwaza and Charminar, was adorned with flowers and saffron flags to honour the arrival of one of India's most prominent Hindu rulers. Madan ensured that Shivrai's journey to the Golconda Fort was smooth and free of difficulties. Upon their arrival, Madan and his men warmly welcomed Shivrai with flower petals and garlands, guiding him to the courtroom where Hassan awaited.

As Shivrai entered the courtroom, he was greeted with a mixture of awe and respect. Hassan, clearly impressed by Shivrai's presence, embraced him warmly and offered him a seat, signalling the beginning of their discussion. Accompanying Shivrai was Pralhad Niraji, while Yesaji and his men stood as his defence, ready to act if necessary.

"Shah Abdul Hassan," Shivrai began, paying his respects to the Qutubshahi ruler. "I am on my southern expedition to defeat the Adilshahi. If we succeed, the Deccan will fall under our control. In this situation, it would be immensely beneficial for the Qutubshahi and the Marathas to form an alliance to combat the Adilshahi."

Shivrai's piercing gaze conveyed the seriousness of his proposal. He anticipated Hassan's response and continued, "Throughout your reign, you have endured relentless Mughal invasions, with your cities being looted and your people suffering. By allying with us, we can together bring an end to the Adilshahi's dominance, and we will be the only remaining force capable of challenging the Mughals."

Hassan's memories of the past were vivid—burning cities, the cries of the wounded, and the atrocities committed by the Mughals. The painful recollections were deeply etched into his consciousness, and Shivrai's words resonated with his long-standing desire for reprisal.

Shivrai's knowledge of Hassan's situation was unparalleled. He understood that Hassan's decision would be influenced by his experiences and aspirations. To further sway Hassan, Shivrai added, "Once we defeat the Adilshahi, the Qutubshahi will benefit significantly from the strongholds we capture."

Hassan envisioned the acquisition of the formidable Vellore Fort, a long-held ambition. Shivrai's assurance that such a victory was possible ignited a spark of hope within him. A smile slowly spread across Hassan's face as he began to contemplate the potential alliance.

On the surface, Hassan believed he had gained the most from the discussions, while in reality, Shivrai had skilfully manoeuvred the terms to secure substantial advantages for the Marathas. The alliance with the Qutubshahi not only promised additional military strength but also provided strategic leverage against both the Adilshahi and the Mughals.

DESPITE BEING miles away from Raigad, Sambhaji had already made a significant impact that reverberated throughout the kingdom. Annaji Datto's corrupt ambitions had been abruptly halted, and the once-steady flow of revenue from Shringarpur and the surrounding Konkan regions was temporarily suspended. Sambhaji's decision was clear: when revenues resumed, they would be directed to Shringarpur itself, ensuring the funds were used for the welfare of the very people who paid the taxes, rather than being funnelled into Raigad's coffers.

"You have done the right thing, Yuvraj," Yesubai said softly, sensing that Sambhaji was deep in thought as he engaged in his daily exercises. She had always been adept at reading his mind, understanding his concerns even before he voiced them.

"Did I, Yesu? Do you truly believe so?" Sambhaji responded, his doubt evident as he suddenly stood up and looked at his wife.

"Yes, Yuvraj. Our existence is for the welfare of the people. We are chosen by God to protect the weak, feed the needy, and rebel against the demons," Yesu replied with a calm assurance that belied her youth. Her words resonated deeply within Sambhaji, making him realize once again how fortunate he was to have such a wise and supportive partner by his side.

Just as Sambhaji was about to resume his exercise, a loud commotion erupted outside. A man on horseback had bolted towards his residence, causing a flurry of activity as people rushed to stop him from entering. The guards at the door had quickly shut the main gate, forcing the man to dismount and restraining the intruder.

"How dare you barge in like that?" one of the guards demanded angrily, tightening his grip on the intruder.

"I know the Yuvraj," the man replied, his breath heavy with exhaustion and fear as the growing mob around him eyed him suspiciously.

Inside, Sambhaji could hear the commotion; his instincts told him immediately that something was amiss. With long, purposeful strides, he made his way to the gate.

"What is happening here?" he asked one of the guards, his voice calm but commanding.

"Yuvraj, someone attempted to force their way into your residence. We've detained him," the guard reported, his tone filled with concern.

"Open the gate," Sambhaji ordered without hesitation.

"But, Yuvraj..." The guard hesitated, unsure if it was wise to comply. His concern for Sambhaji's safety was palpable.

"It's an order," Sambhaji repeated firmly, his expression leaving no room for further debate. Reluctantly, the guard opened the gate, revealing a man being held by several guards, surrounded by an anxious crowd. Sambhaji's curiosity piqued as he wondered who could be behind such a bold attempt to breach his residence.

As Sambhaji pushed through the crowd, many onlookers stepped aside, some bowing and others simply staring in awe at the Yuvraj. His presence alone commanded respect and admiration. Finally, his eyes fell upon the captive, and the tension in his features melted away, replaced by a warm smile.

"Kalashji!" Sambhaji exclaimed with joy upon recognizing

his old friend from Mathura. The guards, confused by the sudden change in Yuvraj's demeanour, released their grip on the man.

"Yuvraj!" Kalash cried out, tears welling up in his eyes as he saw Sambhaji. The overwhelming relief of finally finding his friend after a long and arduous journey was evident.

Sambhaji embraced Kavi Kalash with both arms, memories of their shared past flooding back. "I am so happy to see you," Sambhaji said, his voice filled with genuine warmth.

"As am I," Kavi Kalash responded, still in disbelief that he had managed to find his old friend. His journey from Mathura to Raigad, and then to Shringarpur, had been fraught with challenges, but seeing Sambhaji made it all worthwhile.

The rest of the day passed smoothly as Sambhaji and Kavi Kalash caught up over lunch, reminiscing about old times and discussing the current state of affairs. It was during this time that Kalash expressed his desire to stay with Sambhaji and serve him.

"The Mughals have looted us, destroyed our temples, and made every Hindu's life miserable in Mathura and the surrounding provinces," Kalash lamented, recalling the horrors of mass lynchings and the trampling of innocents by elephants.

"Aurangzeb is a monster," Kalash continued, his voice trembling with anger. "He has no remorse for his vile actions."

"Kalashji," Sambhaji said, placing a reassuring hand on Kalash's shoulder, "You need not worry any longer. From now on, you are safe here. You can stay with me until my last breath."

"Until my last breath," the words echoed in Kalash's mind, creating an instant bond between the two. He knew at that moment that their destinies were intertwined and that they would stand by each other through whatever challenges lay ahead.

Back in Raigad, Annaji Datto was not idle. He kept himself well-informed of Sambhaji's every move, aware that a man named Kalash had joined his side. The growing strength of Sambhaji, along with the people's increasing affection for him, troubled Annaji deeply. He knew he had to act before Sambhaji's influence became too powerful to contain. Soyrabai, too, was anxious.

"That poet has joined him," laughed Soyrabai wickedly, "A

person close to the Mughals is now roaming around with Sambhaji."

Annaji did not understand how to respond. He remained silent.

"Annaji," Soyrabai remarked, "What is history to you?"

"History is shaped by the narratives we create and the stories we tell," Annaji replied.

"Then write something that makes history," Soyrabai looked at him with a spark in her eyes, paused and stressed, "In our favour"

Annaji's smile, tinged with malice, said, "I shall ensure that the history we write serves our purposes."

"Certainly!" Soyrabai responded, "A poet close to Mughals joins the Prince, spoils him... You know what to write, right?"

Meanwhile, in Shringarpur, oblivious to the schemes being plotted against him in Raigad, Sambhaji was focused on rewriting history in his own way. He was determined to leave a legacy that would outshine the deceitful plots of his enemies.

DAYS AND nights merged into one as Shivrai and his loyal men traversed barren lands, dense forests, rugged hills, and crossed over two dozen rivers and lakes. Their journey was relentless, marked by brief halts for rest, where they would set up camp along the riverbanks. The determination in Shivrai's heart was fuelled by the strength and support he had garnered from Abdul Hassan, who had provided both military and financial aid. This newfound strength had Shivrai's eyes set firmly on a new prize: the formidable Gingee Fort.

Within the camps, strategies were meticulously crafted. The best minds of Shivrai's army: Senapati Hambirrao Mohite, Yesaji Kank, Dhanaji, Santaji, Pralhad Niraji, and a few others gathered around Shivrai, forming the core of his advisory council. Shivrai's exceptional foresight and strategic brilliance set him apart from his contemporaries. Unlike many rulers of his time, he studied intensely to understand the political landscape and the background of his enemies before charting a course of action. He knew that the Adilshahi Sultanate was in the throes of political turmoil following the death of Ali Adil Shah. The young heir, Sikander, was too inexperienced to rule effectively, leaving the wazir, Nasir Khan, to make critical decisions in governance and warfare.

However, Nasir Khan's position was precarious. His bitter enemy, Bahlul Khan, who had murdered Nasir's brother, harboured ambitions of seizing control of the Gingee Fort. Complicating matters further, Sher Khan Lodhi, the commander-in-charge of the impregnable Vellore Fort located a few kos northwest of Gingee, maintained amicable relations with Bahlul Khan. This alliance left Nasir Khan vulnerable, with no hope of receiving support from Lodhi in the event of an attack. The Adilshahi forces were divided, and the common people were caught in a web of uncertainty, unsure of whom to support. Shivrai recognized this disarray as an opportunity ripe for exploitation.

"We march on Gingee Fort with full force," Shivrai declared to his commanders, his voice resonating with unwavering confidence. "Nasir Khan will receive no support from Lodhi. Lodhi's desire to see Nasir Khan fall will make him hesitate to come to his aid. Nasir Khan is fully aware of this. Faced with the overwhelming strength of our forces, he will have no choice but to either perish or flee."

True to Shivrai's prediction, the sight of the massive Maratha army advancing towards Gingee Fort left Nasir Khan with no viable option. Overwhelmed and outmanoeuvred, he chose to open the gates of the fort and escape, leaving the fort to fall easily into the hands of the Marathas. The saffron flag of the Marathas soon fluttered proudly atop Gingee Fort, symbolizing yet another victory for Shivrai and his forces.

With Gingee Fort secured, Shivrai left a contingent of his men behind to fortify and rebuild its defences, ensuring it would remain a stronghold for the Marathas. The rest of the army, led by Shivrai and his trusted subhedars, now set their sights on Vellore Fort, situated a few kos to the northwest.

Sher Khan Lodhi, standing atop the fort's walls, watched with mounting dread as the Maratha forces approached. Thousands of cavalrymen, led by the formidable Hambirrao Mohite, advanced with a determined pace that made the ground beneath Lodhi's feet seem to tremble. Panic seized him as he barked orders to his subordinates, "Close the gates!"

Once inside the court, Lodhi anxiously inquired about any news from Bahlul Khan, his supposed ally. The response from his minister, who stood with his head bowed in silence, spoke volumes. Bahlul Khan, it seemed, had chosen not to come to Lodhi's aid.

'Why has Bahlul Khan abandoned me now, of all times?' Lodhi's thoughts raced. He had always maintained a close and friendly relationship with Bahlul Khan. Now, when he needed his friend the most, Bahlul Khan was nowhere to be found.

The cries of 'Har Har Mahadev' echoed in the distance as the first wave of Lodhi's scouting forces fell before the Maratha onslaught outside the fort's walls. In desperation, the Adilshahi archers unleashed a volley of arrows, but they proved futile, unable to reach the Maratha warriors who were just out of range. The Marathas soon encircled Vellore Fort, effectively cutting off all food and monetary supplies. Shivrai's strategy was clear: starve the enemy into submission. Without provisions, it was only a matter of time before the defenders would be forced to surrender.

Inside the fort, Lodhi's hopes of rescue dwindled with each passing day. His morale plummeted further when news arrived of Bahlul Khan's death. The realization that he was now entirely alone sent a cold chill down Lodhi's spine. *'Could the Marathas have been responsible for Bahlul Khan's death?'* Lodhi pondered in despair.

As the days wore on, the fort's grain stores dwindled to dangerously low levels. Lodhi, now faced with the grim reality of the situation, made the painful decision to flee. He bid a tearful farewell to his wife and daughters, embracing them one last time. "If I flee and stay alive today, there's a chance I might return tomorrow. But if I remain here, I will surely die," he told his distraught wife.

"What will happen to us?" his wife asked, her voice trembling with fear.

"Shivrai will not harm you. He has never posed a threat to women and children," Lodhi reassured her before making his escape, accompanied by his personal bodyguards.

As the gates of Vellore Fort swung open, the Marathas surged in, launching a fierce assault. Lodhi and his guards attempted to slip away through a secret route, but Shivrai had anticipated this move. Unwilling to let Lodhi escape and pose a future threat to the Marathas, Shivrai led a small contingent in pursuit.

As the chase unfolded, Shivrai's men closed in on Lodhi's bodyguards, swiftly cutting them down. Lodhi, now desperate, turned his horse to face his pursuers, but it was too late. The cries of 'Har Har Mahadev' echoed from within Vellore Fort as the Maratha flag was hoisted, signalling the fort's capture. Lodhi, realizing the futility of resistance, dismounted his horse in surrender.

Shivrai, seated on his horse, gazed at Lodhi with piercing eyes, the intensity of his stare leaving no doubt about the outcome. Lodhi, now surrounded by Shivrai's men, knew he had no choice but to surrender. Defeated and broken, he lowered his head in submission.

"Capture him," Shivrai ordered, his voice firm and resolute.

THE MAINTENANCE work on the forts had begun in earnest. Saffron flags fluttered high above, and the walls echoed with the resounding chants of 'Har Har Mahadev'. Shivrai's southern expedition had been a resounding success, dealing yet another blow to Aurangzeb's ambitions. The Mughal emperor in the north was now more troubled than ever, particularly by the ongoing difficulties in his Marwar campaign. Aurangzeb had sent multiple letters to his son Akbar, inquiring about the situation, but the responses were far from satisfactory. Akbar repeatedly reported that his forces were struggling against Durgadas's men in the rugged terrains of Marwar, attributing their failure to the Mughals' inexperience with mountainous warfare, as they were more accustomed to fighting on the plains. However, this was only part of the truth. Unbeknownst to Aurangzeb, Durgadas had forged alliances with the Sisodia clans, further complicating the Mughal's campaign.

In the Maratha-occupied Adilshahi territories, Shivrai was fully aware of Aurangzeb's renewed interest in the Deccan. He had received intelligence that Diler Khan had been appointed as the Mughal Subhedar on the north-eastern borders of the Deccan, Shivrai knew he had to be ready for whatever was to come. He was confident that his southern expedition would prove advantageous if the Mughals attempted to invade the Deccan again. Strengthening the forts of Gingee and Vellore provided the Marathas with a strategic fallback position, essentially a second capital, in case they needed to retreat. A fortified southern stronghold would also force the Mughal army to split, making it easier for the Marathas to launch counterattacks.

Additionally, the Marathas now had access to the Chondamandalam coast, opening new trade opportunities with the Malay (Currently Malaysia) and Thai provinces. Their influence in the Bay of Bengal was growing, and with a robust naval base in the Konkan as well, even the British were beginning to worry. They feared that if Shivrai's maritime power in the Arabian sea increased, it could threaten their trading operations and potentially lead to Maratha ships sailing as far as British territories in Europe. Shivrai knew he was on the right path, bolstering both his land and sea power.

As the restoration work on the forts concluded, Shivrai made his way to the temple he had constructed on the fort to seek the blessings of the Goddess. Just as he was about to enter the temple, he noticed Bahirji Naik, the Maratha spy, who was disguised as a priest.

"Yes, Bahirji?" Shivrai said, recognizing him immediately.

"Raje…" Bahirji responded, still in awe of his king's uncanny ability to identify him every time.

"There is bad news," Bahirji continued, his tone grave.

"What is it?" Shivrai asked, giving him his full attention.

"We may have made a mistake by befriending Hassan," Bahirji replied. "The man has been involved in slavery, prostitution, and the slave trade with various provinces in Malay."

This revelation was nothing short of a shock to Shivrai. Realizing the urgency of the situation, he responded decisively, his words both a statement and a warning, "We sever all ties with Hassan. There is no treaty anymore. If he continues with this practice, the Marathas shall march on his fort. The Chondamandalam coast is ours, and we decide what is to be traded."

Shivrai had now become more fearless and invincible than ever before.

Meanwhile, back in Shringarpur, Sambhaji was blessed with a baby girl. He received a letter from Shivrai, which he hadn't expected. Despite being occupied with the warfront, his Abasaheb had not forgotten to congratulate him on the new addition to his family. Sambhaji often found his father to be something of an enigma. Shivrai had sent him to Shringarpur, keeping him away from the warfront, seemingly indifferent to how he would fare there. Shivrai had never inquired about him or Yesu, but now he had written this letter, congratulating Sambhaji on the birth of his child. This gesture made Sambhaji realize that his father hadn't completely forgotten about him. He was still on Shivrai's mind. That day, Sambhaji's joy knew no bounds.

Just as Sambhaji was about to fold the letter and tuck it safely away in one of his lockers, he remembered something else that was mentioned in the letter, something he had overlooked in his excitement and happiness. Shivrai had asked him to meet a priest at Sajjangarh.

THE NEXT day, Sambhaji set out for Sajjangarh, a fort near Satara. As he travelled, a whirlwind of questions and suppositions swirled in his mind. *'Why had Abasaheb asked him to meet the saint?'* The thought nagged at him persistently. *'Was this some kind of political strategy?'* The possibility unsettled him. Sambhaji had hoped for direct, face-to-face conversations with his father, devoid of riddles and veiled messages. The prospect of being entangled in yet another puzzle was far from appealing.

After days and nights of relentless travel, passing through rugged terrains and challenging landscapes, Sambhaji finally arrived at the foothills of Sajjangarh. The exhaustion of the journey was momentarily forgotten as excitement began to build within him. Meeting the saint had always been a source of profound inspiration for Sambhaji. Throughout his life, he had admired and revered Swamiji, whose influence had profoundly shaped his character and beliefs. From his early childhood, his Abasaheb had taken him to Sajjangarh to seek the blessings and guidance of Swamiji. On numerous occasions, Swamiji's wisdom had illuminated the path for both Shivrai and Sambhaji, especially when they faced the most daunting challenges.

Shivrai, in his gratitude for Swamiji's guidance, had even renamed the fort from Parali to Sajjangarh, meaning 'Sajjan,' as a tribute to the saint. This act reflected not only his reverence but also his recognition of the spiritual strength Swamiji brought to their lives.

As the sun dipped toward the horizon, casting long shadows across the landscape, Sambhaji ascended the massive steps of the fort with a sense of purpose. Reaching the courtyard at the summit, he made his way to the Lord Ram temple, a place where hundreds of Swamiji's disciples gathered daily to offer their worship and perform their duties as an act of 'sewa' to Swamiji.

However, as Sambhaji's eyes scanned the area, searching for Swamiji, he was disheartened not to find him. His anticipation began to wane when he crossed paths with Kalyan Swami, Swamiji's senior-most disciple. Kalyan Swami informed Sambhaji that Swamiji had embarked on a holy pilgrimage to worship at a distant temple. The news struck Sambhaji like a blow, and the excitement that had fuelled his journey dissipated in an instant.

The journey, which had taken days and nights, now seemed futile. As he walked, he couldn't help but feel a sense of loneliness, a growing distance from the world he had once been so intimately connected with.

Pausing momentarily, Sambhaji gazed up at the night sky, the stars twinkling against the dark canvas, and wondered what destiny had in store for him. His thoughts were interrupted when, out of the shadows, someone hastily dropped a letter at his feet and disappeared into the bushes before Sambhaji could react. He instinctively pursued the mysterious figure but soon realized the person had vanished without a trace. Returning to where the letter had fallen, Sambhaji picked it up and began to read.

The letter was from Diler Khan, the Mughal mansabdar stationed in the northeast of Deccan:

I am so proud of your valour, Sambha. You have everything within you to be an able Mughal mansabdar. The Marathas do not respect your valour, and with them, you can never conquer the nation. Your place is here. We know how a real fighter must be treated.

Perplexed, Sambhaji reread the letter, his mind racing with thoughts. Sambhaji recalled his earlier days, when Kalash had once mentioned that Shahzada Muazzam, Aurangzeb's other son, wanted to rebel against his father. Diler Khan, the Mughal mansabdar, directly reported to Muazzam. This meant that Muazzam had probably instructed Diler Khan to write this letter. *Was this letter a sign? Was it somehow connected to Swamiji's guidance or his father's intentions? And how had Diler Khan known of his presence at Sajjangarh?*

Sambhaji felt as if he were being pulled in multiple directions, caught between his loyalty to the Maratha dynasty and the tantalizing prospect of aligning with Diler Khan and Shahzada Muazzam against Aurangzeb. In both scenarios, Aurangzeb remained the common enemy, but the path to victory was far from clear. Sambhaji knew that it was far more important to put an end to Aurangzeb's tyranny, and he would go to any extent to achieve his goal, even if it meant befriending an enemy for another enemy for a while.

Sambhaji's instincts told him that it was his father who wanted him to join Diler Khan, and that Swamiji was probably the medium. He also reminded himself of the Purandar Treaty, in which his Abasaheb had himself named him a Mughal mansabdar.

'Was Abasaheb aware of Muazzam's disliking towards his father Aurangzeb?' Sambhaji wondered.

In two minds, Sambhaji had to decide. He decided to trust his instincts, for they had never led him astray. The next day, Sambhaji prepared to join hands with Diler Khan, stepping into a future that was as uncertain as it was promising.

8.

"*MERA SHER ka Baccha*," Diler Khan exclaimed, throwing open his arms in welcome as Sambhaji approached him. After days of arduous travel across the Deccan's rugged terrains on his Kathiyawadi horse and enduring countless nights under the starlit sky, Sambhaji had finally reached his destination. The journey had been relentless, but his determination to ally with an old adversary to challenge a familiar foe had spurred him on. Shringarpur and Raigad remained blissfully unaware of Sambhaji's new allegiance, but it was only a matter of time before the news would spread. The ramifications of this alliance weighed heavily on him. His instinctive decision to side with the Mughals could be seen as treachery by the Marathas, and he was all too aware of how swiftly Raigad could brand him a traitor, altering his legacy for eternity. Yet, beneath his apprehension, Sambhaji harboured a firm belief that his choice was justified.

His father, Shivrai, had once navigated the complexities of political alliances by making Sambhaji a Mughal mansabdar during the Purandar Treaty when he was merely nine. Shivrai had intentionally stayed clear of this role, choosing instead to position his son as a mansabdar to ensure the Maratha kingdom's safety. This astute political manoeuvre had safeguarded the Marathas from Aurangzeb's ambitions, and now Sambhaji hoped his own decision could similarly reshape the Maratha fortunes. Though he was indifferent to the slander that might follow him from Raigad, his primary concern was how his father would perceive his actions. More than anything, Sambhaji wanted to prove his worth as a warrior on the battlefield rather than merely being a figurehead managing revenues and speaking to peasants.

As he prepared to meet Diler Khan, Sambhaji repeatedly pondered his decision. After freshening up in a luxurious Mughal tent, he approached Diler Khan with a sense of resolve and dignity.

"Mera Sher ka Baccha," Diler Khan greeted him warmly, his arms open in a gesture of affectionate embrace. Sambhaji, his face beaming with a genuine smile, reciprocated the embrace, feeling a mixture of relief and apprehension. He then performed the traditional Maratha gesture of joining his hands together before Diler Khan, a symbolic nod to his heritage and warrior spirit. Sambhaji and Diler Khan had first crossed paths when Sambhaji was made a Mughal mansabdar at the tender age of eleven. Diler Khan had taken a liking to the young prince, endearingly referring to him as the "lion's cub, a Chhava!" Time had etched lines of age upon Diler Khan's face, but his warm demeanour remained unchanged.

Diler Khan spared no effort to make Sambhaji feel at ease. The lavish hospitality included an array of delectable dishes, grand tents adorned with vibrant decorations, and an ambience of grandeur. Diler Khan was elated at the prospect of having such a formidable warrior by his side. He saw in Sambhaji the potential to unlock countless opportunities and drive a wedge between the Marathas. A sly grin played on Diler Khan's lips as he envisioned conquering the entire Deccan and earning Aurangzeb's favour.

Amidst the opulent setting, Diler Khan served Sambhaji another round of aromatic biryani, eager to please his esteemed guest. Sambhaji, while savouring the dish, remained guarded. His true intentions diverged from the apparent goodwill. He was not merely there to dine and be honoured; he sought an audience with Shahzada Muazzam through Diler Khan. Sambhaji's motives were layered, driven by his own strategic objectives.

After the sumptuous feast, Diler Khan made a grand announcement in his courtroom. "Sambhaji shall now be the mansabdar of seven thousand horses and seven thousand dhats," he proclaimed.

The crowd erupted in cheers, their joy resonating through the grand hall.

"And as a token of our esteem," Diler Khan continued with a flourish, "Sambhaji shall be presented with a war elephant adorned with a silver howdah."

The declaration was met with jubilant applause once again. It marked a new chapter for Sambhaji—one whose ultimate correctness or error could only be judged by the passage of time. As the celebrations continued around him, Sambhaji remained contemplative, knowing that his future actions would be pivotal in determining whether this bold move would fortify or fracture his legacy. Right or wrong, only time could tell!

RAIGAD WAS alive with celebration. The fort was aglow with festive lights, and the air was thick with the scent of flowers and excitement. Soyrabai's face was radiant with joy as her son, Rajaram, was about to marry Janaki, the daughter of the late Prataprao Gujjar, Shivrai's esteemed Sarnobat. The entire fort was adorned with vibrant decorations, and priests were summoned to officiate the grand occasion. Invitations had been sent out to kings, subhedars, and mansabdars from neighbouring regions, requesting their presence to bless the young prince on his special day. Drums resounded through the air, and shehnais played melodiously as the procession commenced. Hundreds of people had gathered, bearing gifts and well-wishes. Rajaram, still innocent and wide-eyed, marvelled at the spectacle. The mangalashtakas were chanted as Rajaram and Janaki exchanged vows, their union marked by solemn rituals and joyful festivities.

"Kalash ji," said Yesu, consumed with worry about her husband, "Is it true that Yuvraj has joined the Mughals?"

"I do not know what made him do so, but certainly yes," replied Kavi Kalash.

This revelation was a severe blow to Yesu, who found it difficult to process.

"Even if it is true, it must be related to some political strategy," Yesu spoke, "Isn't it?" She kept looking at Kavi Kalash with desperation.

Kavi Kalash, who was grappling with the reasons behind Sambhaji's decision, had no answers. He could understand the mental torment that Yesubai was going through, but could not come up with a solid answer that would give a concrete answer to her worries.

Yesu was restless. She walked to and fro in the verandah before turning back to Kavi Kalash with another worry.

"Could it be another lie spread to tarnish Yuvraj's reputation?"

"I don't know how to put this, but Yuvraj has definitely joined the Mughals. Why, when, and whether by choice, strategically or forcibly, we don't know. This time only could tell."

"It definitely has to be some strategy," she stressed before returning to the privacy of her room, distressed. She sat before a flickering lamp; her thoughts clouded with anxiety. She wondered why her Yuvraj had not communicated this significant shift directly.

Her concern was compounded by the treachery often associated with the Mughals and the unreliable nature of those at Raigad. She feared for Sambhaji's safety from all sides.

Back in Konkan, Shivrai was preoccupied with matters of the Maratha naval expansion. He was at the Khanderi Sea Fort, inspecting its progress. The resources from his successful southern campaign were being invested in fortifying the structure. The Maratha naval presence in the Arabian sea was growing stronger under Shivrai's leadership.

"Raje," Daulat Khan, the Maratha naval Sarnobat, reported, "The English are threatening us. They've warned us to halt the fort's construction."

"So what?" Shivrai replied with defiance, "Are we to cower because an invader dares to disrupt our efforts to fortify our own land? Increase the work, double the investment. I want this fort to be impregnable."

Daulat Khan understood Shivrai's intentions. The Khanderi Fort, strategically positioned between Goa and Bombay, was a critical asset. It posed a threat not only to the Siddhis from Janjira but also to the Portuguese from Goa and the British from Bombay. The Siddhis, who frequently traded between Goa and Bombay and extended their influence to Surat port in Gujarat, were disrupted by Shivrai's control over key territories. The Adilshahis' trade routes to Malay (now Malaysia) were similarly affected. The presence of the Khanderi Fort added significant pressure on the British, Portuguese, and Siddhis, who, allied with the Mughals, were increasingly antagonistic.

"And Maharaj…" Daulat Khan stammered.

"What is it, Sarnobat?" asked Shivrai.

"Yuvraj has joined hands with Diler Khan," Daulat Khan found his words, gathering confidence to speak.

"Jagdamb," Shivrai remarked.

Shivrai wondered why Shambhu had allied with the enemies.

"What if they all unite against us?" Shivrai had to be careful.

Despite his concerns, Shivrai held on to a belief that Sambhaji might have a strategic plan. He knew his upbringing couldn't go wrong. He knew his Shambhu well. He knew he wouldn't align with the enemies for the Maratha throne.

Shrugging off thoughts, Shivrai knew he had to focus on what lay in front of him.

"Strengthen the fort. It is our strongest asset in this region," Shivrai instructed Daulat Khan, his voice strained by bouts of coughing. His cough had been persistent, likely a remnant of the year-and-a-half-long campaign far from home.

"Raje, you should rest," Daulat Khan urged, noticing the distress in Shivrai's voice.

THE NIGHT of Amavasya, devoid of moonlight, enveloped the land in darkness as the Mughal forces descended upon Bhupalgad Fort to the south-east of Khanapur district. This stronghold, held by the Marathas, was conquered by Shivrai after defeating the Adilshahi. Due to its elevated location and strong fortifications, Bhupalgad Fort served as a strong military defence, helping in surveillance and monitoring the enemy movements. Leading the charge was Diler Khan, with Sambhaji, his most prized asset, following closely behind. Sambhaji, now a Mughal mansabdar in command of seven thousand horses, knew precisely what he was getting into. The weight of his actions pressed heavily on his conscience, but he was resolute—this was something that needed to be done.

Ever since Diler Khan had arrived at the northern borders of the Deccan, the locals had been gripped by fear. The mere mention of his name sent shivers down spines, leading hundreds to abandon their homes, fleeing with whatever goods, gold, and revenue they could carry. As they neared the outskirts of Bhupalgad Fort in Sangli province, Diler Khan's eyes gleamed with anticipation. The moment to strike had arrived. To him, the unguarded wealth within the fort was not just plunder—it was the rightful spoils of his impending victory.

Within the fort, Firangoji Narsala, the fort commander, was already preparing for a counterattack. Narsala, a seasoned warrior, had much to prove. Previously criticized for surrendering a fort in Chakan province during Shaista Khan's attack, this was his opportunity to redeem himself. Bhupalgad stood firm atop a hilly plain, its strategic importance underscored by a secret route to the summit known only to a select few.

As Narsala observed the approaching Mughal forces, he knew that his men were not even half of the Mughals, but one thing he was confident about was his men's valour. He had no time to prepare or wait for ammunition or reinforcements. The only advantage that Narsala and his men had was the height of the fort. It put them in the perfect position to take a shot at their approaching enemies.

"We are few in number, but enough of mettle in our steels," ordered Narsala as he strode through the wall of the fort. Narsala knew the fort inside out. The main darwaza of the fort led to a small passage, which widened into steps leading to the top of the fort.

"The main darwaza is vulnerable, and the Mughals shall easily be able to blast it with the cannons. Our only defence and chance of survival is in the small passage that follows. A small unit shall battle out the approaching soldiers and stop them in the passage. At the same time, the archers shall have to precisely aim at the enemy heads from the top of the fort," declared Narsala, looked at his men and continued, "God forbid, if we fail to stop them at the passage, it shall be an easy win for them in the open."

The Mughals, too, did not waste time reacting. The cannons were blasted at the Mahadarwaza. Narsala could hear the loud blasts.

"The Mahadarwaza shall fall any moment," said one of the soldiers.

Narsala immediately ordered his first wave of warriors to take a stance and prepare to counter the invaders.

It didn't take much effort for the Mughals to blast the Mahadarwaza. The Maratha war cries of 'Har Har Mahadev!' pierced the moonless night, echoing through the darkness as swords clashed immediately after. Heads were chopped and abdomens pierced with enough precision that the Mughal soldiers fell to their blades. Despite the initial success, Narsala's satisfaction would definitely remain short-lived.

Sambhaji had visited the fort when he was young and had studied the vulnerabilities. He knew exactly how the Mughals could fail in the narrow passage with heavy armour and elephants. The Marathas were in a strategically favourable position.

Without revealing the secret, Sambhaji requested, "Let me lead the soldiers." This was music to Diler Khan's ears. He wanted the Marathas crushed by their own prince, and immediately agreed, allowing Sambhaji to lead the charge. Mounted on his Kathiyawadi horse, Sambhaji was ready to lead, his grip tightening on the reins. A weight settled in his chest—these were his own people, his fellow Marathas, and yet, fate had placed him on the other side, leading the enemy toward them. He wished he had not been put into this position.

With more forces, the Mughal soldiers began ascending the fort, and Narsala was forced to send another unit to launch a fierce counterattack. The Marathas descended the fort with full charge and loud battle cries. There had to be no margin for error. Narsala took charge into his control. With his dandpatta, he descended upon the Mughals, cutting through the throats of hundreds, slashing them and tearing them apart. The clash was brutal—swords slashed, and arrows flew with deadly precision. It seemed for a moment that the Marathas might prevail, until something unexpected happened.

Narsala couldn't believe his eyes. So couldn't his men. Through the dust and chaos, the silhouette of a lone horseman emerged, galloping swiftly to the top. It was Sambhaji. The entire force was taken aback.

'Was this a dream?' Narsala wondered.

'Or a Yuvraj's lookalike?'

But soon he noticed, it wasn't just him but his entire unit that had witnessed the harsh reality. Narsala, stunned, had no choice but to command his men to halt. The sight of Yuvraj leading the Mughals left the Maratha soldiers in shock. Some were frozen in disbelief, others were gripped by fear, and many were simply clueless about what was unfolding before them. One by one, the Maratha warriors dropped their weapons, unable to comprehend the betrayal they were witnessing. With no further resistance, the Mughals reached the summit and quickly captured the fort. Sambhaji too wanted the Marathas to surrender and did not intend to attack or kill them.

Within an hour, Bhupalgad was under Mughal control. Every corner of the fort was seized, and the once-proud Maratha stronghold now lay in the hands of the enemy. Diler Khan, overjoyed, rushed to embrace Sambhaji. "Mera Sher ka baccha! You have done a great job," he exclaimed, his eyes brimming with pride.

But beneath his stoic facade, Sambhaji was drowning in guilt. This was not who he was, not the man he had been raised to be. His people, his fort—now overshadowed by the Mughal banner—felt like a wound carved deep into his soul. His eyes flickered toward Narsala, bound and restrained by Mughal soldiers. The old warrior's gaze bore into him, searching for answers Sambhaji could not bring himself to give.

The news of Sambhaji's role in the Mughal victory spread rapidly, reaching even Shivrai in Konkan. Upon hearing it, Shivrai closed his eyes and muttered, "Jagdamb!" He prayed fervently, "May the Goddess show him the right path." Joining the Mughals necessarily did not mean leading the attack against his own men.

Meanwhile, Shahzada Muazzam, also known as Shah Alam, the subhedar of Mughal-occupied Deccan, was informed of the success at Bhupalgad. Elated, he praised Diler Khan for his skillful management of the situation and for securing Sambhaji's allegiance. The looting of Bhupalgad meant a substantial increase in revenue, and the Marathas were now on the back foot, and with Sambhaji in their ranks, he was convinced that Shivrai might be forced to surrender, if not for defeat, then for the sake of his son's life.

Eager to solidify this new alliance, Muazzam made his way to Bhupalgad to congratulate Sambhaji in person. "Congratulations on the victory, Sambhaji," he said, embracing him warmly. This was the moment Sambhaji had been waiting for—not for the accolades, which he scarcely heard, but for the opportunity to speak with Muazzam, a man not easily reached.

During the celebratory lunch, Diler Khan continued to heap praise upon Sambhaji's bravery, with Muazzam listening intently. Seizing the moment, Sambhaji said, "With your support, and Shah Alam's backing, we can conquer the entire Deccan."

These words were music to Muazzam's ears. He imagined himself as the conqueror of the Deccan, a feat his father, Aurangzeb, had long dreamt of but never achieved. The thought of accomplishing what his father could not was intoxicating.

"Is that truly possible?" Muazzam asked, his voice tinged with anticipation.

"Without a doubt," Sambhaji replied confidently. "I know the secrets of the Maratha kingdom. With me on your side, there's nothing to worry about, except…" Sambhaji paused, deliberately leaving his sentence unfinished.

"Except what?" Muazzam's curiosity was piqued.

"Even if you do conquer the entire Deccan," Sambhaji continued, "You may never receive the credit you deserve."

Muazzam frowned, "What do you mean?"

"The Badshah in Delhi," Sambhaji explained, "will descend upon Aurangabad to claim your victory as his own. Conquering the Deccan has been his lifelong dream. He will ensure that all glory goes to him, declaring himself the Alamgir—the ruler of the entire nation."

Sambhaji's words resonated with Muazzam, who now began to see the truth in them. Sambhaji pressed further, "If I support you in conquering the Deccan, and you will succeed, then I believe you deserve the credit and the title of Badshah."

Muazzam's expression shifted from joy to contemplation. He glanced at Diler Khan, who seemed encouraging, his own ambitions quietly simmering. Diler Khan knew that if Muazzam became the Badshah, he could rise to the position of the chief of the Deccan, a prospect that excited him greatly.

"I do want to conquer the nation," Muazzam admitted, the greed in his eyes unmistakable.

"But…" Sambhaji hesitated, then added, "I've heard that Akbar has allied with Durgadas and his men to fight against the Badshah. He could be your biggest rival."

Muazzam's hatred for his step-brother, Akbar, was well known. The very thought of Akbar challenging his ambitions ignited a fire within him.

"I'll cut off his head," Muazzam snarled, his voice dripping with venom.

This was precisely the outcome Sambhaji had hoped for. The Mughals were now splintered into three factions: Aurangzeb in Agra, Akbar in Jodhpur, and Muazzam in Mughal-occupied Deccan. The once formidable army was now divided, as were the revenues. The empire, once united, was now a battlefield of competing ambitions—a son eager to betray his father, a brother driven to kill his brother, and a father willing to commit any atrocity to retain his power, just as Aurangzeb had done by executing his elder brother and imprisoning his father, Shah Jahan, in a bid for the throne.

This was the beginning of the end for the Mughal Empire, and Sambhaji knew it. A wicked smile played on his lips as he realized how deeply he had sown the seeds of their downfall.

BACK IN Raigad, things were not normal. Annaji Datto's mind, as usual, was a cauldron of wicked schemes, his tongue itching to spill the venom he had been harbouring. His walk was filled with desperation, his urgency evident as he approached Soyrabai's chamber. Even before he spoke, she sensed his presence. One look at his taut expression told her he had come with news of great importance, or so he believed.

"What is it, Annaji?" Soyrabai asked, her tone measured and calm, though she knew well that Annaji had something to share that would be nothing but an important gossip.

"Have you heard the news?" Annaji asked, his eyes gleaming with a mix of excitement and malice.

"What news?" Soyrabai responded with disinterest, assuming it was another one of his tedious updates. However, Annaji's following words caught her completely off guard.

"Yuvraj has joined the Mughals against us," Annaji announced, his words landing like a blow.

"What!" Soyrabai gasped, springing up from her couch, her face a mixture of disbelief and shock.

"Yes, you heard it right," Annaji confirmed, his lips curling into a sly grin. His pleasure in delivering this news is evident.

"What makes you so happy about this?" Soyrabai demanded, her eyes narrowing at the sight of his glee.

"You don't see it, Rani Sarkar," he pressed. "The Yuvraj has betrayed us. Bhupalgad is in flames, a few of our men killed, our coffers plundered. The people are devastated, their faith shattered. This treachery changes everything—Rajaram is now the rightful heir in the eyes of the Chhatrapati and the people. Don't you see? The path is clear."

His words settled deep in Soyrabai's mind. The weight of what he was suggesting was immense, but so was the opportunity it presented. A power shift was within reach, and she could already envision the future taking shape.

"Annaji," she ordered, her voice sharp and decisive, "Call the scribes. Make sure history remembers Sambhaji as a traitor. Write down how Sambhaji killed our men, fought against his own Abasaheb, disrespected his ideologies and put an end to his dream of Swaraj. This needs to spread far and wide. I want every person talking ill of Sambhaji. It must become the talk of every village, every fort."

As Annaji left, Soyrabai felt a wave of exhilaration. She had to discuss this with Chhatrapati Shivaji Maharaj. She needed to understand his views on the matter and prepare for what lay ahead. She knew it wouldn't be long before the Chhatrapati would return to Raigad, and she waited impatiently for her husband's arrival.

Upon his return, however, Shivrai did not head directly to her chambers. Instead, he visited Putalabai's residence first, much to Soyrabai's frustration. The fort of Raigad was alive with celebration, its people rejoicing in Shivrai's successful return from his military campaign. But despite the victorious homecoming, a shadow loomed over Shivrai's heart. His face was thinner, his complexion pale, and his demeanour sombre. He was consumed by thoughts of his son, Sambhaji, and the choices he had made.

When he finally visited Soyrabai, she wasted no time. She rushed to him; her face streaked with tears.

"How could Yuvraj betray our men like this? He is a traitor!" she cried out, her voice filled with feigned anguish.

"Calm down, Soyra," consoled Shivrai and made her sit.

"I cannot see our child kill our own men; capture the forts you won with your sweat and blood. How can I see our Swaraj get tarnished in the hands of the Mughals?" Soyrabai complained.

Shivrai was all ears to her. Recalling the battles at Bhupalgad and the crushing defeat, his heart ached. He knew something was wrong.

Shivrai wondered how a mother could label her son a traitor so quickly, without first understanding his reasons, but soon shrugged off his thoughts, believing it might have been the queen within her speaking.

Putalabai, on the other hand, had not uttered a single complaint all this while. She had maintained her faith in Sambhaji.

Without comparing the contrasting behaviours of Soyrabai and Putalabai, Shivrai decided to visit his court. There, he found Firangoji Narsala, the fort commander of Bhupalgad, weeping inconsolably.

"Raje…" Narsala sobbed, "The Gods have forsaken us. Our men were slaughtered, and our fort lies in ruins. Not only has our fort fallen, but the Maratha pride has been betrayed as well. We have lost everything."

Sensing that Narsala wished to speak privately, Shivrai signalled and asked the others in the courtroom to leave. Narsala recounted the grim events that had unfolded at Bhupalgad, describing how Diler Khan had manipulated Sambhaji against them. He explained how, under Sambhaji's lead, the Maratha soldiers had found themselves cornered, forced to lay down their arms rather than fight against the Yuvraj they had once sworn to protect.

"This is intolerable," Shivrai remarked, his voice steady but his eyes aflame with emotion.

"Although…" Narsala hesitated, swallowing hard before continuing, "I managed to escape because of Yuvraj. He asked me to deliver a message to you."

Shivrai's eyes widened slightly, a flicker of hope breaking through his anger. His mind was racing with conflicting thoughts.

"Today is a day of dishonour," he announced, his voice ringing out across the hall. "I knew that Shambhu had shaken hands with Diler Khan, but all this while, I had believed it could have been a strategic alliance that Shambhu best knew; probably it still could be a strategic alliance. I had not expected Shambhu to attack us. Bhupalgad is lost not because the Mughals won but because our men dropped their arms, not wanting to hurt Shambhu. Now, I am compelled to declare that, though Shambhu is my son, no mercy should be shown to him. For us, the cause of Swaraj stands above all, even above blood ties. Anyone who aligns with the Mughals shall not be spared. Do not hesitate to wield your swords for the sake of Swaraj," Shivrai steadied himself, his voice strained yet firm. A bout of coughing interrupted him, a stark reminder of the toll the years had taken. But his resolve remained unshaken. With a weary breath, he declared, "The Mughals must learn their lesson."

THE LOUD cries of the Maratha men, mercilessly being slashed to death by the Mughals, echoed incessantly in Sambhaji's mind. Even though he had managed to create a wave of political instability among the Mughal ranks, Sambhaji couldn't help but lament the heavy cost of this gamble. Only a few days earlier, Diler Khan had ordered the imprisonment of all Maratha warriors captured at the fort, condemning them to the dungeons, and the immediate execution of the fort commander, Narsala. In a crucial moment, Sambhaji had deftly intervened.

"We shouldn't be killing this fort commander," Sambhaji had whispered urgently into Diler Khan's ear, his voice steady but his heart racing.

"Why is it so? He is our enemy, and a commander as capable as him must be executed to weaken our adversary," Diler Khan replied, his eyes narrowing with suspicion.

"I understand your reasoning," Sambhaji responded carefully, locking eyes with Diler Khan. "But what is far more strategic is to demonstrate our power to the Marathas. Moreover, they must know that I have joined the Mughals. Most of them will drop their weapons, making it even easier for us to claim victory. Who else would take this news to Shivrai?"

Sambhaji's words caused Diler Khan to pause and think. He cast a critical glance at Narsala, who had been forcibly made to kneel and was restrained by two soldiers. His hands and feet were bound tightly, and a blazing sword, gleaming in the bright sunlight, hovered mere inches from his neck. The soldier holding the sword was poised to execute him the moment Diler Khan gave the signal. Narsala's eyes, burning with rage and defiance, darted from Diler Khan to Sambhaji, wondering what the young prince had whispered into the Mughal's ear.

"Let him go," Diler Khan's voice rang out, clear and unexpected. Narsala released a sigh of relief, his shoulders slackening as tension left his body.

Sambhaji's plan had succeeded. If it hadn't, Narsala would have met his end that very day. Ensuring no one saw them, Sambhaji covertly met Narsala before the latter was released. The burden of the encounter weighed heavily on Sambhaji; he couldn't meet Narsala's questioning gaze, which was searching for answers amidst the chaos.

"I cannot tell you everything right now," Sambhaji stated with a firm tone. "All you need to do is return to Raigad and report that I acted against the Marathas. If the Chhatrapati considers laying down his arms, which is unlikely, make sure he doesn't. No Maratha should lay down their weapons. Ensure they disown me and choose to fight against me, even though I am their own blood. This will further fracture the Mughals."

Narsala was bewildered. Yuvraj's words made little sense to him. Throughout his journey back to Raigad, he was consumed by questions: Why had Yuvraj joined the Mughals and fought against his own men? Why had the same Yuvraj saved him from death, only to then urge him to ensure the Marathas continued their resistance? Sambhaji's strategy seemed bizarre, even unreal.

Days turned into weeks, and Sambhaji anxiously hoped his message had reached Raigad and that his father, Shivrai, would understand the subtext. It was time for Muazzam to depart, and Sambhaji's plans had been unfolding as intended thus far. He had skilfully managed to convince Muazzam to engage in a battle of succession against his father, Aurangzeb, and his step-brother, Akbar. Just as Sambhaji began to believe that his carefully orchestrated strategy was succeeding, he heard a man's scream, then pleas and then the sound of somebody chaining them and dragging them. Sambhaji rushed to the site, and what he saw next was a nightmare.

One by one, all the prisoners held at Bhupalgad were dragged out into the open, forced to stand before hundreds of Mughal soldiers who towered menacingly over them.

"What is happening?" Sambhaji demanded.

Muazzam, his kohled eyes gleaming with a cruel glint, glanced at Sambhaji and said, "Before I leave, I wish to carry memories of our victory at Bhupalgad. And what better than the cries of the Marathas to cherish for months to come?"

"What do you mean?" Sambhaji asked, his voice filled with terror that he felt rising within him.

Muazzam saw the discomfort and concern etched on Sambhaji's face, despite his efforts to maintain a mask of indifference. "You're one of us now. Why should this trouble you?" Muazzam said, a wicked smile creeping across his face.

The prisoners, sensing the impending doom, looked desperately toward Sambhaji for help. Sambhaji could not meet their eyes; his helplessness was evident. The sun's rays glinted off the Mughal swords, making them appear like flaming tongues of death in the bright daylight.

Muazzam lifted his hands to the sky in a show of devotion before delivering the dreaded command. In an instant, hundreds of swords flashed through the air, severing the arms of the helpless Maratha prisoners in one brutal motion.

A chorus of anguished screams tore through the courtyard as blood splattered across the stone, pooling beneath the writhing bodies of the wounded. The ground, once dusty and dry, was now slick with deep, dark red blood.

Mughal soldiers watched with cruel delight, their mocking laughter mingling with the agonized cries of their victims. Muazzam exhaled slowly, savouring the scene before murmuring 'Subhan Allah', his voice laced with chilling satisfaction.

Sambhaji was not only horrified by the grisly spectacle unfolding before him but also felt a burning rage ignite within his soul. He could almost feel the agony his soldiers were enduring. Some of the men died instantly from the intense shock and blood loss. Those who survived were subjected to further torment. Mughal soldiers stomped on their severed limbs, crushing them underfoot. Others were dragged mercilessly and tossed into dungeons where they would bleed out or starve. That day, Bhupalgad became the stage for a brutality no one had imagined.

That night, Sambhaji confronted Diler Khan. "Was all this really necessary?" he demanded.

Diler Khan, unfazed, responded coldly, "This was necessary to keep the Mughal army motivated. The army is trained in a manner that only the enemy's blood, riches looted from their forts, and women taken as slaves keep their spirits high. It must prevail for the glory of the Mughal Empire."

A furious storm of anger brewed inside Sambhaji. This rage was not going to subside anytime soon. His political manoeuvring had worked in some respects; he had succeeded in creating a divide within the Mughal forces, turning them against one another. However, the savagery he had just witnessed made him rethink his strategy. Did the ends justify the means?

9.

SEATED ON his throne in Agra, Aurangzeb had grown increasingly anxious. He hadn't heard from Muazzam or Diler Khan in quite some time. His letters demanding updates had gone unanswered. Meanwhile, the news of the Bhupalgad tragedy had spread like wildfire across the Maratha empire. Contrary to what the Mughals might have hoped, instead of retreating or surrendering, Chhatrapati Shivaji Maharaj had doubled the size of his army. Over time, Diler Khan's attempts to assault other forts met with fierce resistance. The Marathas responded with unyielding force, inflicting heavy losses on Diler's troops.

Diler Khan's campaigns were costly, and he relied heavily on Muazzam for financial support to sustain his military endeavours. Muazzam, who now harboured ambitions of becoming the Badshah, did everything he could to provide Diler Khan with the necessary funds to continue the fight and keep his army's morale high. But with Aurangzeb's watchful eyes on Delhi, the channels for direct support were temporarily closed.

Sambhaji saw an opportunity in this disarray. He knew Diler Khan well, having observed his ways since his days in Aurangabad. He knew Diler Khan to be a man driven by his vices—an insatiable desire for women, alcohol, and opium. Over time, Sambhaji had skilfully befriended Diler Khan, gaining his trust and even indulging in revelries with him. Sambhaji endured the lavish gatherings, understanding they were a necessary step in his larger plan to undermine the Mughal ranks from within.

Diler's parties grew more extravagant under Sambhaji's influence, filled with the finest women procured from the slave markets. Much of the money Muazzam sent to Diler for military purposes was now diverted to fund these lavish gatherings. Over time, Diler Khan's entire army began to mirror his leadership, indulging in luxuries and forgetting their true purpose.

Muazzam, watching his treasury slowly deplete without seeing any substantial victories, eventually sent an ultimatum to Diler Khan, demanding results. It was at this moment of mounting pressure that

Sambhaji decided to strike the next blow in his covert campaign.

"We should attack the Adilshahi," Sambhaji suggested casually over a meal with Diler Khan, the aroma of spiced dishes filling the air.

"Why is it so?" Diler Khan asked, intrigued but cautious.

"If we defeat Bijapur, the pride of the Adilshahi, it will pave the way for us to challenge the Marathas for control of the Carnatic region, which they recently seized from the Adilshahi," Sambhaji explained. He paused, gauging Diler Khan's reaction before continuing, "This move would also allow us to dominate trade routes extending to Malay."

Diler Khan fell silent. His mind churned as he weighed the risks and rewards of waging war on the Adilshahi.

"The Marathas are becoming a thorn in our side," Sambhaji pressed, sensing Diler's hesitation. "An attack on the weakened Adilshahi would only strengthen our position. We could expand our territory and revenues. Not only can we expand our trade with the Malays, but we can also come closer to the Portuguese and the Siddhis. The Marathas would then have three enemies in the west." Sambhaji then leaned closer, lowering his voice to add, "And I've heard there is a princess in the Adilshahi territory renowned for her beauty. The only way to win her over is by defeating her father," Sambhaji laughed.

A sly grin spread across Diler Khan's face.

"And not just her, the Deccan too shall be yours. What more can you ask for?" Sambhaji added.

Sambhaji knew exactly what could grab his attention. If Diler Khan, the commander, hesitated, Diler Khan the womanizer would not.

"Bijapur it is!" Diler Khan declared with newfound enthusiasm.

"But..." Sambhaji interjected with calculated timing.

"What now?"

"According to the Mughal-Adilshahi peace treaty, the Adilshahi princess is promised to one of Aurangzeb's sons. If you inform Muazzam or Aurangzeb about this, you might still be allowed to wage war against the Adilshahi, but you'd have to give up your claim to the princess," Sambhaji explained smoothly.

"Why should we tell Muazzam or the Badshah? Anyways,

neither Muazzam nor the Badshah fights. It's me and my army that always strive on the battlefield. I can do what's necessary," Diler Khan scoffed, already lost in thoughts of conquest and his newfound prize.

With that decision, Diler Khan had unknowingly driven a wedge between himself and Muazzam. In the flickering torchlight, his eyes gleamed with quiet triumph.

Later that evening, as an intoxicated Diler Khan stumbled back to his quarters, Sambhaji took the opportunity to clear his mind with a walk. He wandered through the open verandah of the fort, his eyes scanning the starless night sky.

His feet carried him to a secluded area of the fort, where he spotted a shadowy figure standing in the distance. Sambhaji moved closer, his steps deliberate, his senses alert.

"I have some work for you," Sambhaji said to the man whose face was partially concealed by the cloth wrapped around his head.

"*Ji Yuvraj. Adesh Asava* (Yes, Yuvraj, please order)," the man responded in Marathi, his voice low and steady.

Handing over two letters, Sambhaji leaned in and whispered, "One is for Sikander, the Adilshahi head, and the other is for Shivrai. Make sure they both reach the intended hands."

The man nodded solemnly. Sambhaji glanced around, wary of spies. When he turned back, the man was gone, swallowed by the night. His plan was taking shape, but he knew there were many more steps ahead, each one filled with risk and uncertainty.

DILER KHAN, accompanied by Sambhaji and thousands of his men, marched towards Bijapur with determination etched on his face. They trudged through the winding path along the Torvi River, which was the lifeline of Bijapur, the capital of the Adilshahi sultanate. His mission was clear: to lay siege to Bijapur and bring an end to the Adilshahi dynasty once and for all. As they advanced closer, the air grew tense with the anticipation of battle, and every soldier knew they were on the brink of a major conflict that could reshape the Deccan's power dynamics.

Far from this advancing force, in his camp, Muazza received

disturbing news about Diler Khan's plans. Muazzam was not pleased with Diler Khan's decision to attack the Adilshahi territories. From his position, Muazzam could see the bigger picture: he wanted Diler Khan to focus on destroying Maratha strongholds and not waste precious resources fighting battles against the Adilshahi, who were supposed to be their allies under a peace treaty. Frowning deeply, he penned a letter to Diler Khan, reminding him of the treaty terms.

The peace treaty does not permit the Mughals to attack the Adilshahi, and let us not forget that the Adilshahi princess is meant to marry one of Aurangzeb's sons, which is me or my brothers. We must keep good relations with them if we are to remain united against the Marathas.

Meanwhile, in Bijapur, the air was thick with fear and anxiety. The Adilshahi had already suffered devastating blows at the hands of Shivrai, losing their Carnatic territories. Now, they were without an influential leader or a battle-ready army to stand against the formidable Diler Khan. The current ruler, Sultan Sikander Adilshah, a young and inexperienced sovereign, found himself drawn into a political maelstrom after his father's death. His trusted wazir, Masud Khan, stood by his side, but the weight of the situation was heavy upon them both. Years ago, Masud Khan had witnessed Aurangzeb, then Mughal Subhedar of the Deccan, descending upon their lands with fury and taking them by force.

With Bijapur teetering on the edge of catastrophe, Sikander sought his sister, Shahr Banu, to propose a grim solution. "It is time for you to marry one of Aurangzeb's sons," he urged her with desperation in his voice.

Shahr Banu, known for her fierce independence and sharp wit, looked at her brother with disdain. "What if I don't want to?" she challenged, her voice steady and resolute.

"The nation is at risk of being wiped out!" Sikander pleaded, his face a mask of frustration and fear. "Marrying Muazzam could be our salvation. I've heard he does not support Diler Khan's reckless actions. If we align with him, we might turn him against Diler Khan and gain a powerful ally. This is the only way to defeat Diler Khan's forces."

Shahr Banu's eyes flashed with anger. She felt disgusted that her own brother would use her as a pawn in a political game. She replied firmly, "This is not going to happen. I am not a bargaining chip to be traded for political gain. And above all, how could I marry the son of a man who killed our father and brought ruin upon our land?"

"You don't understand, Shahr. Diler Khan's forces are marching toward us, and we have barely recovered from our losses against the Marathas. We lack the resources, men, and strength to withstand another battle. Even Shivrai's forces could return to challenge us at any moment. We will perish without a strategic alliance."

"I would rather face death than marry the son of the man who destroyed our family and our kingdom," she declared, her tone leaving room for no argument. With a heavy heart, Sikander realized that he could not change her mind and reluctantly decided to drop the matter.

As Sikander turned to leave, Masud Khan hurried towards him, breathless and with urgency in his eyes. "My Sultan, an unknown man delivered a letter for you," he said, holding it out. "Before we could question him or learn who sent him, he disappeared."

Taking the letter, Sikander's hands trembled slightly as he broke the seal and unfolded the paper. His heart pounded as he read, fearing it could bring more bad news.

In the unforeseen chain of events and the looming threat of the complete wipeout of the Adilshahi, I hope this letter finds you in the best of spirits.

As Diler Khan's army advances towards your borders, the only hope for your survival and counterattack lies with the one who holds sway over the Carnatic region. With due respect to the valour, the harsh reality is that the Adilshahis do not have a force that can withstand Diler Khan's army.

Send your men and ask Shivrai for his help. The Marathas consider you an enemy, but they consider the Mughals an even bigger enemy. This is an opportunity for you to amend things with the Marathas before the situation worsens.

Stunned by the letter's message, Sikander weighed its wisdom. The sender clearly understood the region's shifting politics. Perhaps, he thought, Allah had indeed shown him the way. Wasting no time, he ordered a group of Adilshahi scouts to ride for Raigad and seek Shivrai's support.

Meanwhile, in Raigad, Shivrai had also received a letter, and the moment he saw the handwriting, he knew it was from Sambhaji. His eyes grew moist with a mixture of anger and sorrow as he read it. Sambhaji's letter, written with a heavy heart, read:

Dear Abasaheb, I am short of words, and I don't know how you shall react to this, but one thing I can assure you of is that whatever I am doing is for the welfare of our own men. I know everybody, including you, is angry and would want to punish me, but whatever I have done is for the benefit of Swaraj. This isn't the right medium for me to explain the political agenda behind this, but I promise I'll explain it to you in person the next time. Also, I know that my strategies bring a lot of backfire for ages to come, but all of it is only to help our people. I have been successful in parts, but have failed at Bhupalgad, for which I should be criticized. I deserve whatever punishment you choose for me. But the intentions were always pure. Now that Diler Khan and I march onto Adilshahi territory, you can expect a request for help from Sikander and his men, and I would want our men to support the Adilshahis and offer resistance to Diler Khan. I assure you that this is the start of a sad ending for the Mughals.

Shivrai folded the letter and set it aside, his mind a storm of emotions—worry, frustration, but also a flicker of hope. Sambhaji was treading a dangerous path, but perhaps, there was a method to his madness.

It was only a matter of time before Shivrai had guests from the Adilshahi territory asking for help against Diler Khan, as he had expected. Shivrai instantly agreed to support Sikander and his men.

HUGE CONTINGENTS of Mughal cavalry and infantry marched steadily, their presence looming like a dark cloud over the landscape. Diler Khan, the ruthless commander, had given strict orders to raze every village that dared cross their path. His decree was clear: he would spare no one. As the Mughal forces advanced, the once-peaceful village of Tikota became the first to experience the full extent of Diler Khan's barbarism. The cries of men, women, and children echoed through the night as their homes were set ablaze.

Sambhaji, understanding the nature of the Mughals, did his best to mitigate the damage. He had stationed spies across the region, who worked tirelessly to warn villages of the Mughal invasion, giving residents a chance to flee. Despite his efforts, some villagers chose to stay, either out of loyalty to their land or because they underestimated the Mughals' brutality. Those unfortunate souls faced tortured deaths at the hands of Diler Khan and his marauding men. After obliterating Tikota, the Mughal army moved on to the neighbouring village of Athani. It too fell in a matter of hours. Villages were reduced to ashes overnight, leaving no survivors among those who had stayed behind.

As the smoke from burning homes filled the air over Athani, one of Sambhaji's trusted Maratha spies arrived to report.

"Yuvraj, Diler Khan's forces are sparing nobody. Athani is reduced to ashes. Everybody is terrorized. What should we do?"

Sambhaji, his face set with determination, listened intently before issuing his orders. "I want you to alert the Maratha troops stationed nearby," he said, his voice firm. "Diler Khan, before launching his assault on Bijapur, will send a part of his forces with me through Miraj and then to the Panhala Fort, hoping to capture our strongholds. This is the moment we turn their own tactics against them. He believes that I know the forts of Panhala inside out, which I definitely do and wants me to help the Mughals capture the fort. With the Bhupalgad incident, he trusts me more than anybody else. As soon as I lead the huge Mughal forces through the valleys and jungles around Panhala, I want the Maratha swords coming blazing down upon the Mughal soldiers. Let our forces at Panhala be ready to intercept. This is the time for you to surprise the Mughals with our guerrilla tactics and put an end to their dominance in the Deccan. This shall be a huge blow to Diler Khan."

Sambhaji's voice was calm yet authoritative as he continued, "While Diler Khan continues his advance toward Bijapur, I want another unit of our warriors to strike at Mughal-occupied territories in the Deccan. Disrupt them from every side. When I reach Panhala, I will separate from the Mughal forces and proceed alone to Bijapur to meet with Masud Khan, the wazir of the Adilshahi."

The spy nodded, understanding the significance of his mission. Under the watchful command of Bahirji Naik, the head of the Maratha intelligence network, messages were dispatched with remarkable speed and precision. Within days, the Maratha commanders at Miraj and Panhala were fully prepared for a counterattack. Meanwhile, Maratha soldiers disguised as ordinary villagers quietly took their positions in nearby settlements, ready to strike at a moment's notice.

True to Sambhaji's prediction, Diler Khan dispatched a contingent of his forces, accompanied by Sambhaji, to seize control of the Maratha forts near Miraj and the Panhala Fort, which lay only a few kos from Kolhapur. As the Mughal forces approached these villages, the Marathas executed their guerrilla tactics with precision and ferocity. The Mughal soldiers, unprepared for the sudden and relentless ambushes, fell in waves, unable to mount a coherent defence—batches after batches of Mughal soldiers perished under the Maratha onslaught.

Simultaneously, in the Mughal-occupied territories of the Deccan, another Maratha force launched a surprise attack, striking with full force and sowing panic and confusion among the Mughal ranks. The situation became dire for Diler Khan; more than half of his once-mighty army had been decimated either near Miraj or in the effort to protect their territories in the Deccan. Shivrai had hoped that these incursions would force Diler Khan to abandon his campaign and retaliate against the Marathas, but Diler Khan remained obstinate. He was determined to press on toward Bijapur, despite his dwindling numbers and Muazzam's lack of support.

Back in the Mughal camp, news of Diler Khan's catastrophic losses reached Muazzam. Frustrated by Diler Khan's incompetence, Muazzam realized that the campaign had brought more ruin than progress. Sambhaji, instead of aiding the Mughals in conquering the Maratha forts near Miraj and Kolhapur, had only strengthened Shivrai's forces, who now fought with doubled resilience. With time, Muazzam could now understand how Sambhaji had single-handedly destroyed the Mughals on both the financial and strategic warfronts. Muazzam decided it was time to act. Overnight, he declared himself the new Mughal Mansabdar of the Deccan, demoting Diler Khan and cutting off his supplies. Diler Khan was now isolated, his support diminished to almost nothing.

As the dust settled near Miraj, Sambhaji, mounted on his majestic white Kathiawadi horse, set off toward Bijapur. It was time to solidify his alliance with Masud Khan. After days and nights of hard travel, his resolve unwavering, Sambhaji finally arrived in Bijapur. His first task was to meet Masud Khan and relay the Mughal strategies he had overheard. Any other day, even with half their strength, the Mughals would have stood a fair chance against the weakened Adilshahi. However, Sambhaji's intervention had turned the tide. Masud Khan, now aware of the Mughal plans, prepared his forces for a showdown, with Sambhaji standing at his side.

As the Mughal troops reached the outskirts of Bijapur, they were met with a ferocious assault from the Adilshahi forces, bolstered by Sambhaji's guidance. The sound of swords clashing and the cries of battle filled the air as the Mughals were caught off guard. Their initial ranks were cut down before they could even mount a proper defence. Diler Khan, expecting to lay a siege and slowly starve the city into submission, was blindsided by this unexpected resistance. Even before he could lay a siege, he was welcomed by the Adilshahi forces in full force. From the outside, the Marathas encircled Diler Khan's forces. Sandwiched between the two, Diler Khan now had no option but to fight.

"How do the Adilshahi forces know our plans?" he asked one of his subordinates. He added, "Who invited the Marathas?"

Just when his defeat was staring him in the face, he tried looking for Sambhaji, but he was nowhere near him. Seated on his horse, he could see nothing but his soldiers being crushed and slashed by Masud Khan and his men. Excusing himself from the battlefield, with a small unit to his help, he decided to close onto the Bijapur gates, and there he could notice Sambhaji charging towards the Bijapur gates. But neither was he attacking the Adilshahi forces, nor were they causing any harm to him. Soon, the gates opened, and Diler Khan could see Sambhaji enter the Bijapur Fort as the gates closed immediately after him. Diler Khan realized his defeat.

By the end of the day, Diler Khan's ambitions were left in tatters. He had nowhere to turn, no reinforcements from Muazzam, no means to retreat to the Deccan, and no hope of capturing Bijapur or the Maratha forts. Defeated and abandoned, Diler Khan stood on the brink of ruin, his dreams of conquest shattered.

AURANGZEB FELT a sharp, piercing pain in his chest. The news had struck him hard, plunging him once again into a nightmarish state of gloom and despair. His trusted general, Diler Khan, had failed yet again. This was not the first time Diler had disappointed him; years earlier, when young Sambhaji was a Mughal mansabdar, stationed with Diler Khan in Aurangabad, Aurangzeb had ordered Diler to arrest the boy and bring him to Agra. But Diler had not obeyed those orders. Aurangzeb, with the passage of time, had let that insubordination fade from his memory, forgiving his general for that misstep. But now, this time, Diler Khan had committed a blunder far too great to overlook.

Sambhaji had manoeuvred cleverly, outwitting the Mughal forces and turning the tables on them. The news of Sambhaji outwitting Diler Khan and his forces had now reached Aurangzeb. Furious and filled with a sense of betrayal, Aurangzeb took immediate action. He wrote a letter to his son, Shahzada Muazzam, instructing him to halt all funds and provisions to Diler Khan without delay and to sever all ties with the disgraced general. Aurangzeb then summoned Bahadurshah Kokaltash, one of his most trusted commanders, and dispatched him to Burhanpur. This city held a special place in Aurangzeb's heart, as he had once declared it the second capital of the Mughal Empire after Agra. Burhanpur was also a strategic treasure trove, its underground vaults filled with riches looted from various provinces over the years. Bahadurshah Kokaltash was now tasked with safeguarding these assets and the city's strategic importance.

Meanwhile, Muazzam, who had recently declared himself the new Mansabdar of the Mughal-occupied Deccan, received Aurangzeb's letter. Even without the Badshah's command, Muazzam had already planned to take action against Diler Khan for disobeying his direct orders by attacking the Adilshahi provinces, thereby breaching a critical peace treaty. However, what concerned Muazzam even more was how Sambhaji had managed to escape so easily from under their noses. Despite Sambhaji's betrayals, Muazzam found himself strangely admiring the Maratha prince's audacity and wisdom. Deep down, he knew that Sambhaji's moves had shown him a tantalizing glimpse of a possible future, one where he could ascend to the Mughal throne as the next Badshah.

The thought of this had been reverberating in Muazzam's mind for a long time. It was a risky ambition, but one that he knew he would have to pursue one day, whether in the near future or in the years to come. He also knew that if he did not act soon, his half-brother Akbar might beat him to it. Through his network of spies, Muazzam had learned that Akbar had allied himself with Durgadas Rathore, an influential Rajput leader, and was similarly plotting to claim the throne. Muazzam's dislike for Akbar was well known, and with Durgadas on his side, Akbar was becoming a formidable threat. Muazzam realized he needed to act swiftly and strategically.

He decided to engage in some subterfuge to address this new threat. Muazzam had to now use his father's forces to first put an end to Akbar and his dreams. He had to win his father's heart after the mess that he had created in the Deccan. He knew that Aurangzeb had been dissatisfied with what Akbar had been doing in Rajasthan. He had heard that Akbar was not focusing on the campaign and was spending time on leisure and with women. This piece of news had also reached Muazzam. He, being the better of the two in Aurangzeb's eyes, decided to strike gold as he wrote a letter to Aurangzeb, letting him know of Akbar's real intentions, detailing his alliances with Durgadas Rathod and plans to seize the Mughal Empire.

For Aurangzeb, this was another devastating blow, but he did not know whether to believe it. The ground beneath him seemed to be shifting, yet he forced himself to be calm. He could sense how isolated he had become in his old age, with treachery lurking on all sides. Reinforcements had been continuously sent from Agra to Jodhpur at Akbar's request, ostensibly to aid in his battles against Durgadas's guerrilla forces, who had been attacking in the hills and mountains with brutal efficiency. Akbar had cleverly siphoned off a significant portion of the Mughal army from Agra to bolster his own ambitions. Meanwhile, what remained of the Mughal forces had suffered heavy losses under Diler Khan's disastrous campaign, and the few thousand soldiers still loyal were either under Muazzam's command in the Deccan or stationed with Kokaltash in Burhanpur, where they could not be recalled without risking a Maratha takeover of the Mughal strongholds in the Deccan.

Aurangzeb found himself cornered with only a small contingent of personal bodyguards and servants at his disposal, men who had served him only ceremonially and had not seen real combat in years. This was a troubling sign for the ageing emperor, a reality that kept him awake at night. Desperate to know the truth, Aurangzeb decided to send a group of his most trusted spies to Jodhpur to gather intelligence. He had to be doubly sure before he could take an action. Either of his two sons was wrong; he had concluded. If Akbar's intentions weren't bad, then it was Muazzam who wanted to fool him, he believed. In both cases, he knew he had to react and put an end to this. He could see his kingdom falling with the greed lurking around him.

It took a few days for the spies to get into Akbar's cantonment and come up with the reports which confirmed Muazzam's warnings: Akbar had indeed formed his own army with the robust backing of Durgadas, and their forces, strengthened further by alliances with the Sisodia and Kacchavah clans, were preparing to march on Agra at any moment.

The news was indeed very heart-wrenching for Aurangzeb. He couldn't imagine his own flesh turning against him.

'I cannot lose my throne,' Aurangzeb warned himself. He couldn't imagine losing to his own child. All his life, he had been challenged by many rulers, including Shivrai and the Marathas, but he had not cared so much. This time, it was his own son, and he couldn't afford a defeat at his hands. At any moment, Akbar could launch an attack and put an end to everything Aurangzeb had built. Akbar had wisely taken away the major chunk of his army, leaving the remaining with Muazzam. It scared Aurangzeb. His entire life had been consumed by his desire to rule as Badshah, to wield absolute power. The mere thought of losing that power, of being dethroned by his own son, made him sweat with dread. He had to devise a plan – a plan that would be nastier than ever.

RAIGAD WAS alive with celebrations, the entire fortress echoing with the joyous cries of its people. It was as if the stars had descended upon the land, for every home and street was lit up with thousands of lamps, welcoming their Yuvraj, Sambhaji, back home. It was a festival of lights like never before. The common folk sang praises, danced in circles, and chanted blessings for their Yuvraj's return. Shivrai, the great Chhatrapati Shivaji Maharaj, had not questioned his son Sambhaji about his time with the Mughals, nor had he scolded or praised him. This unexpected silence stirred whispers among his subhedars.

Some of them wondered whether Sambhaji's joining the Mughals had been part of a grand, undisclosed plan orchestrated by both Shivrai and Sambhaji. Others speculated that the Chhatrapati was forgiving him because he was his son.

The reactions were divided and varied. The majority were relieved and believed in the possibility of a larger strategy that they weren't privy to. They trusted their leader's wisdom, thinking that if Shivrai had not questioned Sambhaji, it must mean the act was intentional and had a deeper purpose. However, a vocal minority, led by Annaji Datto, were critical. They felt Sambhaji had committed an unforgivable betrayal and should face severe consequences.

In the royal palace, Soyrabai, Sambhaji's stepmother, had kept her distance. She was noticeably sombre amidst the celebrations.

"You don't seem alright, Queen," said one of her househelp.

"Of course, I am not. How can a traitor be set free? He needs to be punished. The bonds of family cannot outweigh the principles of loyalty and duty to the Swaraj."

Meanwhile, within the confines of Raigad Fort, Sambhaji was preparing himself for the inevitable meeting with his father. As he stood before the massive idol of Bhavani Mata, his heart pounded, and his palms were sweaty. His father, Shivrai, stood before him, noticeably frailer than when they last met. Sambhaji was shocked to see how much weight his father had lost. A pallor and a persistent cough now overshadowed his once strong, commanding presence.

"Abasaheb," Sambhaji finally managed to stammer, his voice cracking. His father looked at him, the weight of age evident in his eyes, and replied, "Ji, Shambhu." The voice no longer carried the thunderous command that Sambhaji had always known. It was softer, more vulnerable.

Sambhaji's heart ached at the sight. His father, the lion of the Deccan, was weakened. A sudden thought flashed through his mind: *Was it my actions that have caused this?* The idea gnawed at him. If he was indeed the cause of his father's decline, then he wished for divine retribution. "If it is because of me, then God should punish me," Sambhaji muttered under his breath.

He had been hoping for his father's wrath—a barrage of reprimands, maybe even a harsh sentence. Anything but this suffocating silence. "Abasaheb, won't you ask me why I joined the Mughals?" said Sambhaji.

"Shambhu bala," Shivrai replied softly, "I know to an extent through the letters you wrote."

This is a father speaking, Sambhaji thought, his eyes moistening. Shivrai was showing an unshakeable trust in him, even when he didn't deserve it. He had fully trusted the letters he had written.

"You did what you felt was right," continued Shivrai, his voice interrupted by bouts of coughing, "And I did what I felt was right. My conscience told me to continue the fight against the Mughals, even if it meant opposing my own son even before you sent Narsala to me."

"Abasaheb, I don't care what others think of me or what history will write about me," Sambhaji replied, his voice heavy with emotion. "All that matters to me is what you think of me, whether I have made you proud or let you down."

Sambhaji paused, looking into his father's eyes, which remained steadfast. He continued, "I felt trapped at Shringarpur, sidelined from the battlefield. Joining you in the southern expedition wasn't possible, and returning to Raigad meant entangling myself in politics. So, I thought the best way to serve the cause of Swaraj was to join Diler Khan, divide the Mughal ranks, and turn them against one another. And I succeeded! Diler Khan, who was like a rampaging demon in the Deccan, is now reduced to a mere shell of his former self. Muazzam's resources are depleted, causing instability. Muazzam now thirsts for Akbar's blood to claim the throne, and Diler Khan covets control over the Deccan, clashing with Mughal allies that have turned enemies. The Mughal forces are fractured among three leaders, each vying for dominance."

He paused again, observing his father's face, which remained impassive but attentive. "I didn't have an army of my own to lead. The best I could do was divide their forces and let them destroy each other."

"But at what cost, son?" Shivrai finally spoke, his voice firmer this time. "We lost Bhupalgad, a stronghold of Maratha pride. We lost countless men, and many are now maimed for life. Swaraj is not just about winning battles; it's also about safeguarding our own people and protecting what we already have."

Sambhaji bowed his head in shame, "I understand, Abasaheb. I failed to foresee the massacre and the cruelty that unfolded. I cannot justify the losses. I looked at distant success but not the immediate threats. I am prepared to face whatever punishment you deem fit, but I swear, my intentions were only to gain their trust and divide them from within. I never wished to raise my sword against a Maratha soldier, and contemplating that our people might get killed, I decided to lead the Mughal forces so that the Maratha soldiers could drop their weapons. I needed to act in a particular way to not only safeguard our people but also to win over the Mughal forces' trust in me to divide them later and make them fight against each other."

Shivrai contemplated his son's words, understanding that in warfare, not everything goes as planned. After a long, thoughtful silence, he said, "I understand your intentions, Shambhu, and that is why I have not questioned your decisions. But the reason I sent you to Shringarpur was not to keep you away from the battlefield, but to help you understand the economics and dynamics of revenues and governance."

"I did learn, Abasaheb. I learned that there are traitors and corrupt individuals within our system. I tried to expose them and punish them. I tried my best," Sambhaji retorted.

"Do you think I have never pondered upon this?" Shivrai questioned, his gaze piercing. "Shambhu, I can understand your intentions, but sometimes waiting for sufficient proofs and collecting them flawlessly takes time. One has to consider both sides of the coin, listen to both parties, form a judgement, and then react. With this, I am not doubting your intentions but your temperament. Decisions cannot be taken in haste."

Sambhaji, humbled by his father's wisdom, felt the depth of Shivrai's reasoning. His father's decisions were not driven by anger but by a larger vision for the kingdom.

"Shambhu bala," Shivrai continued, placing a hand on Sambhaji's shoulder and coughing intermittently, "Anger is not the solution to every problem. You are young; your blood boils at every injustice, but remember, anger is like fire. It can burn others, but it also burns the hand that wields it. Anger may work in some cases, but more often, cleverness and sound strategies shall win the day. At Shringarpur, I wanted you to witness greed and corruption and learn how to channel your anger into wise, calculated decisions."

"I have learned a lot, Abasaheb. But where do I go from here?"

"The Mughals have their eyes on you. The best course of action now is for you to go to Panhala. The fort requires some reconstruction. I want it fortified to become our stronghold after Raigad," Shivrai instructed, his voice punctuated by another bout of coughing.

"Are you alright, Abasaheb? You seem unwell," Sambhaji inquired, his concern evident.

"I am fine, Shambhu," Shivrai assured him, "It's just the dust from the battlefields that has taken its toll on me."

10.

"WHO ARE you? What brings you here?" a guard demanded, his voice sharp and unwavering. The guard stood resolutely outside Durgadas's residence, his eyes narrowing as he scrutinized the unknown visitor. His sole duty was to ensure the safety of Prince Akbar, and any unfamiliar face was met with immediate suspicion.

"I am a messenger. The Badshah has sent me," replied the man, his voice wavering slightly as he sensed the tension in the air.

"What is it you want?" the guard pressed, not lowering his weapon.

"I need to meet Prince Akbar," the messenger insisted, attempting to appear calm despite the evident hostility.

But the guards were not so easily convinced. The lead guard swiftly grabbed the messenger by his arms, and two more guards joined him, one seizing him by the neck and forcing him to kneel on the hard ground. They searched him thoroughly, snatching every belonging he carried. There was suspicion in the guard's mind. The guards knew that if this was truly a message from the Badshah, it was highly probable the messenger had mistakenly arrived at Durgadas's camp rather than Akbar's. They were vigilant, unwilling to risk revealing anything about the secret alliance between Marwar and Akbar.

As they searched, one of the guards discovered a letter tucked inside the messenger's garments. "This is for Prince Akbar..." the messenger tried to explain, his voice strained with panic.

"Silence!" barked one of the guards, tightening his grip around the messenger's neck. "Speak another word, and we shall behead you. This is Marwar. We are Durgadas's men."

Fear flashed in the messenger's eyes. He had made a grave mistake, wandering into the wrong camp. Even the Badshah might not spare him for such an error.

The guards hurried to Durgadas, who was resting inside his tent. Emerging into the lamplit night, Durgadas took the letter, lit a torch, and began to read. His eyes widened, and his heart pounded as he absorbed the contents. His breath quickened, and his face darkened with anger and disbelief as he comprehended the letter's shocking message:

My dear son,

I am so proud of you. I adore the way you have skilfully handled every situation for the betterment of our men. Jihad must prevail. While Muazzam and Diler Khan have failed in the Deccan with their reckless aggression, I am jubilant that you have held onto our motives with intelligence. Now that you have ensured that Durgadas, the Sisodias, and the Kacchavah are by your side, march to Agra with them. They trust you blindly. As swords rip them apart and pull out their intestines, slave their children and rape their women, and chaos ensues, we shall arrest those who survive and send them to the dungeons to rot for their entire lives. With this, Marwar shall be erased, and we shall be the sole rulers in Rajasthan. My eyes yearn to see you arrest our enemies and punish them like never before.

The letter bore the unmistakable signature and seal of the Badshah, Aurangzeb himself.

"Who sent you this letter?" Durgadas demanded, his voice a low, menacing growl.

"The Badshah... It was for Shehzada Akbar," stuttered the messenger, trembling in fear. "I am so sorry," he pleaded, sensing the danger to his life.

"Leave him and let him go," Durgadas instructed his guards. "We do not harm messengers. It is against our code of conduct."

Relieved but terrified, the messenger hurried away into the night. Durgadas, however, was seething with rage. He stormed toward Akbar's tent, questions swirling in his mind. If even a fraction of what the letter stated was true, he could not risk having a serpent like Akbar within his camp. Betrayal of this magnitude could not be tolerated.

"Shehzada Akbar!" he shouted outside the tent, his voice echoing in the quiet of the night. But there was no response. Akbar's personal guards were conspicuously absent as well, which only fuelled Durgadas's suspicions.

Meanwhile, several kos away, Akbar was riding through the dark wilderness with a small entourage of his most loyal guards.

His heart raced with a mix of anger and fear. The letter he had received earlier that day had unsettled him to his core. Though he had been staying at Durgadas's camp to strategize their attack, he now feared for his life and had decided to return to his own camp, a safe distance away.

The letter, which had been delivered to him, mistakenly addressed to Durgadas, read: "Life has not been easy for me. Despite being the Badshah of this vast land, I am not blessed with a son's loyalty. Akbar has turned traitor. If you capture the traitor and present him before me, I promise the Mughals shall leave Marwar alone, offering a hand of friendship. All I want is for you to bring the culprit to me so that I can punish him with my own hands."

The words were enough to make Akbar flee. He realized that remaining in Durgadas's camp would only lead to his death.

Back in the Marwar camp, Durgadas's fury knew no bounds. He felt deeply betrayed by Akbar, whom he had trusted. The Sisodia and Kacchavah clans, who had allied with Durgadas primarily due to Akbar's assurance of victory, began to waver in their loyalty. Uncertainty now loomed large, and Durgadas found himself standing alone, his hopes and plans unravelling.

Aurangzeb, however, was not done sowing discord. A third letter had been dispatched, this one to the Mughal commander who was under Akbar's command. It read:

I am fully aware of the treasonous alliances being formed in Marwar. Challenging the Badshah is an act of treason, but I am prepared to forgive you if you withdraw with your forces to Agra. However, if you choose to side with Akbar against me, I promise your wife, daughter, and son will be tortured to death in public for the crime of treason. Before you even reach Agra to challenge my forces, you will be greeted by their beheaded bodies.

The threat was clear, and the consequences dire. Terrified for his family, the Mughal commander ordered an immediate withdrawal to Agra. Confusion spread among the soldiers as they packed up the camp.

When Akbar finally reached his own camp, he was met with a shocking sight—empty tents and a mere handful of soldiers remaining. Bewildered, he learned of the army's sudden retreat to Agra. Agony tore through him as he realized the full extent of his predicament. His dreams of ascending to the Mughal throne had crumbled in an instant. Worse yet, he had made enemies on all sides: his father, who now wanted him dead, and Durgadas, who felt deeply betrayed.

Seated on his grand throne, Aurangzeb wore a sinister smile. He had won a battle without lifting a sword or setting foot onto the battlefield. He had undone his enemies from within.

"Prepare for the attack," he instructed one of his subordinates. "Akbar needs to be taught a lesson."

THE WALLS of Panhala Fort offered little comfort to Sambhaji. His thoughts were constantly drawn back to Raigad and his father, Shivrai. It had been months since he had received any updates from Shivrai, and the silence gnawed at him. The vast, imposing walls that surrounded him felt more like a cage, keeping him away from what truly mattered: the heart of the Maratha empire and his father.

Meanwhile, at Raigad, Shivrai, despite his deteriorating health, continued to focus on the state's affairs. He was deeply engrossed in discussions with his advisers, planning to establish new naval bases in Konkan to strengthen the Marathas' hold in the Arabian sea. Yet, he would find time to discuss Rajaram's wedding plans with Soyrabai. However, his body was beginning to betray him.

One afternoon, after finishing his meal at Soyrabai's, Shivrai made his way to Putalabai's residence. His sudden appearance in her chambers caught her off guard, as he would have usually informed his queens before visiting. The concern in his eyes was unmistakable.

"Is everything okay?" Putalabai asked, immediately touching his feet as a gesture of respect.

"Not really," Shivrai replied, his voice heavy with worry. He sank into one of the couches, his usual vigour visibly diminished.

"What is troubling you?" Putalabai asked, offering him a glass of water, her own heart racing with concern.

Shivrai took the water with trembling hands and gulped it down, his breath ragged and uneven. His face was flushed, and his usually steady gaze seemed distant. Beads of sweat dotted his forehead, and his palms were clammy. His chest tightened as he tried to articulate his fears, his voice almost a whisper. "It all troubles me...," he gasped. "I worry about what will happen after I am gone. Not everyone around here has pure intentions. I fear for Shambhu. These people...," his voice trailed off, his breath catching in his throat as he struggled to find the words.

"You don't look well. Are you alright? Should I call someone?" Putalabai's worry deepened as she watched his pallor worsen.

Shivrai tried to stand, but his legs gave way beneath him. Putalabai quickly reached out to support him, her hand steadying his faltering steps. "You have a fever!" she exclaimed, her voice tinged with panic.

He turned his head slightly to acknowledge her, but before he could respond, a wave of darkness enveloped him. His body went limp, collapsing into her arms.

"Shivrai...Shivrai...Shivrai!" Putalabai called out, her voice rising in desperation. When he didn't respond, she shouted for help. Within moments, the house staff rushed to her aid.

"Call the Rajvaidya, immediately!" she commanded, her voice trembling but authoritative.

The Rajvaidya arrived in no time. Shivrai was laid gently on the bed, as he checked his pulse with a grave expression. A couple of attendants began applying wet cloths to Shivrai's head and feet in an attempt to lower his fever.

"The pulse is weak. His heart rate is too high," the Rajvaidya observed, his brow furrowed with concern.

"Is it something serious?" Putalabai asked, her eyes never leaving the Rajvaidya's face.

"What did he eat?" the Rajvaidya asked, looking around.

Putalabai, at a loss, turned to Soyrabai, who had just entered the room. "He has had a loss of appetite for some time," Soyrabai interjected.

The Rajvaidya, along with his assistants known as Bhishaks,

performed *Nadiparikshan*, an Ayurvedic diagnostic technique to examine the balance of doshas, *Vata*, *Pitta*, and *Kapha*, in the body. His face grew more serious as he concluded the examination.

"It seems Shivrai has been suffering from an underlying illness for quite some time. His three doshas are severely imbalanced. He might be suffering from high fever with desentry," the Rajvaidya announced grimly.

Putalabai's eyes welled with tears. Her limited understanding of Ayurveda only amplified her fears. The Rajvaidya continued, "We should lay the Chhatrapati on the ground, not on a bed."

The weight of his words hit her like a tidal wave. Laying Shivrai on the ground was a ritual for those nearing the end of their journey—a custom meant to ease the soul's departure. Soyrabai, who had been standing strong until now, broke down in tears, retreating to a corner with Rajaram, who clung to her side.

"Why is Abasaheb not speaking?" Rajaram asked, his small voice piercing the heavy silence. Soyrabai hugged him tightly, her tears flowing unchecked, unable to answer his innocent question.

Women from the palace and several of Shivrai's subhedars gathered around, whispering prayers and touching his feet for blessings. Putalabai remained by his side, holding his hand, her own trembling. She only left his side once, desperate to find Soyrabai. As she walked barefoot toward Soyrabai's chambers, a gut-wrenching wail erupted from behind her. She froze mid-step.

"Shivrai..." The cries grew louder and more heartbroken, echoing through the corridors. Putalabai's breath hitched, her body rigid with fear. She didn't dare turn around; she already knew what had happened. Her heart broke into a thousand pieces as the reality settled in.

Slowly, she turned, her eyes meeting the scene she dreaded the most. The Rajvaidya gently closed Shivrai's eyes Putalabai's legs buckled beneath her as she let out a soul-crushing wail. Her mangalsutra snapped and plummeted to the floor, its beads spilling like a cascade of stars, each one hitting the floor with a delicate, heart-wrenching finality, a painful reminder of the end of an era, the end of her beloved Shivrai.

11.

AT PANHALA, Sambhaji's heart quivered with an unexplainable pain. The stars shimmered brightly in the inky sky, but instead of their usual comforting presence, they seemed distant and indifferent to his turmoil. His eyes searched among them, hoping to find a sign, a reason, or some form of guidance to understand the burden weighing down on him. Yesubai, who had accompanied him to Panhala, watched him closely. She could see the conflict raging in his mind, the silent battle against the fear of the unknown and the dread of what he could not yet fathom.

Meanwhile, in Raigad, a sombre air filled the fort as preparations for Chhatrapati Shivaji Maharaj's final rites were underway. The fort, once alive with the sounds of bustling activity and the cheerful shouts of soldiers and citizens, was now wrapped in a heavy blanket of silence. As word spread, people from every corner of Raigad came forth, wanting to see their beloved Chhatrapati for one last time before he departed for his final journey. They brought flowers as a mark of respect and devotion to the great leader who had been the very foundation of the Maratha Swaraj. For them, Shivrai was more than a king; he was a guardian, a protector, and a divine figure whose mere presence promised safety and justice.

Yet, amid the sorrow, Soyrabai stood with a stoic determination. Despite the pain of losing her husband, she remained focused, overseeing the preparations for the last rites with an unyielding resolve. Putalabai, on the other hand, had been rendered almost lifeless by her grief. She had spent days and nights crying, her gaze fixed on Shivrai's empty throne. Often, she would find herself speaking to the vacant seat, as if hoping that her beloved Shivrai could somehow hear her.

As the dawn of the final rites approached, Putalabai, her voice frail but determined, turned to Soyrabai and asked, "Where is Yuvraj? Hasn't he come to bid farewell to his father?"

Soyrabai's response was sharp, almost cutting through the air like a blade. "Traitors like him should not be called. It's better he isn't here," she snapped, her eyes cold and unyielding.

"This is wrong!" Putalabai protested, but her voice was drowned out by the tension in the room, "How can a son not be informed about his father's death?".

Putalabai's heart was aching with every beat. She continued, "Shambhu has the karmic right to light his father's pyre. How can you take that sacred right away from him?"

"It is not I alone who wants it to happen. Even the ministers feel the same," declared Soyrabai.

"Who are these ministers? Not bigger than Shivrai and Shambhu, right? Shivrai himself never complained about Shambhu," argued Putalabai.

Thoughts swirled in her mind, and Putabai resolutely walked towards the pyre, her steps determined. But before she could get too close, Soyrabai intercepted her, grasping her hand firmly and pulling her away towards her own quarters.

"We have to perform the last rites," Putalabai implored, her voice cracking with a mixture of grief and anger.

Soyrabai, however, was unmoved. "Sabaji, his cousin, will do that," she replied flatly.

"How can Sabaji perform the last rites when Shivrai has two sons?" Putalabai argued, her voice rising as her eyes filled with tears. The very thought of such a sacred tradition being broken filled her with anguish.

"Rajaram is too young, and Shambhu is a traitor," Soyrabai retorted with an air of finality.

"Even a three-year-old child can be guided to light the pyre! Rajaram is almost nine now. And if Shivrai did not condemn Shambhu as a traitor, who are we to do so?" Putalabai countered, her voice growing stronger, her eyes blazing with an inner fire.

Avoiding Putalabai's words, Soyrabai turned away and walked to the door. She latched it from the inside, ensuring Putalabai could not leave as the final rites proceeded outside. The heavy wooden door creaked shut, sealing Putalabai away from the ceremony.

"This is not right!" Putalabai cried out in despair, her fists pounding on the door. But Soyrabai stood firm, her voice as cold as stone. "After Shivrai, I am the queen in-charge," she declared. "It is my authority to decide what is right and wrong."

Putalabai's tears flowed freely, her heart shattering under the weight of the injustice. She could do nothing but watch, helpless, as the sacred rites were performed without Shivrai's rightful heir, Sambhaji, present to bid farewell to his father.

LESS THAN a week had passed since Shivrai's demise, and the throne had already begun to feel empty. The news of Shivrai's death had reached the distant corners of the empire, including Aurangzeb's ears. Yet, surprisingly, the news had not reached his own son, Sambhaji. Putalabai was beginning to realize that Sambhaji was being deliberately kept in the dark about his father's passing by those involved in a deeper conspiracy.

Dignitaries from various provinces, Kings, mansabdars, and subhedars, had arrived at Raigad to pay their final respects to their beloved Chhatrapati. Among them was Hambirrao Mohite, the chief of the Maratha cavalrymen. Bowing solemnly before the ashes preserved on the throne, Mohite made his way to his sister Soyrabai's consort chambers.

Upon seeing her brother, Soyrabai burst into tears, overwhelmed with grief. "The bad times have come," she sobbed, her voice trembling with sorrow. Mohite, who had revered Shivrai as a deity, tried to console his sister. Despite his personal grief, he knew that as the chief commander of the Maratha troops, the responsibility of safeguarding the nation now rested heavily on his shoulders. He was, undoubtedly, the most crucial figure at this moment of uncertainty.

"Without Shivrai, the throne looks so empty. The nation's safety is paramount, and we must name our next Chhatrapati," Soyrabai said, looking directly at Mohite.

Mohite was taken aback by her abrupt shift from mourning to politics. He couldn't believe how quickly his sister had composed herself and turned her focus to the succession. "I believe Yuvraj might be on his way," Mohite said, assuming that Sambhaji had already been informed of his father's death.

"Don't take that traitor's name!" Soyrabai snapped, her tone filled with anger. "It's better to have no Chhatrapati than to have one like him, who could align with our enemies at any moment."

Mohite's face turned pale with shock. "You haven't informed him?" he asked, his voice strained with disbelief. Soyrabai avoided his gaze, her eyes darting away from her brother's penetrating stare.

"As the Queen of the Maratha empire," Soyrabai began, her voice faltering slightly, "I want Rajaram to be the next Chhatrapati."

"But..." Mohite tried to interject, but Soyrabai raised her hand to silence him. She continued with a firmness that surprised even herself, "Only you and Annaji have the authority to appoint the new Chhatrapati. Annaji has given his consent, and now I demand yours."

"Yuvraj, being the elder son, deserves to be the king," Mohite argued, his voice steady but filled with concern.

"No!" Soyrabai retorted, her fury boiling over. "His place lies in the dungeons! He must be imprisoned for his treachery. Annaji Datto and Peshwa Pinglay shall leave for Panhala soon. You should take your troops too."

Mohite's expression was a mix of confusion and disbelief. "For what?" he asked, trying to understand the depths of her intentions.

"To arrest Sambhaji," Soyrabai declared, her eyes burning with a mixture of determination and resentment.

A PROFOUND sense of devastation engulfed Sarnobat Mohite. The Maratha kingdom, once a beacon of unity and purpose under Shivrai's leadership, now faced a tumultuous and unsettling political landscape. Mohite had never before encountered such ruthless power plays at the highest levels of authority. The insatiable thirst for the throne and the pervasive hunger for power exhibited by his sister Soyrabai had created deep fissures within the Maratha empire. This fracturing of loyalties and principles threatened to undermine the very foundation of Swaraj that Shivrai had painstakingly built over the years. The situation was dire, and Mohite's internal conflict was only exacerbated by the betrayal he witnessed around him.

As Mohite prepared to leave for Satara to regroup with his troops, he stumbled upon an alarming conversation between Hiroji Farzand and Surnees Datto. This discussion was emblematic of the shifting allegiances and the emergence of new power dynamics within the kingdom.

"We need to imprison that traitor," Surnees Datto declared, his voice brimming with determination.

"Definitely, we have to. Maharani Soyrabai wants it too. He can be a big threat to all of us. If he becomes the king, he shall make sure we are the ones first thrown out from the court, just like he tried doing it earlier," Hiroji Farzand responded, his agreement highlighting the extent to which loyalties had shifted.

The ease with which these men, once loyal to Shivrai, had altered their allegiance was startling. Hiroji Farzand, a man who had been a trusted ally and a significant contributor to the kingdom's victories, was now being manipulated by forces driven by personal greed, minting money and holding power that could be taken away from them only by Sambhaji. Mohite felt a profound sense of loss as he observed the disintegration of the unity that Shivrai had so carefully cultivated. He left for Satara with a heavy heart, uncertain about the future and his role in this evolving crisis.

Meanwhile, in her private quarters, Putalabai was consumed by her grief. From her room, she gazed forlornly at the sky, speaking to her deceased husband as though her words could bridge the chasm of death.

"Shivrai, I am heartbroken to see how things have unfolded," she lamented, tears streaming down her face. The memories of Shivrai's pyre, ignited by Sabaji rather than his own sons, haunted her deeply. The absence of Shambhu and his wife, Yesu, from the ceremony, coupled with the lack of a *bhadagni* performed by the priests, compounded her sorrow.

"The Gods will never be appeased," Putalabai sobbed. "Shivrai, I wish I had the power to correct these wrongs. How can they neglect the rites that a king rightfully deserves? How can they fail to pray for your safe passage to the afterlife?" Her despair was palpable, and her cries echoed through the fort's desolate corridors, a stark contrast to the political machinations outside. In the queen consort's quarters, Soyrabai had seemingly moved beyond her grief, her focus shifting to the practicalities of her new role. The mantle of leadership demanded that she act decisively and prioritize the kingdom's welfare, regardless of personal loss.

"Some decisions are difficult but necessary for the greater good," Soyrabai stated firmly to Annaji Datto. "You are to take 10,000 men and march towards Panhala immediately."

Peshwa Pinglay, who had been silently observing from behind Surnees Datto, listened attentively. When Soyrabai addressed him, she continued, "Pinglay, you and your troops will rendezvous with Sarnobat Mohite in Satara. Together, you will advance towards Panhala. I want the traitor to be captured and presented before me."

Both men nodded in agreement, though Datto harboured concerns. "But there is a complication," he said, his brow furrowed with worry.

"What is it?" Soyrabai inquired, her tone demanding clarity.

"The fort commanders, Vitthal Mahadkar, Janardan Hanmante, and Yuvraj's most trusted Malhoji Ghorpade. Will they not resist our efforts? If they refuse to admit us, are we prepared to confront our own men?" Datto questioned, his anxiety evident.

Soyrabai's eyes sparkled with determination. "You need not concern yourself with Vitthal Mahadkar and Janardan Hanmante. I have already spoken with Hiroji Farzand, and he will handle them. As for Malhoji Ghorpade, if he obstructs our plans, deal with him decisively."

After the two men departed, Soyrabai summoned Balaji Avaji, the scribe renowned for his precise and authoritative writing. Letters drafted by Balaji were considered official and were often viewed as direct orders from the Chhatrapati or the Queen. Soyrabai required two letters: one addressed to Vitthal Mahadkar, instructing him to facilitate the arrival of troops, and another to Sambhaji, misleading him about the situation in Raigad to ensure he did not leave Panhala.

Balaji Avaji, who had been Shivrai's scribe for years, found himself in a moral quandary. "I cannot betray Yuvraj. I have witnessed his growth. I cannot turn my back on Shivrai's son," he implored, clasping his hands in a gesture of supplication before Soyrabai.

Soyrabai, her resolve unyielding, insisted on her demand. "You must comply," she said, her tone leaving no room for negotiation.

Faced with no viable alternative, Balaji Avaji agreed to carry out the task, but with a condition. "My son Khando, whose handwriting is indistinguishable from mine, will draft the letters," he stipulated.

Soyrabai, though reluctant, acquiesced to the arrangement. Balaji Avaji's son would write the letters, maintaining the facade of authenticity while executing Soyrabai's plans.

As Mohite made his way to Satara, the gravity of the situation weighed heavily on him. The political turmoil and shifting allegiances within the Maratha kingdom posed significant challenges. The future of Swaraj hinged on the decisions made in the coming days, and Mohite knew that the path ahead would be fraught with difficulty and uncertainty.

AT PANHALA, as the sun rose, Sambhaji embarked on his routine inspection of the fort. The fortress walls echoed the soft footsteps of the Yuvraj and his trusted companions.

Over the past few days, however, a cloud of unease had settled over Sambhaji's mind. He had been wondering what was happening at Raigad. It had been unusually long since he last heard from his father, Shivrai, which was not like him. His father's letters were usually timely and filled with both guidance and warmth. This silence felt like an ominous void. That morning, he also received news that Hiroji Farzand and Janardan Hanmante had mysteriously gone missing. On further inquiry, Sambhaji was told they had left due to family emergencies. But that didn't sit well with him; his gut feeling told him that something was terribly wrong.

"Who could be this 'family emergency' that's so important they wouldn't inform me?" Sambhaji pondered, his brows furrowed with concern. But before he could dwell on it longer, Kavi Kalash approached him with a new piece of intelligence.

"Yuvraj, my men have witnessed something strange," Kavi

Kalash reported, his tone grave and eyes sharp.

"What is it?" Sambhaji asked, his curiosity piqued.

"Many men from Raigad have settled at the foothills of Panhala."

Behind Kavi Kalash stood Malhoji Ghorpade, a loyal warrior and commander, who nodded in agreement, his face taut with concern.

"Malhoji kaka, I trust no one more than you. Can you personally go to the foothills and check what the matter is?" Sambhaji asked, his eyes fixed on the steadfast commander.

"Of course, Yuvraj," Malhoji replied, his voice filled with conviction.

As Malhoji left to investigate the villages, Vitthal Mahadkar, the fort commander, approached Sambhaji with a letter. The letter was addressed to Sambhaji, supposedly from Raigad. Sambhaji opened it cautiously. It read like any other letter he had received from his father, Abasaheb, over the years, a message detailing the state of affairs at Raigad, mentioning that he was well, and inquiring after Yesu and Sambhaji. However, something about the letter did not sit right with Sambhaji.

Vitthal Mahadkar's face was a mask of calm, but beneath it, his heart was pounding. Moments earlier, he had received a letter from Soyrabai herself, instructing him on how they planned to imprison Sambhaji. The letter now in Sambhaji's hands was a carefully crafted lie, meant to keep him calm and unassuming until the Maratha troops could arrive to capture him.

"Who brought this letter?" Sambhaji asked, his voice tinged with suspicion.

"A messenger from Raigad, Yuvraj," Vitthal Mahadkar replied, his words stammering, betraying his nervousness.

Sambhaji's eyes narrowed as he scrutinized the letter. He glanced from Mahadkar back to the letter, noting the royal stamp indicating it was supposedly official correspondence from Shivrai. His mind raced, his instincts screaming that something was amiss.

"These aren't Shivrai's words, and this isn't Balaji Avaji's handwriting either," Sambhaji declared, his voice filled with certainty.

"No, Yuvraj, it is Balaji!" Mahadkar blurted out, but then stopped abruptly, realizing his mistake.

"Mahadkar, this is Balaji's son Khando's writing," Sambhaji pointed out calmly. "Mahadkar, next time you have a messenger, please make sure you bring him to me in person and not just deliver the letter," Sambhaji said, his tone firm, his eyes piercing with a hidden warning.

After Mahadkar departed, Sambhaji turned to Kavi Kalash and said, "Please keep an eye on Mahadkar. A fort commander delivering a letter himself is highly unusual unless there is something significant about it."

Later that evening, as the shadows grew longer, Sambhaji sat in his chamber with Yesu beside him. His face was drawn, his eyes clouded with worry. "I really don't know what exactly is unfolding at Raigad. Something is terribly wrong there. I can feel it deep within my heart," he confessed.

"Yuvraj, you might be overthinking. You have seen a lot of turmoil lately. Perhaps you are simply tired," Yesu replied softly, her hand gently caressing his arm, trying to soothe him.

But Sambhaji remained resolute. His instincts told him that this was not just his mind playing tricks on him. Something sinister was indeed afoot.

As if to confirm his suspicions, there was a knock on the door. Sambhaji rose immediately and went to see who it was. A man stood at a distance, shrouded in shadows, waiting for him. Sambhaji immediately recognized him as a messenger.

"Yuvraj," the man whispered, glancing around cautiously, "Bahirji Naik has sent me." He stopped, his eyes darting nervously to ensure no one else was listening.

The messenger reached into his robes and carefully pulled out a letter, hidden securely within the folds of his clothing. He handed it to Sambhaji and said, "This is a letter from Putala Rani Saheb for you. Please read it in private."

"Who let you in?" Sambhaji asked, his voice low and measured.

"I trespassed in. The fort commander did not allow me entry," the messenger replied.

This was precisely what Sambhaji had anticipated. Despite his explicit instructions to Mahadkar to bring any messenger to him directly, the commander had not followed his orders. This only deepened his suspicions.

Sambhaji asked the messenger to wait outside his chamber as he went in to read the letter. His hands trembled slightly as he opened it, bracing himself for what it might reveal.

The letter read:

Yuvraj, the situation at Raigad is worsening. You are being kept away from the reality. Shivrai had been ill for a long time and has sadly traversed on his journey to the afterlife. I am caged here within the politics. I do not have powers, and the conspiracies are all against you. The conspires are ensuring that you are labelled as a traitor and punished, thereby actually securing their positions and making Rajaram the new king. More than Shivrai's demise, what hurts me more is that he received a Bhadganani which no king deserves. His own people did not want you to be told about his demise, keeping you away from lighting his pyre. The last rituals were performed without priests, and the pyre was not even lit by Rajaram.

Sambhaji's world came crashing down. The ground beneath him seemed to shift as he struggled to comprehend the magnitude of the news. His father, his guide, his hero, gone, and he had not even been allowed to bid him farewell. His legs shook, and he found himself needing to sit as his hands trembled with grief. He continued reading, eyes blurred with tears:

Your Abasaheb was always concerned about you even in his last days. He used to talk about you. He told me once that you are the future of the Maratha Samraj. He said, Putala, it would be our son Shambhu who would fulfil my dreams of Swaraj after me. I had nodded to him that day. He believed in you and he feels you shall ensure our freedom as a rightful heir. Least did he know that his own people shall turn enemies in fulfilling his dream. In his last days, he was mentally tormented and worried about the politics around you. He wanted to tell me something but collapsed before he could. I cannot get over the last moments that keeps replaying. I am dying everyday. The last hope I have is you. He too wanted to see you, but these greedy people have kept you away from your own rights. You had the right to see your Abasaheb and light his pyre. They are calling you a traitor, which I cannot tolerate anymore. Sinister plans are being made, which I am completely unaware of. I have heard Soyrabai asking a few men to head to Panhala and imprison you. Almost everything is being governed by her. Raigad is in disgrace. Swaraj's foundations are shaky. This isn't the Swaraj your Abasaheb had dreamt of. Your place is on this throne. You have to fulfil your Abasaheb's dreams. You are needed here to channelize the mindsets and show our men the correct direction. The day is not far away when the Mughals shall take advantage of this and descend upon us. We need a capable Chhatrapati to govern us And I see it in you.

Your life is at threat too. Not just the Mughals and our enemies but our very own people too. Trust nobody! Almost everybody is involved. Like your Abasaheb said once, you are a lion's cub awaiting it's time to roar. You are his Chhava! This is the time to roar and rebel for your rights. I want to see you victorious and seated on this throne, your Aausaheb Putala.

Sambhaji's hands continued to tremble as the letter slipped from his grasp, falling to the ground. His mind was overwhelmed with memories of his father, from his childhood, playing in Shivrai's arms, to their last meeting when his father had looked frail. Regret flooded his heart: he wished he had spoken more, asked more questions, been there more often. Now, these would remain mere memories, haunting him.

Gathering his resolve, Sambhaji met with the messenger and instructed him, "Tell Aausaheb in person that I have received her letter. Assure her she need not worry about me. It's just a matter of time before I shall be back at Raigad!"

12.

THE HORSES neighed and galloped through the green terrains, splashing through rivers as Malhoji Ghorpade and his men raced back to Panhala. The urgency was evident in their swift movements; Malhoji needed to reach the fort before the approaching army did. His heart pounded as he desperately wanted to warn Yuvraj about what he had witnessed. Behind him, in the distance, a formidable force of 10,000 Maratha soldiers was charging towards Panhala, led by Annaji Datto. Another division of several thousand men, led by Peshwa Pinglay, had regrouped with Sarnobat Mohite in Satara, all heading in the same direction.

As Panhala came into view, Malhoji shouted to his men stationed at the gates, "Open the gates!" His voice carried an urgency that left no room for delay. As he approached the fort, he dismounted his horse and hurriedly ensured all the gates were secured and closed behind him. He then climbed the fort's steep steps, his breath ragged and heavy. He ran through the open ground to the front of the fort, grossed the main chamber and the gate up until he reached the courtroom where Sambhaji was seated along with his subordinates, discussing work.

"Yuvraj... Yuvraj..." Malhoji panted, his chest heaving.

Sambhaji, noticing his distress, gestured to one of his subordinates to fetch water for Malhoji.

"Yuvraj," Malhoji began urgently, still catching his breath, "We have been deceived. They are coming for us, not in hundreds but in thousands, to imprison you. Our own men are marching against you!"

Sambhaji, who had already sensed a conspiracy forming against him, was taken aback by the sheer scale of the threat. He hadn't anticipated an army of thousands turning against him.

"This is disgraceful," Kavi Kalash, Sambhaji's trusted adviser, remarked with a deep frown. "Is this what Shivrai envisioned for Swaraj?"

"Yuvraj, you must leave," Malhoji pleaded. "There is a secret route. You can escape while I, along with the men here, will defend the fort to our last breath."

Sambhaji turned to him, a pained expression on his face. "Defend against whom, Malhoji?" he asked, his voice tinged with sadness. "These are our own men. If they win or we win, it is our blood that will be shed. Swaraj would be jeopardized, leaving us vulnerable to our enemies, giving them a chance to defeat us."

"But Yuvraj," Malhoji tried to protest, but Sambhaji cut him off, his voice firm. "If imprisoning me serves their purpose, I am ready for it. Let them come in. No one is to counterattack. Even if I perish, Swaraj must not be sacrificed. The freedom of our land and the safety of our people matter to me more than my own life."

"They didn't even tell you about our Chhatrapati's demise. This is a crime," Malhoji's eyes filled with tears. Sambhaji, sensing his inner turmoil, placed a reassuring hand on his shoulder, said, "I have been informed by Putala Aausaheb recently about Abasaheb's demise," Sambhaji stopped, his Abasaheb's face flashing in his mind, before he continued, "When I have men like you Malhoji to protect our lands against our enemies, I am sure the nation is safe. It does not matter, whether I lead or Rajaram leads. It is people like you who shall be deciding the future of this nation"

"Raje…" Malhoji was teary eyed.

"I am not your Raje, yet," Sambhaji said.

"That's what I see in you – a capable leader," replied Malhoji.

Sambhaji embraced Malhoji. There was a moment of silence. Nobody spoke.

"The good news, Yuvraj," Malhoji continued, "is that many people from Raigad have settled at the foothills of Panhala. After Shivrai's passing, they no longer feel safe in Raigad. They look to you as their protector. They wish to see you as Shivrai's rightful successor."

A flicker of hope ignited in Sambhaji's eyes. He walked to one of the fort's walls and gazed out into the distance. From a wall of the fort, he could see the Maratha forces rapidly advancing toward the fort. He recognized the familiar faces of Peshwa Pinglay, Annaji Datto, Sarnobat Mohite, and many others leading the army.

To his surprise, Janardan Hanmante and Hiroji Farzand reappeared before him. They had returned just in time, ahead of the Maratha invasion, as part of a well-orchestrated plan to help the forces infiltrate the fort.

"Welcome back, Hiroji and Janardanji," Sambhaji said, greeting them with a cordial tone.

A sly smile crept across their faces.

"What emergency in your family called you away so urgently?" Sambhaji asked, his tone deceptively light.

"A close relative," Janardan replied cautiously, while Hiroji, after a moment's hesitation, added, "My cousin passed away."

"I feel sorry for both of you," Sambhaji replied, his tone laced with an undercurrent of contempt. "And how is Shivrai? Did you meet him?"

"Perfectly fine," Janardan lied with confidence.

Sambhaji laughed bitterly, knowing the truth. Kavi Kalash and Malhoji stood by, witnessing the deceitfulness of these men.

As the Maratha army approached Panhala, Sarnobat Mohite's mind was a battlefield of its own. Doubts and fears clashed within him. Was he making the right choice by siding against Yuvraj Sambhaji, who had always trusted him? Sarnobat Mohite was close not only to Shivrai but also to Soyrabai, Shivrai's queen, and Sambhaji's stepmother. As a military chief, his duty was to follow orders, but his heart was conflicted.

After Shivrai's death, he had listened to two contrasting stories: Soyrabai's, which branded Sambhaji a traitor, and Putalabai's, which spoke of Shivrai's understanding of Sambhaji's motives. If Shivrai had not punished Sambhaji for joining the Mughals, maybe there was more to the story than met the eye. It could have been a strategic decision that Shivrai was aware of. Which version was true? Which path should he follow?

As the Maratha forces reached Panhala, Mohite expected resistance. To his astonishment, the gates of Panhala opened, welcoming the troops inside. Mohite had anticipated a fierce counterattack, but instead, Sambhaji had chosen to face his men with open arms. As Mohite and his men climbed the steps of the fort, up to the open ground in front of the courtroom, he recalled Shivrai's words: that the most vital person after the Chhatrapati was the Sarnobat, the military commander. The king might give orders, but it was the Sarnobat who fought the battles. Both were indispensable. Rajaram, still a young boy, was not ready to take on such responsibilities. Shivrai's words now made perfect sense to Mohite.

"Who can truly lead the Marathas?" Mohite wondered as he ascended the steps. "An experienced Sambhaji or an adolescent Rajaram?"

When Mohite reached the top of the fort, he witnessed a sight that was both unexpected and striking. The soldiers stood before Sambhaji, with Malhoji leading them, forming a protective line. Sambhaji stood behind them, but none of the soldiers attacked Mohite and his men. Behind Mohite were Peshwa Pinglay and Surnees Datto, who appeared to be brimming with confidence, believing they had already secured victory.

"Before you imprison me, may I speak?" Sambhaji's voice rang out, calm yet commanding. "If you are imprisoning me for joining hands with the Mughals and labelling me a traitor, then so be it. But what of the treachery you all committed by denying a son the right to see his father one last time and perform his final rites? You hid the truth of Abasaheb's death from me. Even enemies allow their foes to meet their families in death. And what of the indignity of Shivrai being given a *bhadagni* instead of a *mantrangani*? How do you justify this crime?"

The soldiers, unaware of the bhadagni, were taken aback. They had revered Shivrai as their God, and now they felt outraged. A bhadagni was a pyre lit without the mantras being chanted. In contrast, mantrangani was believed to be offered to the king: a pyre lit by one of his sons, in the presence of the pandits chanting Vedic mantras, to aid the peaceful transition of the departed soul. A king deserved a mantrangani.

"How do you know?" Pinglay demanded.

"He is right," Mohite interjected, breaking his silence.

Pinglay and Datto were stunned. "What are you saying?" they asked in disbelief, trying to remind Mohite of his supposed allegiance.

"Don't you dare question a Sarnobat. You do not have the authority," Mohite retorted sharply.

Sambhaji, Kavi Kalash, and Malhoji were taken aback by Mohite's sudden shift. Mohite had been battling his thoughts and his decision to imprison Sambhaji all the while, until he remembered Shivrai's words.

"I have seen everything with my own eyes. If you have Soyrabai on your side, I have Putalabai on mine," Mohite continued. "As the Sarnobat, it is my duty to ensure the Maratha army's welfare, to protect our men, and to expand our territories against our enemies."

Turning to Pinglay and Datto, Mohite declared, "Though I was confused for a time about what was right and wrong, deep down, I always knew the truth. My country needs Yuvraj."

Fury flared in Mohite's eyes as he commanded, "If you can commit treason, so can I. Arrest these two!"

Pinglay and Datto were caught off guard.

"Soldiers," Pinglay shouted, "Arrest the Yuvraj," but his shouts went in vain. The army stood silent. In front of them was not only the Yuvraj but also Sarnobat Mohite, who was the chief of the military. The army did not move an inch.

"You fools!" Datto shouted at the soldiers who still did not react.

Mohite laughed at the two of them and signalled the men, who quickly overpowered them, forcing them to their knees.

Bowing before Yuvraj, Mohite said, "Yuvraj, forgive me for my errors. I had no choice but to feign allegiance to them until I could discern the truth. Once I knew, I was clear on what needed to be done."

A smile spread across Sambhaji's face. He placed his hand on Mohite's shoulder in a gesture of trust and gratitude.

As they all descended from the fort, the sun began to rise. It felt as though a new dawn was breaking not just for the Marathas but for the entire Swaraj. The soldiers erupted into chants and roars, their spirits lifted, and morale was restored.

Pointing towards the vast army, Mohite said, "The entire army belongs to you now, Yuvraj. Raigad is devoid of an army. Up until reaching Panhala, I was in two minds until I made up my mind. Later, I had to pretend to be on their side to bring the entire army to you. If Raigad disowns you, you are free to set up your capital here in Panhala with the entire army by your side and I as your shied."

A loud cheer echoed in the walls of Panhala as the army cheered for Mohite.

Sambhaji's eyes glistened with tears as he rode down the steps, looking upon his men who stood cheering him on. '*This,*' he thought to himself, '*is the Swaraj my Abasaheb had envisioned.*'

Mohite continued, "Shivrai might have gone on his next journey, but we have his own blood, his own son with us. You are our Chhatrapati."

"*Chhatrapati Sambhaji Rajencha Vijay aso,*" hailed the army in unison.

"Har Har Mahadev," the hails continued as a sense of pride ran through the entire army.

"This is a new beginning. A beginning of a new chapter of the Maratha dynasty," declared Mohite to the army as Sambhaji looked at him from a distance.

"Shivrai is gone," he continued, "But…we have with us…" Mohite paused and added, "Shivrayancha Chhava!" as the hailing grew louder and the hooting intensified.

Sambhaji, the Chhava, was now ready to roar.

FOUR EYES remained fixed intently on the Mahadarwaza, the grand entrance of Raigad Fort, their breaths held in anticipation of who would pass through its formidable gates. Two of those eyes belonged to Putalabai, who desperately wished to see Sambhaji return, marching through those gates in victory and glory. The other two eyes belonged to Soyrabai, who fervently hoped to see her brother Pinglay and her trusted ally Datto arrive bearing the news that Sambhaji had been captured, shackled, and imprisoned far away from the fort's commanding heights.

Over the past few days, Soyrabai had been tirelessly consumed with preparations for Rajaram's coronation. She had been meticulous, leaving no detail unattended. The palace was adorned with flowers, garlands, and colourful flags; every corner of the fort was prepared to breathe in the spirit of celebration. Invitations had been sent to close relatives and trusted allies, summoning them to witness her son Rajaram's ascension to the throne. As the days passed, Putalabai began to realize the cunning stratagem behind Shivrai being given a bhadagni instead of the traditional mantaragni during his funeral rites. Had Rajaram performed the rites and the priests chanted the sacred mantras during the pyre ritual; the Bhosale family would have entered a state of 'sutak'—a period of ritual impurity following a death. During this time, no auspicious events or celebrations could be conducted, which would have indefinitely delayed Rajaram's coronation. By ensuring a bhadagni instead, Soyrabai had shrewdly sidestepped the sutak, clearing the path for Rajaram to be crowned without any religious or ceremonial hindrances. With Sambhaji now possibly imprisoned and far away from the fort, she believed she had complete control over the kingdom and its destiny.

Soyrabai's anxious eyes searched the horizon, longing to catch a glimpse of her brother, Sarnobat Mohite. She knew that once he returned with the news of Sambhaji's capture, he would perform the necessary rituals and formally declare Rajaram as the next Chhatrapati of the Maratha Empire. Days of waiting seemed like an eternity, but finally, news reached her that the Maratha army was returning to Raigad. Her heart quickened with a mix of anticipation and triumph. She hurried to the bastions and could see in the distance a vast procession, thousands of cavalrymen and infantry marching toward the fort like an unstoppable wave. Her heart swelled with joy, believing that her plans had succeeded. Elated, she rushed back to her quarters, ensuring she was dressed in her finest, and prepared a welcoming thal filled with a lit diya, fresh flowers, and sweets to greet her brother and allies.

As the Mahadarwaza opened wide to welcome the returning soldiers, flower petals were showered on the warriors, honouring their bravery and valour. Her eyes searched eagerly for her brother, and soon enough, she spotted Sarnobat Mohite at the front, leading the march with the authority and confidence of a seasoned warrior.

Her heart leapt with joy, and she was on the verge of stepping forward to greet him when something stopped her in her tracks. From behind Mohite emerged a figure she had not expected to see, a man dressed in a white Angarkha and a striking saffron turban. He was tall, muscular, and his presence commanded attention. It was Sambhaji. The radiant smile on Soyrabai's face vanished within moments, replaced by an expression of shock and disbelief. Her heart sank like a stone, and the thal nearly slipped from her grasp. She stood there frozen, her mind racing to comprehend what had gone wrong.

Putalabai, who stood nearby in her widow's white saree, had tears welling up in her eyes, her hands trembling as she clasped them together in silent prayer. She silently thanked the Almighty, her heart overwhelmed with gratitude. Her son was safe; he had returned unharmed. That was all she had prayed for in these turbulent days, amidst all the political conspiracies and threats that had surrounded him.

The people of Raigad, who had gathered to witness the spectacle, erupted in cheers, their voices echoing off the massive stone walls of the fort. The air was filled with fervour, anticipation, and the realization that Sambhaji had not only returned but had returned triumphant.

In the courtroom, as Sambhaji made his way to the throne, he walked with a purpose that exuded confidence and authority. The crowd sensed that he would soon declare himself the rightful Chhatrapati, ending all doubts and disputes over succession. As he approached the throne, he paused to bend down and touch Putalabai's feet, seeking her blessings with reverence. Her face softened, her eyes filled with tears of joy and relief.

Then he turned towards Soyrabai. Her heart was a cauldron of bitterness and disappointment. She could not contain her rage and disbelief. As Sambhaji bent down to touch her feet, she abruptly turned away, muttering under her breath, "This is not done. This cannot be true." Her voice was filled with an edge of defiance, but also a realization that her carefully laid plans had crumbled to dust.

"I respect your motherly affection towards Rajaram, and

Rajaram is truly blessed to have received it, which I shall always be devoid of," spoke Sambhaji, "I wish and I know, someday, Rajaram shall definitely be the Chhatrapati of this kingdom, but at the moment, for the benefit of Swaraj, I am forced to go against you. Please bless me with your blessings."

Soyrabai was adamant. She did not respond and walked away, harshly.

"I have always considered you my Aausaheb," spoke Sambhaji from behind, which fell on Soyrabai's deaf ears.

Young Rajaram, who had been excitedly watching his elder brother's return, broke into a run and rushed to embrace him. Sambhaji wrapped his arms around Rajaram, hugging him tightly with genuine affection. Before the moment could linger, Soyrabai rushed back, pulling Rajaram away by the arm, her eyes flashing with a mixture of anger and fear. She quickly led him away, locking themselves in their chambers, perhaps to console him or to vent her frustration at how things had turned out.

Later, the priests began their chants, their voices resonating through the fort, filling the air with sacred hymns as flowers were offered to the deities, and the drummers beat their drums with vigour. The *powadais*, the traditional Maratha ballads celebrating heroism, were sung with pride and energy as Sambhaji ascended the empty throne, which seemed to have been waiting eagerly for its new king. The throne, draped in rich silks and adorned with precious gems, shone under the sun, casting a regal aura. He was asked to take his vows before the holy fire, and he did so with solemnity and conviction.

"I, as the Chhatrapati, shall follow my sacred duty to protect and uphold the Swaraj established by Shivrai. I shall safeguard our land from all enemies, uphold justice, and ensure that no subject of this kingdom suffers oppression. Strength and righteousness shall guide my rule, and the welfare of my people shall be my foremost concern. Let knowledge flourish, let prosperity reach every home, and let no injustice go unpunished. Swaraj shall not only endure but expand, for it is not just a kingdom… it is the embodiment of our people's courage and sacrifice," Sambhaji vowed, his voice firm and resolute, echoing through the fort. His words were met with thunderous applause and cheers from the crowd who had gathered to witness the coronation.

Following tradition, Sambhaji donated gold equal to his weight to the common people, symbolizing his commitment to their welfare. He was then bathed in milk, honey, and flowers as part of the sacred rituals, a symbolic purification and rebirth as the new Chhatrapati. Sarnobat Mohite gifted him a golden dagger, studded with precious gems, as a mark of respect and acknowledgement of his new role as the king. The crowning moment came when Mohite, who had been a loyal servant of Shivrai, placed the royal crown on Sambhaji's head. The crowd cheered again, their enthusiasm undiminished.

Yet, amidst all the jubilation and euphoria, there was a weight that bore down on Sambhaji's heart. While he had the love and support of the common people, he was acutely aware that not all within his court shared the same sentiment. Many of the top subhedars and ministers remained sceptical of his leadership, questioning his intentions and abilities. Five of them, in fact, had been imprisoned at Raigad after being brought from Panhala: Peshwa Pinglay, Annaji Datto, Janardan Hanmante, Hiroji Farzand, and Vitthal Mahadkar, the fort commander of Panhala. Each of them had once been the pride of the Maratha kingdom, celebrated for their valour and service to the empire. Yet now, they were bound by suspicion, their loyalty questioned.

For days, Sambhaji had been deep in thought, pondering his next steps as the Chhatrapati. He knew that to govern effectively, he needed not only the loyalty of the people but also the cooperation and respect of his ministers and commanders. Before departing Panhala, he had made strategic decisions, appointing Malhoji Ghorpade as the new fort commander, rewarding him with a dagger, and ensuring that the army was paid from the revenues of Panhala rather than Raigad. He understood that maintaining a strong army required a steady flow of revenue, and in a region where politics could turn allies into enemies overnight, this was a calculated move. He needed to ensure that the soldiers, who formed the backbone of the Maratha resistance, trusted him as they had trusted his father, Shivrai.

"Where do we stand? What is the latest news from the Mughals?" Sambhaji asked Maratha's head spy, Bahirji Naik. It was Sambhaji's first day at the court after his coronation, and he was accompanied by Sarnobat Mohite, Kavi Kalash, and a few other ministers.

"The news from Marwar is grim," Bahirji began, his expression serious. "Aurangzeb has managed to break the coalition of Durgadas, the Sisodia, the Kacchavah clans, and the Akbar-led Mughals. More than half of Akbar's Mughal army has returned to Agra, leaving him with a significantly reduced force. This makes him vulnerable to attacks from both Durgadas and Aurangzeb. Since the death of Mirza Raja Jai Singh, the Mughals have faced one setback after another in the Deccan. Aurangzeb's eldest son, Mohammed Sultan, has died of depression, and his second son, Muazzam, has parted ways with Diler Khan. That was, in fact, thanks to your efforts, Raje."

Bahirji continued with a hint of admiration in his voice, "Diler Khan is now without funds and reduced to nothing, while Muazzam, who dreams of becoming the next Badshah, is lost in his addictions to women and alcohol. Frustrated with the constant failures, Aurangzeb dispatched Bahadurshah Kokaltash to Burhanpur, but even he had been distracted, more focused on his own marriages than on the Mughal campaign, much to Aurangzeb's displeasure. As for Shaista Khan, who once terrorized the Deccan, he has refused to return here, still fearing the Marathas after Shivrai slashed his fingers. He remains content in Bengal. Moreover, with our peace treaty with Adilshahi, there is little cause for immediate concern."

"We would be fools to believe this." Sambhaji interrupted, his voice stern. "Aurangzeb will not stay silent for long. If he finds no general capable enough to fight against us, he will come himself, leading his army. And if that happens, we must be ready. We have lost significant revenues from Bhupalgad, and the income from Panhala is insufficient to keep our forces motivated. Should Aurangzeb descend upon us, his first move would be to create divisions within our ranks, bribing our soldiers and offering them positions of watandars and mansabdars. We must ensure we have enough revenue to sustain a prolonged conflict."

Standing at a distance, Sarnobat Mohite listened, feeling proud of his decision to prioritize Swaraj over familial ties. Shivrai's words echoed in his mind: "*A Sarnobat can fight wars with valour, but only a wise and seasoned king knows when, where, and how to wage them.*" He realized Rajaram, still in his teens, would not have been able to take such a decisive stance.

"What do you suggest, Yuvraj?" Kavi Kalash asked.

Sambhaji turned to Bahirji Naik, who had intimate knowledge of both Maratha and Mughal territories, for an answer.

"Burhanpur is the key," Bahirji declared confidently.

"But Burhanpur could be too risky," Kalash warned, aware of the dangers involved. Burhanpur was close to Aurangzeb's heart, a place he had established as the second capital of the Mughal province. All the wealth the Mughals had accumulated over the years was stored there.

"Attacking Burhanpur means directly challenging Aurangzeb," Kalash continued. "He will come after us."

"And that is precisely what we need," Sambhaji said with determination. "An invasion of Burhanpur would send a loud and clear message to the Mughals that while Shivrai may no longer be with us, the flame of Swaraj still burns brightly in the hearts of every Maratha."

Turning to Bahirji, Sambhaji added, "Bahirji kaka, I want you to go to Burhanpur with your spies, study the terrain, and come up with an actionable plan."

"Yes, Raje," Bahirji replied, bowing as he left to execute his orders.

Although everything seemed to be falling into place for the Marathas, Sambhaji appeared troubled by something else. Noticing this, Kalash gently inquired, "What weighs heavily on your mind, Raje?"

"We might succeed in looting Burhanpur," Sambhaji replied, "but our strength, our experience, and our valour are already diminished with our five heroes locked up in prison."

"But they committed treason," Sarnobat Mohite pointed out.

"Yes, under the queen's orders, likely under pressure," Sambhaji admitted. "Yet, what matters to me more than the reason behind their actions is having them back so they can continue to serve our cause. Their expertise will be crucial in winning future battles and establishing Swaraj."

"Bring them here," Sambhaji ordered.

"No, Raje! Whatever is done is done. They have backstabbed you," said Kalash.

"They deserve nothing but imprisonment," added Sarnobat Mohite.

"So does Soyra Aausaheb then," Sambhaji came straight to the point, "Whatever is done is done, is what I am saying too. Everybody deserves a second chance."

Sambhaji again commanded his subordinates to bring the imprisoned warriors to the court. The five men, bound in chains, were brought in, taking cautious steps and shivering with fear. They looked around, their eyes darting across the room filled with ministers, Pralhad Niraji, Rahulji Somnath, Balaji Avaji, Khando Ballal, Kalash, Sarnobat Mohite, Abaji Sondev, and many others. As they saw Sambhaji seated on the throne, Annaji Datto's heart sank, fearing the worst. He bowed deeply, hoping for mercy.

Addressing the five men, Sambhaji began, "The Maratha kingdom has never seen warriors and ministers of your calibre, who have brought honour to our land time and again. What you have done to me is unjustifiable, but your contributions to our Swaraj have been unparalleled and invaluable. At this moment, our nation needs skilled warriors like you to help guide and protect us, as you have always done. Thus, I order your release."

Annaji Datto let out a sigh of relief while Hiroji Farzand, overwhelmed with emotion, bowed before Sambhaji, tears streaming down his face.

"In this new chapter, for the smooth functioning of the kingdom, I will assign new roles to each of you," Sambhaji continued, pausing to let his words sink in. Turning to Pralhad Niraji, he said, "Your wisdom in dealing with the Qutubshahi has proven invaluable to us. You shall oversee the judicial affairs of the nation."

Facing Annaji Datto next, Sambhaji stated, "You may have

made errors in handling revenues, and I have challenged you many times before, but I still have faith in your mathematical prowess. You are reinstated as the treasurer. Abaji Sondev shall take up the role of surnees."

"Balaji Avaji," Sambhaji said, making Balaji tense with the memory of his deceit, "You will continue as our scribe. I am willing to forgive you, despite you depriving me of the right to know about Abasaheb's condition, concealing his death, and fabricating those letters."

"Hiroji Farzand," he continued, "Your bravery is what Shivrai admired most. As a doppleganger, you lay on the bed in Agra, helping Abasaheb and me escape from Agra when Aurangzeb had captured us. Indebted to your valour, I shall forgive you, and you shall continue to fight against the Mughals, stationed alongside Bahirji Naik in our upcoming campaigns. Janardan Hanmante will serve as our diplomat during negotiations."

Taking a moment to address the assembly, Sambhaji added, "Rahulji Somnath and Vitthal Mahadkar will guard the foothills of Raigad, and Pinglay shall remain our Peshwa. I am willing to forget all past mistakes, and I expect you all to believe that I have not committed treason by joining hands with the Mughals. It was part of a strategy; one I may never be able to justify or explain fully."

A heavy silence settled over the court as Sambhaji's words hung in the air. Some bowed their heads in guilt, while others felt a sense of relief at having escaped severe punishment. What was evident, however, was that this was the beginning of a new chapter for the Maratha empire, a chapter that generations to come would remember with pride.

DURGADAS'S MEN were everywhere, combing the hills and valleys in search of Prince Akbar. The prince had been in hiding, constantly on the move to avoid being captured, not just by his father Aurangzeb's men but also by Durgadas's warriors, who had set out to find him for his betrayal. Yet, circumstances had changed. Over time, Durgadas, through his network of spies and informants, had uncovered the truth: Aurangzeb had cleverly deceived both Akbar and Durgadas, sowing discord between them and breaking their fragile alliance. Durgadas had begun to wonder whether Akbar had any idea of his father's cunning manipulation. What had started as a hunt to eliminate the rebellious prince had now shifted to a mission to find and protect him from the wrath of the Mughal emperor.

Determined to locate Akbar before Aurangzeb's forces did, Durgadas had travelled across many lands, following every lead, speaking to every spy and sympathizer. After days and nights of relentless searching, he finally succeeded in tracking him down. Finding Akbar hiding among the hills, he tried approaching him but was stopped by Akbar's men.

'We cannot let you in," said one of his guards to Durgadas and his men.

"It is very important for us to meet the Shehzada and clear the misunderstandings," replied Durgadas.

Akbar could overhear the voices from his tent. He decided to confront Durgadas. Either he shall mend things or he shall kill Durgadas Rathod is what he believed and walked out with his sword.

"Shehzada Akbar," remarked Durgadas from a distance upon seeing him. Akbar stood at a safe distance, gauging what Durgadas had to say. Durgadas continued, "Everything has just been a big lie. The Badshah ensured we were divided. The letters were written and forcibly planted in such a way that we both believe them. My sources have told me that it was a part of Aurangzeb's plan. He is far more wicked than he seems," Durgadas said firmly to Akbar, hoping to make him understand the gravity of the situation.

Akbar's eyes narrowed with suspicion. "How can I believe you? This could just be yet another plan of Badshah's and yours to capture me."

Durgadas raised his hands slowly in a gesture of peace. "Please do not get mistaken. People of Marwar never backstab. We are known for keeping our words. I assure you that we desire to tarnish the Badshah and shall help you become the next Badshah," he said, placing his dagger on a large stone beside him, adjusting his turban with a calm, deliberate motion. Akbar sighed, his gaze still wary. "I do not have enough men with me now," he complained, glancing at Durgadas. "How do we plan an attack?"

"The Badshah won't spare your life. If he succeeds in killing you and penetrating our provinces, we might perish as well," Durgadas responded gravely. "Moreover, after the Badshah sent those deceitful letters, the Sisodia and Kacchavah clans believed them to be true and backed off. Convincing them and bringing them back into the fold seems impossible at the moment. We are on our own."

"We cannot win the battle," Akbar said, frustration evident in his tone.

"We cannot win, but we can still survive until we find an ally," Durgadas said, his eyes steady.

"In whom? The Sisodias?" Akbar interrupted, his doubt growing.

"No," Durgadas declared with determination. "The Marathas!"

Akbar stared at him, clearly sceptical. The idea seemed absurd to him. '*Why would the Marathas, so far away and embroiled in their own struggles, help us here in Marwar?*' he wondered silently.

"The Marathas shook hands with the Adilshahi and helped them against Diler Khan's invasion," Durgadas explained, sensing Akbar's hesitation. "With Sambhaji, the new Chhatrapati of the Marathas, we could convince them to support us in our fight against Aurangzeb. The enemy of the enemy can be our friend."

Akbar mulled over Durgadas's words. Everything seemed uncertain, and he had doubts about how these plans would unfold. However, he realized he had little choice. If he had any hope of survival and reclaiming his rightful place, he needed to take risks. And right now, the only person around him who seemed trustworthy was Durgadas.

Reluctantly nodding his agreement, Akbar decided to follow Durgadas's lead. Along with Durgadas and his men, he set out on a cautious journey toward the Maratha territories, his mind racing with thoughts of what lay ahead and whether the Marathas could indeed be the unexpected ally they so desperately needed.

13.

"I HAD expected life to change but not so quickly," wept an inconsolable Putalabai, her voice breaking as she spoke to Yesu and Sambhaji in private. The moment she saw her son safely return to Raigad, her heart swelled with immense joy. That joy only grew when she witnessed him being coronated, ascending to the same throne where Chhatrapati Shivaji Maharaj had once proudly sat. The memories of Shivrai's coronation were still vivid in her mind, as if they had happened just yesterday. Those were her last genuinely happy days, she felt, for after that, life had taken a steep descent into sorrow and uncertainty.

Following Shivrai's coronation, a series of tragic events unfolded, leaving indelible marks on Putalabai's heart. Jijau Mata's demise had cast a long shadow of grief over the kingdom, followed by Shivrai's relentless campaigns on the battlefield. Then came Sambhaji's estrangement from the family, Shivrai's untimely demise, and the treacherous betrayal that nearly led to Sambhaji's capture. Each event had plunged her deeper into despair, leaving her to question the whims of fate. And yet, despite the heartbreak, the sun had peeked through the dark clouds, bringing some light back into her life with Sambhaji's coronation. For a fleeting moment, Putalabai's heart felt whole again, as if her life's purpose had come to fruition.

On the other hand, Soyrabai had confined herself to her quarters for days on end. She had shut herself away from the world, allowing only her most trusted housemaids to attend to her needs. Sambhaji had tried on several occasions to see her, to offer comfort or perhaps to confront her, but his attempts had failed. She had resolutely refused to see his face. For Putalabai, Soyrabai's self-imposed isolation was of little concern. She felt a deep sense of fulfilment and peace in her heart as she softly said, "Now, I feel that the nation is in safe hands." She reached out and placed her hand gently on Sambhaji's face, her fingers tenderly brushing through his hair with maternal affection.

"Shambhu bala," she began, her voice quivering with emotion, "Would you fulfil my wish?"

"Yes, Aausaheb. Is that even worth asking? What do you want?" Sambhaji responded.

"Now that I have seen most of my life unfold before me, I want to reunite with my God, my Chhatrapati, and be his forever," Putalabai replied, her words drenched in the pain of longing. A tear slipped down her cheek, glistening in the soft light as it fell, a tear born of love and remembrance for Shivrai.

Sambhaji and Yesu exchanged puzzled glances; they could not understand the whole meaning of what Putalabai was saying.

"Aausaheb, what are you saying?" Yesu asked, moving closer to her, her concern palpable.

Placing her hands on Yesu and gently caressing her face, Putalabai continued, "Shambhu bala is now fully capable of leading the nation, and you, Yesu, are more than capable of being his queen, handling every aspect of life with strength and grace. I remained alive to see you both happy, to see this day. But the Putala inside me, the woman who truly lived and loved, died the day Shivrai breathed his last. Now, the time has come for me to join him in his afterlife and be blessed to accompany him on every journey he takes."

Putalabai's eyes met Sambhaji's. She saw the alarm in them, the silent plea for her words not to be valid. But she pressed on, her voice steady with the resolve of a woman who had made her peace with her fate. "I want to perform sati and seek your blessings for my next journey with Shivrai. I want you to light the pyre as I make my way to the afterlife."

The ground beneath Sambhaji seemed to vanish. He looked at Putalabai, his eyes wide with disbelief. "This is not going to happen, Aausaheb. Don't you want to live with us?" he pleaded, his voice breaking. Tears began streaming down his face, and Yesu, too, was overcome with emotion, her body shaking with sobs.

Putalabai pulled them both into a comforting embrace. "I have lived my life to the fullest. Seeing you become Chhatrapati fills me with pride. But it's time for me to reunite with Shivrai. This is my promise, my last wish, that you light the pyre and seek my blessings in this noble cause."

Sambhaji, though deeply distraught, realized how resolute

Putalabai was. Her determination left him no choice but to consider her wish, though it tore at his heart. It took days of emotional persuasion and countless pleas, with Putalabai even swearing upon herself, before Sambhaji finally agreed.

On a bright, sunny day, the wood for the pyre was carefully laid out. Sambhaji and Yesu stood nearby, awaiting the inevitable with heavy hearts. Dressed like a bride in her wedding saree, Putalabai emerged from her residence, her steps slow but purposeful. The priests began chanting mantras as a young Rajaram watched the scene unfold from a distance, his eyes wide with fear. He clung to Soyrabai, who had come out of her chambers for the first time in days, drawn by the gravity of the moment.

Putalabai took measured steps toward the pyre, each one heavy with the weight of her decision. She closed her eyes as she neared it, her mind filled only with the thought of Shivrai. The mantras faded into the background, becoming mere murmurs in her ears as she immersed herself completely in her final act. She sat on the pyre, calm and composed. The priests then instructed Sambhaji to light the fire. His hands shook, his eyes brimming with tears, but he remembered her last wish. Summoning his strength, he lit the pyre.

The flames caught quickly, the fire climbing steadily up the wood toward Putalabai. Sambhaji offered water and walked around the pyre, his steps heavy with grief, as per the rituals. The fire began to engulf Putalabai, yet she did not flinch; her mind was beyond the pain. She was already on her journey, one step closer to her beloved Shivrai. Slowly, the fire consumed her, taking her from this world to the next, where she believed Shivrai awaited her.

SAMBHAJI HAD to confront the burdens that had long weighed on his soul and embrace the challenges that destiny had laid before him. The transformation was sudden, leaving him feeling isolated within the mighty walls of Raigad Fort. Despite being king, loneliness crept in. His once-large family was reduced to just his wife, Yesu, and their young daughter. Memories of better times haunted him; moments shared with Abasaheb, Jijau Mata, and Putalabai within these very walls still felt fresh, deepening his solitude. Yet, Sambhaji knew he could not afford to dwell in the past. He had to rise above his emotions, standing tall and resolute to face the trials ahead. His mind also turned to the political intrigues unfolding behind his back while he was away fighting battles. To safeguard his reign and legacy, he needed to make decisive, strategic choices.

In a court filled with ministers and nobles, Sambhaji officially acknowledged Yesubai as queen, granting her the authority to make decisions for the nation's welfare during his absence. This decision, however necessary, stirred unrest in some quarters, particularly with Soyrabai, who had already seen her influence wane. The announcement effectively stripped her of the remaining power she held, and overnight, Yesubai was recognized as the true queen.

"This was really not needed, Yuvraj," Yesubai said to Sambhaji once in private, her voice tinged with concern.

"It is necessary, Yesu," Sambhaji responded, his tone firm yet reassuring. "To win battles on the warfront, we need sound and peaceful governance at home. Your leadership is essential in maintaining that balance."

Meanwhile, the court was once again abuzz with discussions about the upcoming campaign in Burhanpur, a key Mughal stronghold. But this time, the planning was conducted with the utmost secrecy. Only a select few were privy to the details: Sambhaji, Kavi Kalash, and Sarnobat Mohite. Bahirji Naik, the legendary spy, had recently returned from his mission, having scouted the territories surrounding Burhanpur. With his sharp memory, Bahirji had meticulously mapped out the region, presenting his findings to Sambhaji and his advisers.

"Looting Burhanpur is far more challenging than I initially thought," Bahirji Naik declared, his voice heavy with the weight of his reconnaissance.

"What makes you say that?" Sambhaji inquired, his curiosity piqued.

"Burhanpur is a gold mine for the Mughals in the Khandesh region," Bahirji began, his tone measured as he laid out the complexities of the situation. "It shares borders with Surat in Gujarat and Rajasthan. The Mughals used Burhanpur as a critical trade hub, from where they controlled a portion of the Arabian sea to export goods and slaves. Aurangzeb has entrusted Bahadurshah Kokaltash with overseeing the Deccan, and Burhanpur falls under his jurisdiction. However, Kokaltash seldom visits Burhanpur, preferring to indulge in the luxuries the city offered while staying in Aurangabad. He has appointed a wazir to manage Burhanpur in his stead. Both the Wazir and Kokaltash are so engrossed in their own wealth and comforts that they neglect any ambitions of territorial expansion. Their sole focus is defending Burhanpur and reaping its rewards. They don't even send the full revenues to Aurangzeb, keeping a substantial portion for their personal use. Occasionally, when Aurangzeb questions their progress, the wazir stages a few raids on nearby territories, extorts jizya taxes, and incites bloodshed in the name of jihad, just enough to keep Aurangzeb and his army content and distracted. With a large army stationed at Burhanpur and the wazir's constant presence, this region seems nearly impregnable."

A heavy silence fell over the room as Sambhaji absorbed the information. Bahirji then unrolled the map he had prepared, spreading it out on the table for Sambhaji and Mohite to study.

"I expect a solution, Bahirji kaka," Sambhaji finally said, turning to the seasoned spy with a mix of expectation and trust. He knew that if anyone could find a way to breach Burhanpur's defences, it would be Bahirji Naik.

"Do you have a solution in mind?" Mohite asked, his voice tinged with both hope and anxiety.

"Of course, I have a plan," Bahirji replied confidently, though his tone suggested a need for discretion. "But it must remain a closely guarded secret."

"And that's why we are already in a private meeting, Bahirji kaka," Sambhaji said, encouraging him to reveal his strategy.

Bahirji cleared his throat, preparing to speak. "The plan is as follows: My men will disguise themselves as traders and station themselves in Burhanpur, where they will closely monitor the activities there. Meanwhile, thousands of our soldiers will be mobilized towards Surat, under the guise of planning an attack to loot the city. Even our own troops should believe they are headed to Surat to maintain high morale. The news of our army's movement towards Surat will be deliberately spread by our disguised agents in Burhanpur, ensuring that it reaches Kakar Khan, the commander in Burhanpur. With Bahadurshah Kokaltash's son's wedding approaching, Kokaltash will be preoccupied in Aurangabad and will pay little attention to Burhanpur. Most of his forces will be with him in Aurangabad, leaving Kakar Khan with only a fraction of the troops to defend Burhanpur. Upon receiving word of our supposed attack on Surat, Kakar Khan will undoubtedly send his forces to intercept us. As Surat has been a target of Shivrai's raids multiple times in the past, there will be no reason for him to doubt the news. While Kakar Khan's forces are en route to Surat, our troops will halt their advance and return. Simultaneously, a second unit led by Sarnobat Mohite will strike Burhanpur, catching it defenceless and looting it thoroughly, aided by our spies who are already inside the city. The plan is foolproof, and if executed correctly, it will result in a significant victory for us."

Kavi Kalash, who was witnessing Bahirji's strategic brilliance for the first time, was deeply impressed. He finally understood why Shivrai had been so successful in his campaigns. Bahirji Naik had always been the guiding light for the Marathas, a master of espionage and strategy.

"This is brilliant, Bahirji kaka. But…" Sambhaji said.

"What is it, Raje?"

"As much as I trust this plan, we must prepare for the aftermath," Sambhaji began, his tone grave. "Burhanpur is more than just a strategic asset to the Mughals. It is a symbol of their power in the Deccan. Losing it would not only be a strategic loss for Aurangzeb but also a deep wound to his pride. No one has ever dared to attack Burhanpur, fearing the retribution that would follow. If we succeed in this raid, Aurangzeb will be enraged, and he will stop at nothing to retaliate. I believe his counterattack will come from the northwest, through the Baglan province. The Baglan forts are our stronghold and the first line of defence, situated between Burhanpur and Surat."

"Why do you think he will attack from the northwest and not from Aurangabad?" Mohite questioned.

"Because," Sambhaji explained, "Aurangzeb's main objective will be to regain control of Burhanpur. The most effective way for him to do that would be by capturing our forts in Baglan, which he could then use as base camps for further operations. Among these forts, Ramsej is the most vulnerable; it is the easiest to access because it sits on a plain. Salher, on the other hand, is the tallest and strongest, and it will be the most difficult for them to conquer."

For the first time, Bahirji and Sarnobat Mohite, both seasoned warriors who had served Shivrai for years, felt a sense of awe towards Sambhaji. He was no longer the impulsive, instinct-driven youth they had known. He had matured, and his strategic thinking now mirrored that of his legendary father, Shivrai.

"Sarnobat Mohite," Sambhaji commanded, "I want you to visit each of these forts and ensure that restoration work begins immediately, particularly at Ramsej. Make sure we have ample ammunition, provisions, and food supplies to sustain the garrisons for at least a year. Inform Suryaji, the fort commander at Ramsej, about these preparations and instruct Keso Trimal to head to Trimbak Fort to oversee the supplies for Ramsej."

Trimbak Fort, located a few kos away from Ramsej, was strategically important for reinforcing and resupplying the defences during an attack. Sambhaji understood that having this support would be crucial in the coming conflict.

A sense of pride and determination filled the room as Sambhaji concluded, "Just as they attempted to conquer our Baglan forts before, only to taste defeat at Shivrai's hands, we too will make them taste dust like Shivrai did."

UNDER THE diligent supervision of Sarnobat Mohite, the restoration of the forts had been completed. Sambhaji, satisfied with the progress, knew that the preparations for the next phase of his plan were in place. Meanwhile, Bahirji Naik and his men, disguised as textile traders, had positioned themselves around

Burhanpur, befriending nearly everyone in the bustling town. With their strategy in motion, they won the trust of Kakar Khan, the Mughal commander. Bahiriji Naik, along with his men, had managed to get themselves invited to his court and presented him with luxurious silk *jamas* and *choghas*. This act of flattery allowed Bahirji's men to study the interior layout of Kakar Khan's residence, gathering crucial intelligence for the imminent attack.

As part of the deception, Maratha troops set off towards Surat, and soon enough, word of their movement reached Kakar Khan. Alarmed, he quickly dispatched his forces in that direction, convinced that the Marathas were once again planning to plunder the wealthy port city. "Ya Allah, these kafirs!" Kakar Khan had exclaimed in frustration. "The Marathas and their love for Surat! This time I won't spare them." Confident that he had acted swiftly, he did not bother to inform Bahadurshah Kokaltash, who was preoccupied in Aurangabad.

The Mughal troops reached Surat and waited in anticipation for the Maratha invasion. However, no such attack occurred. Days passed, and Kakar Khan grew increasingly anxious. He had received no further updates about the Marathas' movements, and his instinct, honed over years of military experience, warned him that something was amiss. Just as suspicion began to settle heavily in his mind, loud cries filled the air one evening as the sun dipped below the horizon. From his vantage point, he saw a blazing market, with thousands of Maratha soldiers pouring into Burhanpur, looting the province with calculated precision.

Burhanpur, a treasure trove for the Mughals, had everything, from food grains to precious stones and wealth looted from Hindu temples during their ruthless campaigns. Huge sums collected as jizya tax from Hindu families were hidden away in a storehouse that was now engulfed in flames. Kakar Khan's heart pounded as he stood in his chamber, watching the inferno spread, casting a ghastly glow over the once-prosperous market.

The beating of war drums echoed through the night, summoning the startled Mughal soldiers to arms. Kakar Khan, donning his armour, took a position atop a strong, elevated house to assess the chaos unfolding below. The sight was a nightmare. Shops were blown open with cannons, and gold, diamonds, and pearls were hastily stuffed into massive sacks and loaded onto donkeys and oxen, ready to be transported back to Maratha territory. Sarnobat Mohite, leading the charge, swung his sword with deadly precision, cutting down the Mughal soldiers who attempted to resist. Witnessing the fierce Maratha onslaught, many of the Mughals dropped their weapons and surrendered, realizing the futility of further combat. Remarkably, despite the widespread panic among the residents, the Marathas strictly adhered to their code: no innocents were harmed, and no houses were set ablaze.

"Your men are either dead or held captive. Kakar Khan, better surrender!" Sarnobat Mohite shouted from atop his horse, his voice carrying over the clamour of the battle.

"The Badshah won't spare you!" Kakar Khan yelled defiantly from the terrace of the house where he stood.

"First ask your Badshah to enter the battlefields himself rather than sitting in luxury at Agra and ordering others to fight," Sarnobat Mohite retorted with a mocking laugh, striking a nerve.

"How dare you mock us?" Kakar Khan's pride was stung, but his bravado masked his growing dread.

"Isn't your Chhatrapati dead?" Kakar Khan sneered. "Who are you fighting for? A territory ruled by nobody? No successor?" He paused, gauging Sarnobat Mohite's reaction, but the seasoned warrior remained unfazed. "Better join us," Kakar Khan continued with a sly grin. "You would gain power as well as respect."

Sarnobat Mohite chuckled, replying, "What power are you talking about? You don't even have the power to defend yourself at this moment! Your Burhanpur is burning. No ruler has ever dared to do what we have done today. Perhaps the Mughals need better spies if they are unaware of our new Chhatrapati. Unlike your Badshah, our king fights alongside his men!"

Just then, a striking figure emerged from the smoke and chaos, riding a magnificent white Kathiawadi horse. Young, muscular, and radiating authority, Sambhaji appeared, his sword slicing through the enemy lines with lethal grace. 'Har Har Mahadev!' The Maratha war cry rose in unison, growing louder as Sambhaji dismounted his horse. For Kakar Khan, this was the first glimpse of the formidable young Maratha king, a man whose fiery eyes, commanding presence, and lion-like gait left no doubt that he was ready to crush his enemies. Sambhaji held the saffron flag of the Marathas high and planted it firmly in the heart of the market, a bold declaration of victory that could not be ignored.

Seeing the tide of battle turning irreversibly against him, Kakar Khan knew he had only one option left: escape. He slipped away through the back door of the building, abandoning his men to face the wrath of the Marathas. But this was precisely what Sambhaji wanted, Kakar Khan alive to recount the tale of their defeat to Bahadurshah Kokaltash and ultimately, to Aurangzeb himself. The Marathas had arrived in full force, and this was just the beginning. Their message was clear: the days of Mughal dominance were numbered as the Maratha supremacy was dawning over the Deccan.

TRAVELLING THROUGH the arid deserts of Rajasthan, Akbar faced relentless challenges. The searing heat made every moment a battle against exhaustion, and the constant thirst a harsh reminder of their dire circumstances. Sleep eluded him as the shadow of death loomed over him and Durgadas. Despite the harsh conditions, their resolve to reach the Maratha region remained unshaken. With a small band of loyal men, Akbar and Durgadas pressed forward towards Raigad, determined to complete their mission.

Aurangzeb, enraged by the loss of Burhanpur and the renewed alliance between Durgadas and Akbar, intensified his campaign of retribution. He dispatched Shahabuddin Khan with a large contingent to hunt down the fugitives. Shahabuddin, with his ruthless nature, left a trail of destruction in his wake, burning villages and slaughtering innocents under the guise of jihad. The brutal campaign was part of a broader strategy to crush any opposition and instil fear among those who dared to defy him.

In a bid to consolidate his power and eliminate potential threats, Aurangzeb also issued an ultimatum to Shahzada Muazzam, demanding his return to Agra. Akbar's sister, Zebunnissa, who was suspected of conspiring with her brother, was arrested and imprisoned in the dungeons of Salimgarh Fort. Additionally, Akbar's wife and children were taken captive, their fates unknown but presumed grim.

Akbar, tormented by the knowledge of his family's captivity and likely suffering, felt a deep-seated hatred towards his father. He was convinced that only Sambhaji could provide the support he needed to navigate this perilous situation. Yet, a nagging doubt lingered in his mind; would Sambhaji truly come to his aid, or would his plea go unanswered?

THE LOOT from Burhanpur was immense, a testament to the wealth that had been amassed through years of exploitation. It took days for the Maratha forces to transport the spoils from Burhanpur to Raigad and Panhala. The sheer volume of treasure was staggering, with thousands of oxen, donkeys, and horses working tirelessly, yet only managing to carry less than half of what Burhanpur had to offer. The rest remained beyond their reach.

"What do we do with the rest?" Sarnobat Mohite inquired, his brow furrowed with concern.

"Burn it, destroy it, do whatever you must, but ensure the Mughals get hold of nothing," Sambhaji instructed resolutely.

The message was clear and unmistakable to everyone, including both Marathas and Mughals: Sambhaji was determined to retaliate against any form of injustice. The wealth of Burhanpur had been accumulated through centuries of Mughal oppression and exploitation in the name of jihad.

Upon arriving at Raigad, Sambhaji prioritized paying compensation to the families of those who had died or been injured during the Bhupalgad attack. The remaining loot was allocated for the restoration and fortification of the Maratha forts or saved for future campaigns. Yesu welcomed her husband's return with joy, and the people of Raigad celebrated their king's victory with exuberance, showering him with flowers and beating drums.

Meanwhile, Aurangzeb, stung by the defeat at Burhanpur, was consumed with rage. He realized he had underestimated the Marathas after Shivrai's death. None of his mansabdars had succeeded in overcoming the Marathas; they had either failed or been preoccupied with their own indulgences. Determined to rectify this, Aurangzeb resolved to take charge himself. He appointed Shahabuddin Khan to study the entire Deccan region and work under him in the forthcoming attack. Aurangzeb also ensured that Sikander, the ruler of the Adilshahi, was warned and requested to assist the Mughals. Sikander was promised restored friendly relations in exchange for his aid against the Marathas, with the threat of Mughal aggression should he refuse. Khan-E-Jahan, a Mughal mansabdar, was directed to move towards the Maratha borders, while Ranmat and Rahullah Khan were tasked with heading towards the Konkan region. Hussan Ali Khan was ordered to ravage the villages in Kalyan within Konkan.

"Where do we start?" Shahabuddin asked, meeting his master in Agra.

"Baglan!" Aurangzeb declared, pointing to the map before him. This was precisely the strategy Sambhaji had anticipated.

Back at Raigad, Sambhaji was fully aware that the Mughals would likely launch their attack on the Baglan provinces, with Ramsej being the first among the 14 forts to face a significant invasion. The Marathas were prepared. Sambhaji took every precaution, ensuring that all necessary measures were in place through his regular court meetings.

One day, during a routine meeting, a messenger from Durgadas's forces arrived. Kavi Kalash brought the envoy to the court, where he stood before Sambhaji.

Bowing before Sambhaji, the messenger spoke, "Durgadas Rathod and Shehzada Akbar bow before the Chhatrapati of the Marathas and request an alliance against the Mughals. Shehzada Akbar wishes to seek refuge in the Maratha territories. In return, Shehzada Akbar promises to assist the Marathas against Aurangzeb and his tyrannical rule."

"We don't need your friendship," Hiroji Farzand retorted, "We have no interest in forming any alliance with the Mughals."

The messenger spoke, "Shehzada Akbar-led Mughal soldiers are different in ideologies from the Aurangzeb-led Mughal forces."

"It doesn't matter," replied Hiroji.

"Hiroji," Sambhaji said, asking him to stop and intervene, "If Akbar can be of any importance to the Marathas in the fight for Swaraj, we may consider it. Our fight is against Aurangzeb and his Mughal injustice, and not against Shehzada Akbar. Our fight is also not against a specific religion. It is a fight against injustice."

"But Raje, Akbar has it in his blood. After all, he is Aurangzeb's son. Mughals are known to backstab," replied Hiroji Farzand.

"Hiroji, we have nothing to worry. He is coming to our land, seeking refuge. It is not the other way round. If he decides to backstab us, we shall dig his grave here."

Turning towards the messenger, Sambhaji said, "Tell Shehzada Akbar that the Marathas shall welcome him with open arms."

Sambhaji's response took Hiroji and the other ministers aback.

Sambhaji continued, addressing Hiroji, "I will personally welcome Shehzada Akbar. Hiroji, you shall accompany me and ensure that our guests receive the best hospitality."

The date was set, and preparations were made. Tents were erected in the south of Raigad for the forthcoming meeting between Durgadas, Akbar, and Sambhaji. Sambhaji, followed by Hiroji and the Maratha troops, headed towards Pali, where Akbar and Durgadas were stationed. Upon seeing Sambhaji, Akbar was immediately captivated by his presence. The two embraced warmly.

"Welcome, Badshah," Sambhaji greeted Akbar, deliberately choosing the title to appeal to the Shehzada's ambitions. Aware of Akbar's desire for the throne, Sambhaji's gesture was carefully calculated, and it did not go unnoticed. A pleased smile flickered across Akbar's face, acknowledging the unspoken understanding between them.

"The king of kings, the pride of the Marathas, the lion's cub," Akbar praised Sambhaji, bowing before him and added, "I am pleased with your hospitality all this while. Your men ensured that I was safe and had no problem in living in this new land, awaiting our meeting."

"*Atithi devo bhava*!" Sambhaji acknowledged Akbar's gesture with a smile.

"Chhatrapati," Akbar continued, "I wish to avenge my father and put an end to his tyrannical rule. I would request you to help me with an army so that I can charge over Agra and put an end to all of this."

"Shehzada Akbar, I acknowledge your courage, ambitions and your emotions," Sambhaji stopped to sense Akbar's reactions before adding, "But the Marathas shall not spill their blood for anybody else's motives. It shall be us who shall decide when and how to fight the battles and whether to ascend upon Agra or not. Even if we decide to attack Agra, it shall be under the leadership I shall decide."

Sambhaji's words had a sense of warning, letting Akbar know that he should not let his people fight under the leadership of any outsider.

"However, you may join us in our fight for Swaraj," Sambhaji added.

"Certainly, Chhatrapati," replied Akbar, who had no other choice but to accept Sambhaji's offer.

The two embraced as Sambhaji was about to leave.

"Feel safe here. Aurangzeb's shadow also will not fall on you," assured Sambhaji and left.

For the first time in months, Akbar felt a sense of security and refuge, free from his father's looming threat. Hiroji, along with his men, escorted Akbar to a residence at the foothills of Sudhagad. The residence, built from bricks and clay, was lavishly appointed with silk curtains, a long verandah, a private chamber with a red carpet, a small throne for meetings, and an array of Maratha coins, gold hons, diamonds, pearls, and silk robes. Though not a palace, Akbar found the residence charming and comfortable. Hiroji bowed before Akbar, making him feel like royalty once more, before taking his leave.

Durgadas was assigned a residence a few kos away from Akbar. Hiroji ensured that Durgadas's accommodation was comfortable and well-appointed before returning to Raigad. Upon his return, Hiroji was welcomed with unsettling news: Peshwa Pinglay had passed away.

14.

PESHWA PINGLAY'S death in an ambush near Burhanpur had left a profound void in the Maratha leadership. His son, Nilakanth Pinglay, was swiftly appointed as the new Peshwa to oversee affairs at Raigad. The timing of the Mughal attack was almost too precise, aligning with Sambhaji's predictions of their impending descent. The Mughals had reached Shivneri under the command of Hussain Ali Khan, but the most concerning issue for Sambhaji lay further west, the Konkan coast.

Daulat Khan, whom Shivrai had appointed as the head of the Maratha naval forces, approached Sambhaji with grim news.

"Maharaj," he began, his voice tinged with frustration and sorrow, "the Portuguese and the Siddis have formed an alliance and are relentlessly plundering the western coast. Worse, the British have permitted them to use Bombay as a base to anchor their ships. From there, they abduct women and girls, selling them into slavery in foreign lands. The peasants are suffering terribly, held captive by the Portuguese and tortured for days. They are mutilated, bled to death with barbed wires, rods, spikes, knives, hammers, and chains. Their dominance has only grown since Shivrai's passing. Under his command, they feared us. But now... I don't know what to do anymore."

Sambhaji absorbed the painful truth in silence. He remembered the alliance the Marathas had signed with the British and the Portuguese years ago, when he himself had negotiated it. He had strictly warned them of the prohibitions of the trade in the Maratha territories. The alliance was now broken. Daulat Khan's account was only a fraction of the growing turmoil. The Portuguese and Siddis were no longer allies bound by diplomatic ties, and their merciless actions showed no sign of restraint. Before Daulat Khan could continue, Sambhaji's mind had already begun formulating a plan of action. He summoned Sarnobat Mohite to the court and outlined the gravity of their situation.

"The Mughals are advancing, and now we have enemies gathering strength on our western coast," Sambhaji began, his tone unwavering. "I suspect the Mughals may have prompted the Portuguese and Siddis to attack us, hoping to divide our attention. It wouldn't surprise me if Sikander and his Adilshahi troops align with the Mughals soon. We must be prepared for all fronts."

Sambhaji paused, hesitating briefly. "I want you to take full control of the strategic planning against the Mughals. I will be away for some time, dealing with this new threat."

"Where are you going, Maharaj?"

"Janjira"

Sarnobat Mohite's eyes widened with disbelief. "Raje, that fort is invincible! No ruler has dared to challenge it. Attacking Janjira is like walking into a death trap."

Sambhaji chuckled. "Wasn't Burhanpur supposed to be invincible too?" His eyes gleamed with the fire of determination. "History is written by those who defy the odds. Let our enemies think from this day forward that the Marathas are invincible."

The next morning, Sambhaji set out for the sea fortress of Janjira, accompanied by Daulat Khan and a select group of ministers. Upon arriving near the towering granite walls of Janjira, Sambhaji began a thorough inspection of the fortress. The fort was formidable — 15 guz high with cannons mounted strategically along its ramparts. The vast Arabian sea surrounded the fort, and the tides served as defencesl barrier. The massive cannons, with their long range, could sink any ship approaching the stronghold in mere minutes. Even with the Marathas' strength, they lacked the ships and firepower to break through Janjira's defences.

Sambhaji summoned Kondaji Farzand, the person-in-charge of the Maratha province around Janjira.

"What have you been doing Kondaji, all this while? Wasn't it your duty to look after this province? Why are the women and children unsafe here?" Sambhaji blasted.

"Raje..." Kondaji stammered. Sambhaji's subordinates and people from the villages watched Sambhaji yell at Kondaji. This was unusual for the localites

"I shall hereby free you of all your duties," declared Sambhaji.

"Raje, I am sorry," begged Kondaji.

"Please reconsider your decision, Raje. Kondaji Farzand is an expert and most valued senapati of ours. He had helped Shivrai in most of the prominent battles and won us many single-handedly," whispered Daulat Khan to Sambhaji.

"My decision is final, Daulat Khan," declared Sambhaji.

Kondaji Farzand was removed from the Maratha army, taking away the possesion of all his weapons and documents he had over the years. People around had began talking of how Kondaji had been stripped off of his duties.

The news had immediately reached the Siddis. In the Siddis court, stood Kondaji Farzand, bowing before Qasim.

"What brings the Maratha warrior of much accolade to our court?" asked Qasim.

"Insult and revenge," replied Kondaji, the spark in his eyes to tarnish the Marathas, evident to Qasim.

Qasim exactly knew the benefit Kondaji brought to the Siddis with his experience. He made sure Kondaji felt comfortable in the Siddi camps. Later, he was given the authority to lead a small unit of the Siddis.

"Kondaji Farzand has joined the Siddis," Daulat Khan complained to Sambhaji.

"Jagdamb!" Sambhaji closed his eyes.

Days passed as Sambhaji and his men inspected the area. They made sure they left no stone unturned in studying the enemy fortress.

Sambhaji devised his strategy. "We need small frigates," he told Daulat Khan. "They must be swift enough to approach the fort undetected and close enough to strike."

Daulat Khan hesitated, knowing the magnitude of the task. "We will need to construct them from scratch."

Sambhaji's response was resolute. "You can, and you will."

He knew the Marathas might not completely capture Janjira, but his goal was to cripple the Siddis enough that they would no longer be a threat to the Marathas nor of any assistance to their Portuguese and British allies.

Over the next few days, the Marathas began constructing their fleet of small, agile frigates. Sambhaji summoned Dadaji Raghunath Deshpande to lead the mission, alongside Durgadas Rathod, who joined with his Rajput troops. Sambhaji inspected the development of the work, everyday.

One day, seated in his tent, a man dressed in the costumes of a farmer arrived. He wished to meet Sambhaji in private and was stopped by the Maratha guards. The message was passed onto Sambhaji who then allowed the man to be sent to his tent.

"The Siddis have a double dozen cannons, more than five hundred war ships, an ammunition centre to the southern part of the fort that has enough arms and ammuntion to suffice for the entire year. To the north-eastern side of the fort lies the food supply for the Siddis," the man told Sambhaji. He then handed over a map to Sambhaji which had the minute details of the entire Siddi fortress.

Sambhaji signalled the man to leave before he could summon Daulat Khan and others.

'Thank you Kondaji kaka,' Sambhaji thanked Kondaji Farzand after the man had left. 'You shall truly remain the unsung hero of this attack,' Sambhaji spoke to himself.

Kondaji Farzand's defection to the Marathas and joining the Siddis had all been planned. A part of the strategy only known to Sambhaji and Kondaji, the Siddis had believed it all. Sambhaji and Kondaji had faked the insult, allowing the latter to gain Siddis' trust and access to the fort. Janjira had a huge Maratha navy to the outside and the real hero inside, planning the next move.

Once the frigates were complete, the Maratha soldiers embarked on their swift vessels, sailing through the rough waters of the Arabian sea in zigzag patterns. The Maratha warships to one side and the Siddi warships to the other, the battle of the navies broke in. Meanwhile, the frigates sailed across to the walls of the fort.

Qasim ordered, "Fire the cannons," upon seeing the approaching frigates but the artilleries had stopped fucntioning. None of the artilleries fired. Qasim exactly knew what had happened.

To a distant, stood Kondaji Farzand, his sword out now. The man had secretely damaged the artilleries, making them non functional.

"You traitor," Qasim with a dozen of soldiers charged towards Kondaji Farzand, who knew his end was near. Kondaji with his sword slashed the soldiers, amputing their arms, piercing their abdomen and pulling out their intestines.

"Har Har Mahadev," Kondaji shouted, his sword doing the talking until he was taken by surprise by Qasim with a dagger from behind. He attacked Kondaji multiple times, until the man fell to the floor.

"Raje...*akhri mujra swikarava* (King...please accept my last bow)," the man muttered remembering Sambhaji, as he breathed his last.

Meanwhile as the frigates reached the fort's walls, the Marathas launched their mobile cannons, sending cannonballs soaring high into the air and crashing into Janjira's interior. The explosion sent shockwaves through the fortress. The Siddi leaders, Yaqub, Qasim, and Kahiriyat, were caught off guard. They quickly rallied their men to mount a counterattack with bows and arrows, now that the cannons were dysfunctional, but the Marathas were too swift, their frigates darting away before the Siddis' could retaliate.

From his frigate, Dadaji Raghunath Deshpande directed a second wave of attack. The Marathas fired repeatedly, the frigates rotating in and out of range to avoid the enemy's arrows. Durgadas Rathod led another squad, aiming directly for the fort's storehouses, where food was stored. From the southern side of the fort, the Maratha ships countered attacked the Siddi ships as Sambhaji on his frigate charged towards the enemy ammunition centre. Launching the cannons, Sambhaji and his men set the ammunition centre ablaze.

With their fort crumbling around them, the Siddis scrambled to respond. Qasim, in particular, was furious. His arrows were useless against the Maratha frigates, which stayed too close to the fort walls for an effective shot. In desperation, the Siddis decided to turn to guns, but it was too late for them as Sambhaji had already destroyed the ammunition centre.

As the fort burned, Sambhaji got on a warship and turned towards the enemy ships, ordering his men to fire cannons, destroying many of the enemy ships. By the end of the prolonged assault, many of the Siddis' men lay dead, their warships sunk, and the fort left in ruins. Qasim and Kahiriyat were both gravely wounded, and the once-proud fortress of Janjira was left in devastation.

Sambhaji had achieved his objective. The Marathas withdrew, leaving the Siddis crippled and unable to assist the Mughals in future battles. Days later, a letter reached Aurangzeb from Janjira. In it, Yaqub admitted defeat, explaining that the Siddis could no longer support the Mughal campaign against the Marathas. They were broken, their forces shattered.

The Maratha navy, once considered inferior, had now proven their might on the western coast. Janjira had not fallen entirely, but its spirit had.

AURANGABAD WAS now a sea of green, with Mughal flags fluttering proudly across the city as Aurangzeb arrived with his massive army of cavalrymen and infantrymen. The news of Akbar joining the Marathas and Sambhaji helping his son had not gone well with Aurangzeb.

Removing his crown, Aurangzeb vowed in the Agra court, "I shall not wear my crown until the Deccan bathes in Sambha's blood."

The last time the emperor had come to the region was years earlier when he had attacked the Adilshahi sultanate. Later, he forged a peace treaty with them, a fragile peace that Diler Khan had shattered by launching another attack. Aurangzeb, now in disfavour of Diler Khan's recklessness, had disowned him. Still, the people of Aurangabad remembered all too well the cruelty and barbarism the emperor had unleashed on them during his previous visit. The sight of his army reawakened old fears.

Upon reaching Aurangabad, Aurangzeb wasted no time and immediately summoned his commanders and subordinates for a strategy meeting. He briefed them on his plans for the upcoming campaign, determined to crush his enemies and reclaim lost pride.

Meanwhile, at Raigad, unbeknownst to Sambhaji, treachery

was brewing. Following the attacks on Janjira Fort, Durgadas Rathore had left to meet with Prince Akbar. It wasn't long before Sambhaji received word from Durgadas that Akbar wished to have a private meeting with him. Sambhaji agreed and made his way to a village near Pali where the meeting had been arranged.

Both Durgadas and Akbar seemed hesitant when they finally met. "Raje," Durgadas hesitated, "I don't know how to put this up, but... your Swaraj is..." Durgadas stopped. Their reluctance to speak caught Sambhaji's attention.

"Please, don't hesitate. Tell me what is troubling you," Sambhaji urged.

"Maharaj," Durgadas began cautiously, "as soon as I arrived here and met Akbar, we had a guest from Raigad. The man claimed he had an important message to deliver on behalf of the Maratha Sultanate."

Sambhaji's eyes narrowed as he struggled to understand where this conversation was headed.

"The man gave me a letter," Durgadas continued, "claiming it was a communication from your court. The letter proposed that the Maratha kingdom would assist the Marwar province and support Akbar in his struggle for the throne by attacking Aurangzeb's forces at Aurangabad."

Sambhaji's confusion deepened. "But I never ordered any such letter to be sent," he interjected.

"Yes, it was never from you. Somebody else, a parallel government," Akbar chimed in. "That's why we sought this meeting in private."

Sambhaji's mind raced. The Marathas were in no position to meddle in a succession war between Akbar and Aurangzeb. His foremost responsibility was to protect his own kingdom, not to engage in someone else's ambitions.

"The man seemed to sound weird. There was a sense of fear in his tone, as if, he was hiding the information from many," Durgadas added, "He urged us not to support your battles and instead to make an alliance that served their cause."

Sambhaji's heart sank. "And what was their condition?" he asked, though part of him dreaded the answer.

Durgadas hesitated, sensing Sambhaji's mounting impatience. "The condition was... that we help make Rajaram the new king and imprison you or kill you."

The shock hit Sambhaji like a hammer blow. Betrayal was not a new experience for him, but this treachery cut deeper than any blade. He had thought the days of internal conspiracies were behind him, but it seemed his battles with his own people were far from over.

"Was this all written in the letter?" Sambhaji asked, trying to steady his voice.

Durgadas nodded solemnly and retrieved the letter, which he had hidden under his turban "I kept the letter safe. You never mentioned any intention to attack Aurangabad, and I didn't want to support a cause that could weaken the Maratha empire."

Sambhaji appreciated Durgadas's prudence. He took the letter, and as his eyes scanned its contents, his suspicions were confirmed. He recognized the handwriting immediately, and the man behind the treachery was one all too familiar to him.

"Who brought you this letter?" Sambhaji inquired, already dreading the answer.

"Annaji Datto," Durgadas replied.

"That man!" This betrayal was the final straw. Sambhaji thanked both Durgadas and Akbar for their honesty and loyalty before departing for Raigad. There would be no mercy this time.

Upon his return to Raigad, Sambhaji wasted no time. He immediately summoned the conspirators to the court, beginning with Annaji Datto, who was dragged into the courtroom in shackles.

"How many times must I forgive your treachery, Annaji?" Sambhaji thundered, his voice echoing in the grand hall. "You have conspired against me repeatedly. What personal grudges do you hold that drive you to betray me?"

Annaji Datto quaked in fear, unable to meet the king's fiery gaze. Behind him, Balaji Avaji, the court scribe, stood with his head hung low.

Sambhaji turned to Balaji, his tone softer but still commanding. "I know, Balaji, that you bear me no ill will. You served my father,

Shivrai, faithfully, writing countless letters in his name. But this... this is your handwriting, though the words are someone else's."

Balaji's composure broke. Tears streamed down his face as he fell to his knees. "Maharaj, I do not wish to betray you, but I was compelled. I deserve whatever punishment you deem fit."

Sambhaji's heart clenched. "It would be kind of you, Balaji kaka, to name the true culprits."

The names were no surprise to Sambhaji. Those implicated in the conspiracy were summoned to the court: Janardan Hanmante and Hiroji Farzand. Only one person Sambhaji couldn't touch: Soyrabai, whom he still regarded as his mother, despite her role in the treason.

The accused stood before Sambhaji, once trusted men who had now betrayed the very empire they had helped build. The courtroom was tense with silence as everyone waited for the king to speak.

"You all have served the Maratha empire well in the past," Sambhaji began, his voice strained with emotion. "Some of you were my father's favourites, and you contributed greatly to our cause. But now, you have committed crimes so heinous that they cannot be forgiven. An example for treachery has to be set here."

Sambhaji's mind drifted back to the Agra escape, where Hiroji Farzand had risked his life to impersonate Shivrai, allowing his father and young him to flee the Mughal emperor's clutches. But those days of loyalty were long gone.

As the room fell into a heavy silence, Sambhaji's heart ached with the weight of the decision before him. He recalled how, after the last conspiracy, he had shown mercy. This time, though, mercy would be a weakness. If he pardoned them again, it would send a message that betrayal was tolerated in his reign. He thought of his father, Chhatrapati Shivaji Maharaj, and what he would have done. The answer came swiftly. Shivrai would have shown no mercy, even to his own kin.

"Guards!" Sambhaji's voice rang out. The sound reverberated through the vast courtroom, each syllable carrying the finality of his judgement. "Capture these traitors and..."

He paused, letting the weight of his words settle in the air. The tension was palpable, hearts raced, and breaths were held. Annaji Datto trembled, nearly fainting, and Balaji Avaji knew that his crime was beyond forgiveness.

Sambhaji cleared his throat, pain evident in his voice as he forced himself to continue. "And... throw them under the feet of an elephant till death."

The court gasped as the finality of Sambhaji's words sank in. There was no going back. Betrayal would not be forgiven.

WHILE SAMBHAJI had been engaged in the fierce battles at Janjira and navigating the treacherous politics at Raigad, Sarnobat Mohite and his forces were busy fighting the mighty Mughal army. Under the command of Rahullah Khan, the Mughals had managed to outwit the Marathas and claim a decisive victory at Kalyan, a crucial region in the Konkan. This defeat forced the Marathas to retreat, and the news quickly reached Aurangzeb, giving him renewed confidence and motivation. Eager to capitalize on his momentum, the emperor prepared for his next major assault, this time targeting Ramsej Fort, located in the Baglan region. However, little did he know that the Marathas were already bracing themselves for the impending confrontation.

Leading the Mughal forces to Ramsej was Zulfikar Khan, who commanded a formidable army of cavalrymen, infantrymen, and artillerymen. As they approached the fort, Zulfikar's desperation to seize Ramsej grew stronger with each passing moment. The pressure to match the success of Rahullah Khan at Kalyan and further please Aurangzeb weighed heavily on him.

Inside the fort, Suryaji Jedhe, the fort commander, observed the approaching Mughal army. With him were two of his most trusted warriors, Rupaji Bhosale and Manaji More, both seasoned veterans who had earned great respect within the Maratha ranks. They were well aware that the odds were heavily stacked against them. Suryaji had prudently ensured that the fort was well-stocked with food and water, anticipating a prolonged siege. But what truly worried him was the sheer disparity in numbers: the Marathas had only six hundred men to defend the fort, whereas the Mughal army boasted a staggering 40,000 soldiers.

Adding to Suryaji's concerns was the unexpected sight of massive cannons being transported by the Mughal forces. As Manaji More, a skilled strategist, calculated the potential damage, he remarked grimly, "The cannons are enormous, and their cannonballs can easily penetrate our walls. They will make short work of our defences."

Rupaji Bhosale, watching the Mughals erect scaffoldings in their camps, voiced his concern, "They're preparing to bombard us. If we don't act swiftly, they'll break through in no time."

Suryaji, sensing the growing anxiety among his men, maintained his composure. "Do not panic," he said firmly, addressing his subordinates. After a moment of contemplation, he added, "We may not have cannons, but we can create something just as effective. Hollow out tree trunks, and we can fashion makeshift cannons. Fill them with gunpowder and stones, and we can cause significant damage."

Manaji quickly gathered his men and began working on these non-traditional weapons, while Suryaji wrote an urgent letter to Sambhaji, detailing the dire situation at Ramsej. He also sent letters to nearby forts, requesting immediate supplies of timber and other resources.

Within a few days, the letter reached Rai. Upon reading it, Sambhaji it, dispatched reinforcements from Raigad without delay. But Sambhaji had a more unconventional plan in mind. He penned another letter, this one addressed to Bahirji Naik, the Maratha master of espionage. Sambhaji wrote, "Whenever threat stares at the Maratha armies and we find ourselves in a situation where things can go wrong, one man that comes to my mind is you, Bahirji kaka. The Mughals have laid siege to Ramsej Fort, and in this critical moment, it is only you and your men that can now help us. I want you to infiltrate the Mughal camps with your spies, disguised as Mughal soldiers."

Sambhaji knew that this tactic, if executed correctly, would play a pivotal role in turning the tide of the siege.

As days turned into weeks, the Mughal army laboured tirelessly to construct their scaffoldings. At the same time, Suryaji and his men, working around the clock, had completed their wooden cannons. These makeshift weapons, filled with gunpowder and flammable materials, were now ready for deployment. Meanwhile, Bahirji Naik's spies, now embedded within the Mughal ranks, closely monitored every move the enemy made.

Back at Raigad, there was a momentary respite from the chaos of war as Sambhaji welcomed his newborn son. The priests named the child 'Shahu,' and the family rejoiced. Yet, despite the joy of fatherhood, Sambhaji's thoughts remained with his men at Ramsej. Months had passed since the Mughal siege began, but no direct assault had been launched on the fort. Sambhaji's instincts began to gnaw at him.

'Why haven't the Mughals attacked yet?' he pondered. *'Are they planning something far more devastating?'*

His suspicions weren't without merit. Hundreds of miles away, Francisco de Tavora, the Portuguese war general, sat in his opulent chamber, savouring a cigar. As he enjoyed his indulgence, a letter from Aurangzeb arrived.

In the letter, Aurangzeb wrote:

I admire the power and control that the Portuguese Empire has established over the Arabian sea. From Europe to Goa, your dominance is evident in trade and naval strength. However, with the recent setbacks faced by the Siddis, I am aware that the trade routes between Mumbai as we call it or Bombaim for you and Goa have been disrupted, primarily due to Maratha influence in the Konkan. My forces have managed to deal a blow to the Marathas in Kalyan, but I offer you a proposition. Allow my Mughal ships to dock at your ports and grant us safe passage for trade in Goa and its surrounding regions. In return, I promise you military support in both Kalyan and Baglan as we crush the Maratha forces. Together, we can overwhelm them from multiple fronts, and the Marathas, with their new and inexperienced Chhatrapati, will have no choice but to surrender or be annihilated.

Tavora smiled as he read the letter. The prospect of expanding

Portuguese territory by partnering with the Mughals excited him. He was ready to strike.

That same night, another letter from Aurangzeb arrived at the hands of Henry Oxenden, the British commander in Mumbai. Like Tavora, Henry saw an opportunity to align with the Mughals and assert greater control over the region.

As tensions rose on multiple fronts, the Marathas found themselves facing not just the Mughal Empire, but a coalition of foreign powers eager to exploit their moment of vulnerability.

"MAHARAJ, THE Portuguese have joined hands with the Mughals," informed one of Bahirji Naik's men to Sambhaji.

The Maratha spy network was renowned for being one of the most efficient in the land, with information travelling at lightning speed. Even before Francisco de Tavora, the Portuguese governor in Goa, could organize his forces for an attack, Sambhaji was already making moves to counter their plans. His strategy was bold and swift, driven by a fierce desire to send a message to the Portuguese and any other powers daring to conspire against his kingdom.

Sambhaji and his Maratha troops set out for Korlai Fort, a small but significant island fortress controlled by the Portuguese, located in the Arabian sea. With a determination that brooked no delay, the Marathas travelled for two days and nights without rest, fuelled by Sambhaji's impassioned words urging them forward. The night was calm as they arrived, but the atmosphere was thick with anticipation. The moonlight shimmered off the waters, casting a silver glow on the fort's stone walls.

Under the cover of darkness, a small group of Maratha soldiers made their way into the fort, using narrow paths and secretive routes, while Sambhaji and another group laid siege to the nearby city of Chaul. The inhabitants of Chaul were thrown into disarray by the sudden arrival of the Marathas, but Sambhaji ensured that no harm came to civilians. His focus was on strategic victory, not wanton destruction.

Meanwhile, another Maratha force advanced on the Bassein

Fort to the north. At Korlai, the Portuguese garrison had no warning of the impending attack. The Marathas descended upon them with the ferocity of a storm, their war cries of 'Har Har Mahadev' echoing off the fort walls. Armed with swords, daggers, and the lethal dandpatta, the Marathas overwhelmed the Portuguese before they could even fire their guns. In the confusion and chaos, the Portuguese soldiers fell in droves, unable to hold back the wave of Maratha aggression. Soon, the saffron flag of the Marathas was hoisted high over Korlai Fort, signalling their victory.

At Bassein, the situation was equally dire for the Portuguese. Though they were met with resistance led by General Damanial Lobudsilver, the Marathas inflicted significant damage on the fort's defences. The Portuguese managed to hold the fort, but at great cost. Their storehouses were set ablaze, and the destruction was so severe that it would take months for the Portuguese to recover fully.

Back in Chaul, Sambhaji tightened his grip on the city, strategically reinforcing the Maratha presence by constructing scaffoldings and fortifications. Chaul, a hub of sea trade, was now firmly under Maratha control. The Portuguese trade routes and influence were dealt a heavy blow.

Tavora, sitting in his quarters in Goa, was enraged when news of the Maratha strikes reached him. His plan to join forces with Aurangzeb had been thwarted before it could even begin. Furious, he slammed his fist on the table, cursing his luck and the speed with which the Marathas had outmanoeuvred him. He quickly ordered his men to prepare for an attack on Ponda Fort, another Maratha stronghold. Tavora was determined to exact revenge and restore his wounded pride.

Meanwhile, in Aurangabad, Aurangzeb was also growing impatient. He had received no response from the Adilshahi, whom he had asked for assistance. His frustration boiled over as he summoned Asad Khan, one of his most trusted generals. "Take a thousand men and teach the Adilshahi a lesson," Aurangzeb commanded. "Remind them who the true Badshah is. They will regret their disobedience when they realize they should have heeded my orders, not aligned themselves with Sambhaji."

Back at Ramsej Fort, the Mughal forces under Zulfikar Khan were on edge. The massive scaffolding structures they had built for their cannons were ready, and the long wait had only served to heighten their impatience. Zulfikar, itching for a decisive victory, decided it was time to act.

"Load the cannons!" Zulfikar's voice rang out, and his soldiers scrambled to obey. The massive cannons were aimed at Ramsej Fort, the symbol of Maratha resistance.

Inside the fort, Suryaji Jedhe and his men were ready. They had been preparing for this moment for months. As the first Mughal cannon fired, Suryaji gave the order, "Attack!"

The Marathas launched their makeshift cannons, constructed from wood and animal skin, packed with gunpowder. Though crude in design, they were effective. As the fiery cannonballs arced through the air, they struck the Mughal scaffolds, which burst into flames almost instantly. The Mughal camp was thrown into chaos as fire spread rapidly, consuming their supplies and tents. The cannons launched by the Mughals hit thew walls of the forts but the walls were strong enough to sustain the attack as they had been reconstructed months ago, just when Sambhaji had predicted the Mughal invasion.

Zulfikar watched in horror as his well-laid plans went up in smoke. "Attack!" he ordered again, sending his infantrymen rushing toward the fort walls. But Suryaji was prepared for this too. The Marathas unleashed a volley of arrows, raining down death upon the advancing Mughal soldiers. Zulfikar's men fell by the hundreds, unable to breach the Maratha defences.

In a desperate bid to regain control, Zulfikar ordered his remaining forces to storm the fort directly, attacking the gates with swords and bows. But the Marathas had anticipated this as well. Using slingshots and more flaming projectiles, they repelled the attack with ease. By the time the battle ended, the six hundred Maratha defenders had completely decimated Zulfikar's army. Thousands of Mughal soldiers lay dead or wounded, their hopes of capturing Ramsej dashed.

Zulfikar himself barely escaped with his life, fleeing to safety, humiliated and defeated. The cries of 'Har Har Mahadev!' echoed in his ears as he retreated, a reminder of the Maratha victory and the bravery of their warriors.

THE ATTACK on Ramsej was a devastating blow to the Mughals, not only in terms of resources and manpower but also in morale. Aurangzeb was livid. He entrusted Bahadur Shah Kokaltash with the responsibility of continuing the siege at Ramsej. Kokaltash, after the humilation at Burhanpur, awaited to seek his revenge.

Kokaltash arrived at Ramsej with a fresh set of troops. He spent several weeks meticulously studying the landscape, assessing the Maratha defences, and planning his next move. The siege had dragged on for months, and while the Marathas were still holding firm inside the fort, Kokaltash knew that it was only a matter of time before their supplies would run out. However, unknown to him, Sambhaji, had a plan of his own. He sent a message to Bahirji Naik's spies, who were embedded within the Mughal army.

The letter was passed discreetly to Bahirji's man, a Maratha spy disguised as a Mughal soldier. The spy quickly deciphered the message and set the next phase of the plan into motion. Another letter was written to Suryaji, updating about the strategic plan. Meanwhile, Kokaltash, unaware of things building around him, focused on his strategy to bring down the fort.

As the Mughal forces worked on restoring their camp and preparing for a renewed assault, Kokaltash was approached by one of his subordinates.

"What is it?" Kokaltash snapped, irritated by the interruption.

"Apologies, Huzur," the soldier bowed, "but a holy saint from Calcutta has arrived and seeks to meet you."

Kokaltash, a devout believer, was intrigued. He had always placed great faith in spiritual leaders, and the idea of a holy man visiting at such a crucial time piqued his curiosity. Despite his scepticism about the sudden appearance of this saint, he agreed to meet him.

The saint, draped in black robes, his forehead marked with

angara and adorned with rudraksh beads, entered Kokaltash's tent with a mysterious air about him. His voice was calm, yet filled with authority as he spoke, "Your army has been cursed by divine wrath, which is why your thousands of men fell to just six hundred Marathas in the last battle."

Kokaltash was taken aback but didn't interrupt. The saint continued, "But there is a way to lift this curse. I can perform a ritual that will guarantee victory. I have done this for other rulers who have triumphed in impossible situations."

Desperate for a win, Kokaltash leaned forward, his eyes filled with hope. "What do we need to do?"

The saint smirked and replied, "I will need specific items for the ritual: a beheaded hen, a live snake, the bones of your dead soldiers, and some other materials I shall provide you a list of. On the night of Amavasya—when my powers are strongest—I will lead your men through a secret passage into the fort. I will create an invisible shield that will render the Maratha weapons useless against your soldiers. Victory will be yours."

Kokaltash, though eager, was momentarily suspicious. How did this saint know of the secret route into the fort? His thoughts raced, but the saint responded before he could voice his concern.

"Wondering, how I know the secret route right? Never question the power of a saint. I can see things than normal people cannot," the saint said confidently.

This answer, paired with Kokaltash's desperation, placated his doubts. A broad smile stretched across his face as he imagined the glory awaiting him after the Marathas were crushed. The promise of victory, paired with the idea of finally winning back Aurangzeb's favour, filled him with determination.

Elsewhere, Sarnobat Mohite, the Maratha chief of army, was leading his cavalry on a covert mission. They spotted a convoy of Mughal soldiers transporting supplies and ammunition through the dense forest to reinforce their siege at Ramsej. Sensing an opportunity, Mohite's men surrounded the convoy in the dead of night, their battle cries of 'Har Har Mahadev!' echoing through the trees as they ambushed the unsuspecting Mughals. The skirmish was swift and brutal; the Mughal soldiers were cut down, and the supply train was captured. The Marathas rerouted the supplies through their secret passage into the fort, bolstering their own reserves while leaving the Mughal camp in further disarray.

As Kokaltash pondered why the Marathas seemed to have an endless supply of food and ammunition despite being besieged for months, the night of Amavasya finally arrived. The Mughal camp buzzed with anticipation. Kokaltash, eager for his long-awaited triumph, had rallied his troops with speeches of jihad, convincing them that this was a divine mission to crush the infidels.

The saint led the Mughal soldiers through the dark forest, carrying his ritual items: the beheaded hen and a live snake, along with other macabre objects. After an hour of silent marching, they arrived at the narrow secret passage that led into the fort. The passage was so tight that only two or three men could squeeze through at a time. The saint walked confidently at the front, muttering incantations under his breath as the Mughal soldiers followed closely behind.

But as the passage widened into an open ground, the saint abruptly stopped. His lips curled into a sly smile as he saw Suryaji and his men standing in wait.

"Thank you, we shall take it ahead from here," said Suryaji as the saint stepped aside and the Maratha warriors launched their ambush.

The Mughals, packed tightly in the narrow passage, were caught entirely off guard. They were easy prey for the Marathas, who cut them down with swords, spears, and arrows. The Mughal soldiers were slaughtered in the dark, unable to see or defend themselves in the chaotic melee. Terrified, some tried to flee back through the passage, but they ran straight into Sarnobat Mohite and his cavalry, who had arrived at the other end.

The massacre was swift and complete. Kokaltash, waiting anxiously in his tent, heard the distant sounds of battle but nothing of the victory he had been promised of. A lone Mughal soldier, bloodied and breathless, was allowed to escape by the Marathas. He returned to Kokaltash, stumbling into the tent and recounting the horrors of the night.

Kokaltash's face turned red with fury. Realizing that he had been duped by the saint, he grabbed his sword and, in a fit of blind rage, decapitated the soldier who had brought him the news. "There is no mercy for the weak," he muttered as the lifeless body hit the ground.

Meanwhile, inside Ramsej, Suryaji and Sarnobat Mohite were congratulating the saint, the Maratha spy who had infiltrated the Mughal camp and orchestrated the perfect trap.

"We're proud of you," Suryaji said, clapping the spy on the back.

The spy nodded, "I should get going."

"To where?" asked Suryaji.

"To my master, Bahirji Naik," the spy replied, a satisfied grin on his face.

AURANGZEB SAT on his throne in a state of disbelief, his mind reeling from the recent defeat at the fort of Ramsej. This loss was not just another military setback; it was a blow that had cost him heavily in terms of both lives and resources. The fort of Ramsej had bled his coffers dry, and the casualties were staggering. The humiliation of two consecutive defeats, first Burhanpur and now Ramsej, gnawed at his resolve, and for the first time in a long while, a shiver of doubt crept into the emperor's heart. Aurangzeb, the once-unstoppable force that had stretched the Mughal Empire far and wide, felt the bitter sting of failure.

To regain his lost pride and maintain control over the ever-rebellious Deccan, Aurangzeb devised a new strategy. He turned his sights to the Konkan region, a strategic stronghold of the Marathas, known for its unforgiving terrain and fierce warriors. Determined not to suffer another defeat, he ordered his son, Muazzam, to lead a massive Mughal force and attack the southern Konkan provinces. Simultaneously, he commanded Zulfikar, who had recently tasted defeat at Ramsej, to march from Pune and attack the northern Konkan regions. This two-pronged assault was meant to crush the Marathas once and for all.

Aurangzeb's focus was now firmly on Konkan, a region vital to the Maratha's power and influence. With Hussain Ali Khan's recent success in the Kalyan region, Aurangzeb believed that seizing the entire Konkan was within reach. However, not all his generals shared his optimism. Asad Khan had already left for the Adilshahi territories, while Bahadurshah Kokaltash was still recovering from his defeat at the hands of the Marathas. One man, however, watched the emperor's plans unfold with a sense of foreboding: Diler Khan, a seasoned warrior and once a trusted commander.

Diler Khan, who had been a silent observer of the Mughal court's growing disarray, was deeply concerned. The respect and power he had once commanded were now distant memories, but his strategic mind remained sharp. He could see what others could not—that Aurangzeb was underestimating the Marathas and their fierce loyalty to their homeland. The Sahyadri mountains of the Konkan were not just a geographical feature; they were a fortress in themselves, a natural defence that the Marathas had mastered. Much like the Rajputs, who used the arid deserts of Rajasthan to their advantage, the Marathas thrived in the treacherous hills of the Sahyadri, experts in guerrilla warfare and surprise attacks.

Diler Khan believed that Aurangzeb was making a grave mistake, and he was determined to make his voice heard. He set out for Aurangabad to warn the emperor, hoping to share his insights before it was too late. But when he arrived at the Mughal court, he was met with ridicule.

"I want to meet the Badshah," demanded Diler Khan.

"You are not allowed to," said one of Aurangzeb's ministers.

"I have a message for him. Something important," said Diler Khan. The minister told Aurangzeb that Diler Khan wishes to meet him.

"If the man steps into my court, I shall order his execution," shouted Aurangzeb, "Tell Diler Khan to thank the Almighty that it is Friday today and I don't want to kill a Muslim."

The message was immediately passed on to Diler Khan, who was still adamant.

"Throw this man out," said the minister, irritated by Diler Khan's behaviour.

The soldier grabbed Diler Khan by the arms and dragged him out of the court premises.

"You are making a mistake," shouted Diler Khan, his voice falling on deaf ears, "The Badshah is underestimating the Marathas. The Konkan province is invincible. I have lived my entire life in the Deccan, and I know how to deal with the hilly regions."

"We don't need your advice," shouted the minister.

"The Mughals shall repent," shouted back Diler Khan, his voice fading, as he was thrown out of the Mughal cantonment.

Insulted and humiliated, Diler Khan left Aurangabad in despair. Once a man of great stature, he now felt stripped of his dignity, his years of loyal service reduced to nothing. The weight of his defeat, both on the battlefield and in the Mughal cantonment, became too much to bear. Depressed and drowning in shame, Diler Khan took his own life, unable to live with the ignominy that had befallen him.

While internal tensions brewed within the Mughal ranks, Zulfikar moved forward with his invasion of northern Konkan, unleashing a reign of terror upon the people. His forces demolished homes, desecrated temples, and looted villages, sparing no one. Men were killed, women were raped, and entire communities were wiped out as the Mughal army swept through the land. Meanwhile, Francisco de Tavora, the Portuguese viceroy, allowed the Mughal forces to pass freely through his territories in Daman, further strengthening their position.

At the same time, Muazzam had reached southern Konkan through Belgaum, bringing the same destruction and terror to the people. Tavora, who had recently suffered a defeat at the hands of the Marathas at Chaul port, now directed his forces toward the Ponda Fort, a strategic outpost on the Maharashtra-Goa border. The fort was garrisoned by a small force of six hundred Maratha soldiers under the command of Yesaji Kank and his son, Krishnaji. With the Portuguese advancing rapidly, the situation inside the fort grew tense.

"They are coming in huge numbers," Krishnaji said, his voice betraying a hint of panic as he looked to his father for guidance.

The Marathas had not anticipated an attack of this scale. The fort's defences were not prepared for a prolonged siege, and supplies were running dangerously low. They lacked the weapons, ammunition, and provisions needed to withstand a full-scale assault. Even the fort's walls had not been reinforced, leaving them vulnerable to the Portuguese cannons.

"Close the main gate of the fort," Yesaji commanded, his voice calm despite the dire circumstances.

Krishnaji quickly relayed the order, and the soldiers rushed to secure the massive iron gate. Meanwhile, Yesaji hurried to his workroom, where he grabbed a blank piece of parchment and began writing a letter in haste. His hand moved quickly across the page as he penned a message to Maharaj, knowing that their only hope for survival lay in reinforcements.

He called for one of his most trusted men and handed him the sealed letter. "Take this to Maharaj," Yesaji said urgently. "Make sure it reaches him, and no one else."

The messenger nodded and, under the cover of darkness, mounted his horse and sped away, riding swiftly toward Chaul port, where Sambhaji was stationed after his recent victory over the Portuguese. The hope was that Sambhaji would receive the letter in time to send reinforcements before it was too late.

"The gate is secured," Krishnaji reported, his voice steady now. After a moment's hesitation, he added, "But the Portuguese have cannons with them."

Yesaji's face darkened. The situation was becoming more critical by the minute. As the commander of the fort, the weight of responsibility fell squarely on his shoulders.

"If the letter reaches Maharaj, we might still get help," Krishnaji suggested, trying to maintain a sense of hope.

"Yes, but it may be too late by then," Yesaji replied gravely. "The Portuguese haven't come here to lay siege or negotiate. They're here for a quick battle, and we have to be prepared for whatever happens next with the little we have. Gather all the soldiers immediately."

In no time, the soldiers assembled in the fort's courtyard, their faces grim but resolute.

"We are facing an enemy with greater numbers and better weapons," but they do not have what we have: our courage, our honour and land, and we carry within us the spirit of Chhatrapati Shivaji Maharaj. The Portuguese may have cannons and guns but they do not have what we have: our courage, our honour, and our unbreakable will."

The soldiers stood tall, their chests swelling with pride as they listened to their commander. Yesaji's words cut through the fear and uncertainty, filling them with a renewed sense of purpose.

"Not long ago, six hundred of our brothers stood against a far larger Mughal force and emerged victorious at Ramsej. We are no different. We carry the same blood, the same spirit, and we fight for the same cause. Let the Portuguese come. We will fight them to our last breath. We will not surrender, and we will not allow them to take this fort. We are Marathas, and we will die with our swords in our hands before we let them defeat us. Will you fight with me?"

"Yes!" the soldiers shouted in unison, their voices echoing off the fort's walls.

"Har Har Mahadev!" Yesaji cried, raising his sword high.

"Har Har Mahadev!" the soldiers roared, drawing their swords as they prepared for the coming battle.

Yesaji ordered his men to take their positions around the fort. He knew that with their limited numbers, a confrontation would be suicide. Their only chance of victory lay in guerrilla tactics, using the fort's narrow passages and hidden spots to ambush the Portuguese forces. The Marathas were known for their guerrilla warfare, which meant hiding in places where the enemy would least expect them, letting the enemy approach closely and take them by surprise, only to cause damage or kill them and then run away. The soldiers doused the lamps, plunging the fort into total darkness.

At the base of the fort, Tavora watched, puzzled by the lack of resistance from the Marathas. He ordered his men to fire the cannons, bombarding the fort's walls and gate with a relentless barrage of cannonballs. The explosions echoed through the night, yet the Marathas still did not retaliate.

Tavora furrowed his brow. Could it be that the fort was abandoned?

"Keep firing!" he ordered, growing impatient.

For hours, the Portuguese pounded the fort's defences, but the walls held strong, refusing to crumble. The massive iron gate, though battered, remained intact. Tavora cursed under his breath. He had expected an easy victory, but the Marathas' defences were more resilient than he had anticipated. As the sky darkened and heavy rain began to fall, Tavora's frustration mounted.

"The Gods are with us," Yesaji whispered to his men as they listened to the rain pour down from the safety of their hiding places within the fort.

Drenched and determined, Tavora's men continued to fire the cannons, undeterred by the downpour. The rain, however, played to the Marathas' advantage, cooling the fort's walls and preventing them from sustaining significant damage. But the gate could only hold for so long. After two days of continuous bombardment, the gate finally gave way.

"We have finally made it," Tavora shouted in triumph as the gate crashed open.

Still, there was no sign of the Marathas. Tavora, convinced that the fort had been abandoned, sent a small unit of a few hundred men inside to survey the area before the rest of his army could advance.

Inside the fort, Yesaji and his men waited in silence, their swords drawn and their hearts steady. They could hear the footsteps of the Portuguese soldiers approaching. The tension was palpable as the enemy entered the dark, seemingly empty fort.

Just as the Portuguese soldiers began to relax, thinking they had secured an easy victory, the Marathas struck. Emerging from the shadows, they attacked with the ferocity of lions, their swords flashing in the dim firelight. The Portuguese, caught off guard, fell in droves as the Marathas slashed and stabbed their way through the enemy ranks.

Outside, Tavora, unaware of the massacre taking place within the fort, ordered another round of cannon fire. A thunderous cannon blast shook the fort. One of the cannonballs struck the wall near Yesaji's position, sending debris flying in all directions. Amid the chaos, Yesaji spotted a soldier lying motionless beneath a pile of rubble. Yesaji ran towards his man as a few others tried removing the bricks over him. The man was deeply wounded, his skin burnt and entire body soaked in blood. Yesaji bent down to give his arm, but soon stopped upon seeing the man. His heart now skipped a beat as his hands froze, legs trembled, and throat dried up. It was his son Krishnaji.

"If Maharaj arrives, tell him that I died a warrior's death."

YESAJI'S GRIP on Krishnaji's lifeless body tightened as tears blurred his vision. The battle-worn father could barely contain his sorrow as he cradled his son, his heart heavy with the weight of grief.

"Krishna," Yesaji whispered, gently patting his son's face in a desperate attempt to awaken him. The soldiers surrounding fetched water, but it was too late.

As grief threatened to consume him, something else began to rise within Yesaji—a burning, furious resolve. His son's death would not be in vain. The Portuguese would pay for every life they had taken. The sound of the relentless rains crashing against the fort walls seemed to fuel his rage. The Portuguese cannons had fallen silent, unable to fire through the downpour, and now, they were advancing on foot, determined to seize the fort.

Yesaji grabbed his dandpatta, the double-edged sword gleaming under the flashes of lightning. With a fierce cry, he charged forward, shouting, "Har Har Mahadev!" The Marathas, though dwindling in numbers, were relentless, matching their leader's ferocity. They slashed through the advancing Portuguese soldiers, cutting them down despite the overwhelming odds. The battle turned bloody, with rain mixing with the blood of the fallen, soaking the ground beneath their feet.

The Portuguese, with their muskets and guns, fired from a distance, but the Marathas, skilled in close combat, managed to close the gap. Yesaji's dandpatta cut through enemy after enemy, his sword swinging with the fury of a father who had lost his son. Yet, even as they fought valiantly, the Maratha numbers were quickly dwindling. Less than a hundred soldiers now stood, and the Portuguese forces began to tighten their grip on the fort.

Among the Portuguese ranks was Tavora, the viceroy, armed with a musket. He advanced with a menacing grin, firing shots that struck down the few remaining Maratha soldiers. The tide of battle had turned, and Tavora's confidence grew with each step. The bullets he fired pierced through the Maratha men, making them fall to the ground. Tavora's forces surrounded Yesaji and the last of his men, but Yesaji was not ready to surrender. He charged towards Tavora and his men, cutting through the Portuguese men. Yesaji, charged up, swayed his dandpatta towards Tavora but missed by inches as Tavora bent down, only to punch Yesaji in the abdomen. With the butt of his musket, Tavora hit Yesaji's abdomen as the other men held Yesaji from behind.

"That's how battles are won," Tavora boasted, a smug expression on his face as his men held Yesaji by his arms and Tavora aimed his musket directly at Yesaji. Yesaji, still reeling from his son's death, stood frozen, knowing the end was near. He remembered Shivrai and then Sambhaji. He closed his eyes, ready to meet his fate, his mind drifting to his family and the Almighty as Tavora pointed his musket at him.

Suddenly, a sharp crack echoed through the stormy air. Tavora screamed in pain as a bullet pierced through his arm, causing him to drop his musket. Blood poured from the wound as he clutched his arm in disbelief. The pain was unbearable, but even more shocking was the sight that greeted him when he turned around.

Through the rain, Tavora saw a figure advancing on horseback, a matchlock gun in hand. It was Sambhaji, the Maratha king, leading a cavalry of hundreds of reinforcements. Tavora's heart sank at the sight of the fierce warrior-king, his presence on the battlefield turning the tide in an instant. The Portuguese, who had moments earlier believed they were victorious, were now caught between Yesaji's remaining soldiers and the overwhelming force of Sambhaji's army.

"Raje!" Yesaji cried, his heart filled with mixed emotions of pride and grief. His king had arrived to his rescue.

"That's how battles are won," Yesaji repeated Tavora's statement, punched the Portuguese soldiers around him, grabbed the Dandapatta and yanked it at the Portuguese soldiers, beheading them. He charged at Tavora and attacked his arm where the bullet had struck, amputating it.

The Marathas charged with renewed vigour, and the Portuguese soldiers, who had been confident in their win, now found themselves trapped. They were slaughtered mercilessly by the Maratha cavalry, who showed no mercy. Tavora's world crumbled as he watched his men fall one by one, their bodies littering the ground, and he himself in deep pain.

They were outnumbered now. Tavora knew he had to escape, or he would meet the same fate as his men. With a frantic glance at Sambhaji, who was cutting through his forces like a storm, Tavora mounted his horse and fled. His amputated arm was bleeding, but the fear of death pushed him forward. He galloped down the fort's slopes, dodging the relentless attacks of the Maratha soldiers who pursued him.

As Tavora raced through the dense forests that led toward Goa, he dared to believe he had escaped. The forest, drenched in rain, offered some cover, and his horse galloped with all the speed it could muster. Tavora's heart pounded in his chest, and his arm throbbed as he looked over his shoulder, convinced he had left the Marathas behind.

But Tavora's brief moment of relief was shattered when he heard the unmistakable sound of hooves behind him. His heart skipped a beat, and fear clawed its way back into his chest. He turned around, and his blood ran cold at the sight that greeted him.

Sambhaji was still pursuing him.

Galloping through the rain, with eyes full of fury and determination, the Maratha king was not about to let Tavora escape so easily. Tavora's pulse quickened as panic set in. He was in no state to fight Sambhaji. He urged his horse to go faster, but the forest terrain and the storm hindered his escape. The once-confident viceroy was now reduced to a desperate man, fleeing for his life.

Sambhaji's horse drew closer, the distance between them shrinking with every passing second. Tavora knew there was no escape. His chest tightened as he realized that the Maratha king, relentless and unforgiving, would not stop until he took his revenge.

Sambhaji was determined to teach Tavora a lesson, even if it meant chasing him till the ends of the earth.

TAVORA HAD narrowly escaped Sambhaji's pursuit, but the Maratha king's unyielding determination remained. No matter the outcome of this momentary evasion, Sambhaji was not the sort of ruler who allowed his enemies to go unpunished. Alongside him were Khando Ballal, his skilled and diplomatic adviser, Kavi Kalash, a trusted lieutenant with deep knowledge of strategy, and a vast force of Maratha warriors, all marching toward their next objective: Goa, the jewel of Portuguese control in India.

Before setting out on this ambitious campaign, Sambhaji took a moment to reflect on the great sacrifices that had already been made, particularly that of Yesaji's son Krishnaji, one of his most devoted and courageous commanders. The loss of Krishnaji weighed heavily on Sambhaji's heart, and in a gesture that showed his respect for loyalty and valour, he personally honoured the warrior's memory. Sambhaji addressed the family of Yesaji, offering yearly pensions as a means of ensuring that they would be taken care of, a reminder that the Maratha kingdom would always stand by those who gave their lives for the nation.

The march toward Goa was not an idle one. Sambhaji made use of every moment, constantly discussing the geography and strategic importance of Goa with Khando Ballal and Kavi Kalash during their brief stops. As they journeyed through the vast landscape, they pored over every detail of the region they were about to invade. Goa was well fortified, thanks in part to its natural geography. To the north, the Mandovi River split into two rivulets, one of which led to an island known as Santo Estevao. There, a Portuguese Fort stood, poorly defended and isolated. Sambhaji realized that this fort would make an ideal first target. Capturing it would not only give the Marathas a strategic foothold but would send a clear message to the Portuguese: their days in Goa were numbered.

"The river flows into the sea," Kavi Kalash noted during one of their many planning sessions. "We must wait for the right time when the tide is low, or our forces will be trapped."

Meanwhile, in Goa, Tavora's mind was consumed by fear. His close escape from Sambhaji had not come without a cost. His injuries were severe, his arm amputated, and the phantom pains of his lost limb haunted him as much as the thought of Sambhaji's vengeance. He knew that the Maratha king would not rest until he was captured or killed. His desperation grew with each passing day, driving him to write a letter to Aurangzeb, pleading for assistance. He wrote, 'Please accept my heartfelt apologies, my dear Alamgir. We, as a unit, failed in assisting the Mughals in this dire situation. The Marathas are all over the place, their valour unchallengeable and their honesty unquestionable. In this critical situation, where the future of Portuguese seems bleak and my survival is at stake, only you can save us. If your army helps us, it may weaken them and save us from their attacks. The fortunes of Goa lie in your hands. I would be indebted to you, all my life, Alamgir.'

But Tavora's plea for help went unanswered. Aurangzeb, who had initially sought an alliance with the Portuguese to aid his own war against the Marathas, had long since grown distrustful of his European allies. The Portuguese were proving to be more of a hindrance than a help, and with the Siddis weakened and the Adilshahi dynasty offering no support, Aurangzeb realized he had to fight the Marathas alone. His forces were already stretched thin, with Azam at the borders of Bijapur and Muazzam advancing through the Konkan region. Goa's fate was of little concern to him now.

Back in the Maratha camp, Kavi Kalash's patience had paid off. After carefully studying the lunar cycles and the tides, he knew the perfect time to strike had arrived. "Maharaj, it's time we move on the island," he declared one evening, his confidence bolstered by the knowledge that the tides would soon be low enough for the Maratha forces to cross the river without difficulty. To make matters even more advantageous, the Portuguese on Santo Estevao were in the midst of a festival. They were celebrating, dancing, drinking, and feasting, their guards lowered by the revelry.

Sambhaji seized the opportunity. With a small but capable unit of soldiers, he made his way toward the island. Sambhaji's horse was trained to cross a river while the others made use of ropes to cross over the river. At the base of the hill leading up to the fort, Khando Ballal and Yesaji Kank waited with four hundred Maratha warriors, ready to provide reinforcements at a moment's notice.

As the sun sank beneath the horizon, Sambhaji and his unit quietly ascended the hill. The Portuguese soldiers inside the fort were intoxicated, barely able to stand, let alone defend their post. The gates were locked, but the guards stationed there were too drunk to notice the Marathas scaling the walls. Under the cover of night, Sambhaji and his men slipped into the fort undetected, waiting for the Portuguese to wake from their drunken stupor so that they could engage them in battle.

By the time the Portuguese soldiers roused themselves, it was too late. Sambhaji's forces struck swiftly and with lethal precision. The Maratha blades flashed in the torchlight, cutting down the Portuguese defenders with ease. The battle for the fort was short, brutal, and decisive. Once the fort was under Maratha control, they fired a cannon to signal Khando Ballal and his waiting forces, who had been hidden in the shadows, ready to join the fray.

Meanwhile, in the heart of Goa, panic erupted. The sound of cannon fire shattered the stillness of the night, and the people of the city rushed from their homes, only to be met with the horrifying sight of the island fort engulfed in flames. The Marathas had not only captured the fort, they had set it alight, sending a fiery message to Tavora and the Portuguese leadership.

Tavora, already physically weakened and emotionally drained, stepped outside to witness the devastation. His fort was burning, his soldiers defeated, and his pride shattered. The humiliation was unbearable. He quickly assembled his remaining troops, rallying them to prepare for an immediate counterattack. His infantry captain, a grizzled veteran of many battles, gritted his teeth in anger.

"The Marathas are nothing but pests. We'll put an end to this once and for all," the captain growled, lifting his prized shotgun, a gift from a Persian ally.

The Portuguese forces moved with haste, crossing the Mandovi River toward Santo Estevao. But Kavi Kalash's meticulous planning was about to bear fruit. The tides were beginning to turn, and the Portuguese, who had crossed the river easily, would soon find themselves trapped on the island with no way to retreat.

As the Portuguese soldiers neared the fort, they were met with fierce resistance from Sambhaji's troops. Khando Ballal, Yesaji Kank, and their four hundred hidden soldiers surged forward from the shadows. The Marathas unleashed a thunderous battle cry, 'Har Har Mahadev!' as they charged into the fray. Their swords, sharp and swift, cut down the Portuguese with ruthless efficiency.

The Portuguese were outnumbered, outmanoeuvred, and outmatched. Their initial bravado quickly gave way to panic as they realized the extent of their mistake. The infantry captain, determined to salvage the situation, locked his gaze on Sambhaji. With a roar, he charged, firing his shotgun at the Maratha king. But Sambhaji, ever the warrior, raised his iron shield, deflecting the bullets with practised ease. The captain fired again and again, but his shots were futile.

Frustrated and desperate, the captain drew a second gun, firing wildly at Sambhaji as he advanced. But the Maratha king was undeterred. Slowly, steadily, he closed the distance, his shield absorbing the volleys of gunfire. When Sambhaji was within striking range, he hurled his shield with all his might. The heavy iron struck the captain square in the chest, knocking him off balance.

Sambhaji wasted no time. He leapt into the air, his sword raised high. The captain looked up in horror, but it was too late. Sambhaji's blade came down in a powerful arc, slicing clean through the captain's neck. The decorated Portuguese officer collapsed in a pool of blood, his body lifeless at Sambhaji's feet.

Tavora, witnessing the death of his most trusted officer, was gripped by terror. With both his pride and his forces shattered, he had no choice but to flee. His injuries made running difficult, but fear drove him onward. He raced down the hill, heading for the safety of the city, leaving his soldiers to fend for themselves.

As Tavora made his escape, Sambhaji picked up the fallen captain's gun and aimed. With careful precision, he fired, hitting Tavora in the shoulder. The Portuguese viceroy howled in pain but kept running, his fear outweighing his agony.

Sambhaji leapt into the river in pursuit. But the tides had grown stronger, and even the mighty Maratha king struggled against the current. The water surged around him, threatening to drag him under. Khando Ballal, seeing his king in danger, did not hesitate. He spurred his horse into the river, extending his hand just in time to grasp Sambhaji's arm and pull him to safety.

Tavora also struggled to cross over the river. Taking the help of his soldiers, he managed to escape once more. He stumbled into St Xavier's Church, collapsing at the altar in a fit of sobbing. He vowed never to cross the Marathas again, begging the Almighty for forgiveness and mercy.

With Khando Ballal's rescue, Sambhaji had carefully crossed the river. All this while, Smabhaji had kept an eye on Tavora. He had seen him enter the church at a distance. Embarking on their horses, Sambhaji and his men laid siege around the church.

Outside the church, Sambhaji waited, his sword in one hand and gun in other. "Tavora, surrender yourself!" he called out, his voice resonating through the quiet streets of the city. Sambhaji respected the sanctity of the church, but he would not rest until Tavora was brought to justice.

Tavora emerged from the church. His face was pale, his body weak from blood loss. He fell to his knees before Sambhaji, tears streaming down his face. "Please, spare me," Tavora begged, his voice barely above a whisper. "I will never oppose the Marathas again."

For a moment, the night was silent. The fate of Tavora, the once-powerful Portuguese viceroy, now lay in the hands of the Maratha king.

15.

AZAM, WITH his formidable army, laid a siege to Bijapur, the Adilshahi capital. Sikander, the young ruler of the Adilshahi Sultanate, had been frantically trying to placate the Mughal prince. He tried sending emissaries bearing lavish gifts, gold, silver, and priceless ornaments, hoping that these offerings would soften Azam's stance. But Azam remained unyielding, unmoved by wealth or promises. His sole focus was to punish Sikander and bring the Adilshahi sultanate to its knees. There would be no mercy; his stand was clear.

Meanwhile, in another part of the subcontinent, Muazzam, with his enormous forces, advanced through the treacherous hilly regions of southern Konkan. His troops encountered considerable difficulty traversing the rugged terrain, but Muazzam was unwavering. Determined to leave destruction in his wake, he relentlessly marched toward Sawant Wadi, located on the outskirts of Goa. Along the way, he had already seized two Maratha forts, looting and capturing them, and now he regrouped with Hassan Ali Khan, who was stationed in the southern Konkan. Together, they formed a massive force that threatened the entire region.

Simultaneously, Zulfikar Khan, another powerful Mughal commander, advanced through Kalyan in North Konkan, a territory that had already fallen under Mughal control. Zulfikar planned to meet Muazzam and Hassan Ali Khan at Raigad, where they would join forces and lay siege to the Maratha capital. The Mughal strategy was to encircle Raigad, Zulfikar Khan from the north and Muazzam from the south, ensuring a decisive strike that would crush the heart of the Maratha empire.

However, this news of impending Mughal invasion reached Sambhaji through his network of spies. The Maratha king, who had been focusing on eliminating the Portuguese threat, was now forced to shift his attention back to his homeland. The situation is dire; Sambhaji understood that the Mughals' coordinated assault posed an existential threat to the Maratha capital.

Gathering his trusted advisers, including Kavi Kalash, Yesaji

Kank, and others, Sambhaji pondered his next move. Though he desired to rid the Konkan region of the Portuguese, he knew that the defence of his own capital must now take precedence. Sambhaji realized that the Marathas, with their limited resources and stretched army, could not afford to fight on multiple fronts. Reluctantly, but with the future of his kingdom in mind, he decided that he would have to negotiate a peace treaty with the Portuguese.

"Kaviji," said Sambhaji, "The Mughals pose a threat to Raigad, and I must move towards Raigad. I am entrusting you with the duty of negotiating the peace treaty with the Portuguese. Akbar shall join you, too."

"Ji Maharaj," Kavi Kalash bowed before Sambhaji, "Do not worry about the Portuguese. I shall take utmost care of them."

Sambhaji placed immense trust in Kavi Kalash. Bidding him goodbye, Sambhaji, with his soldiers, set towards Raigad. Soon, Kavi Kalash was joined by Akbar to ensure the discussions proceeded smoothly.

In the court of the Portuguese, the negotiations with Tavora, the Portuguese viceroy, commenced. The discussions were intense, stretching for hours as both sides tried to secure favourable terms.

"This is the best we can do," said Kavi Kalash to Tavora. He glanced at Tavora and added, "We have already spared your life, which is no less than a negotiation already."

"I am indebted to you for that," said Tavora.

The Marathas had agreed to return the forts they had captured from the Portuguese and release their prisoners. In exchange, the Portuguese had promised to stay out of Maratha affairs and to refrain from forming any alliances with the Mughals or the Desais, local Konkan rebels who had been seeking Portuguese support against the Marathas.

The peace treaty was signed and sealed. Tavora bowed before Kavi Kalash for saving his life, but Kavi Kalash stopped him.

"Bow before our Maharaj. It is he who saved your life," said Kavi Kalash before leaving.

Tavora was filled with gratitude as he saw the Maratha forces leave. Seated on his horse, as Kavi Kalash left the Portuguese province, he knew that the Marathas had put an end to the Siddis and the Portuguese. Confident and determined, he now hoped to put an end to the Mughals.

However, Kavi Kalash was unaware of a private conversation between Akbar and Tavora. Akbar, who had his own ambitions, had approached Tavora with a separate request: "I want to go to Persia," he said, his voice calm but firm. "Can the Portuguese help me?"

WITH THE success of the Maratha-Portuguese treaty, Kavi Kalash returned to Raigad, where he was reunited with Sambhaji. However, despite this diplomatic victory, a heavy burden weighed upon Sambhaji's shoulders. The threat from the Mughal Empire loomed large, and he knew swift decisions had to be made to protect his kingdom. He summoned his trusted ministers to court.

"We should take on the Mughals in the Konkan region," said one of the ministers.

"We should let them reach Raigad and battle them out once and for all with full strength," said the other.

"Why not attack Aurangabad? That's where Aurangzeb stays. Let's put an end to him," said an adviser.

"It's easier said than done," replied Kavi Kalash, aware of Aurangzeb's strength. "He is not alone in Aurangabad. He has a huge army surrounding him, and the terrains of Aurangabad are not hilly like the Konkan provinces, making it easier for Aurangzeb's army to battle us out."

Each minister voiced concerns, offering their perspectives on how best to tackle the Mughal invasion. Finally, after hearing everyone out, Sambhaji rose and addressed the court.

"The Mughals have been too strategic in their movements. While we were engaged in our battles with the Portuguese, they seized the opportunity to advance against us," Sambhaji began, his eyes scanning the room. "This is indeed a grave challenge, but we are prepared to face whatever consequences come our way. One thing is certain: we will not surrender."

His words, filled with resolve, boosted the morale of his

ministers. He continued, "Kavi Kalash has done a remarkable job in securing the treaty with the Portuguese. For this achievement, I declare him the Chandogamatya."

A murmur spread across the court, as few had anticipated this announcement. The title of Chandogamatya was an honour bestowed only upon those whom the king trusted completely. It gave Kavi Kalash the authority to act on behalf of Sambhaji, travelling to other lands and making decisions that carried the weight of royal decree in the king's absence.

Kavi Kalash, caught off guard by the honour, bowed deeply before the king. "Thank you for the honour, Maharaj," he said with humility.

"Kavi Kalash," Sambhaji said, "You shall now leave for Panhala to lead the battle against the Mughals. I have stationed the hazaris to counterattack the Mughal forces: Naruji Bhosale in Satara, Dadaji Narasaprabhu in Sangameshwar, Sarjerao Jedhe in Maval, and Rupaji Bhosale in Ramsej."

The king then turned to address the rest of his ministers. "For their contributions to the defence of Ramsej Fort, Suryaji and his men will be rewarded with gold. Suryaji shall continue to hold command and protect the fort from the Mughal onslaught."

The ministers nodded in agreement, welcoming the king's decisions. Sambhaji continued, "Yesaji Kaka, you will take charge at Ponda Fort and strengthen our forces there."

"Yes, Raje," Yesaji responded without hesitation.

Turning next to Pralhad Niraji, one of his most trusted ministers, Sambhaji spoke with urgency. "I have received news that the Mughals are being supplied by Surat and assisted by the Siddis. We managed to silence the Siddis for a while, but they are back, helping Muazzam by sending shipments to Konkan. I want you to intercept these supplies. Ensure they never reach the Mughal forces."

Sambhaji paused for a moment, then added, "I know Muazzam from my time in the Mughal army. He is a man easily provoked and often acts rashly. He has underestimated the treacherous terrain of Konkan, and the monsoon rains will only add to his troubles. His forces are dragging along elephants and cannons through hilly terrain that will soon become impassable. Make sure none of their supplies get through. The Mughals will starve before they even reach our lands."

Pralhad Niraji understood the urgency in the king's words. He bowed, realizing exactly what needed to be done.

Sambhaji then turned his attention to Sarnobat Mohite. "You will be stationed at Wai. If the Mughals intend to reach Raigad, they will have to pass through there. Be prepared for them."

The king's careful assignment of tasks reflected his deep understanding of the battlefield and his enemies. But beyond strategy, Sambhaji also believed in rewarding those who had fought for the Maratha cause. In the court filled with ministers, he honoured Khando Ballal, the son of the late Balaji Avaji. To the surprise of many, Sambhaji removed a gold bracelet from his own wrist and handed it to Khando Ballal.

"This is for saving my life," Sambhaji declared.

Khando Ballal, who had witnessed his father being sentenced to death by the same king for treachery, now stood in the same court, receiving one of the honours for his bravery. The atmosphere in the court shifted as smiles spread across those present.

Yet, one issue still troubled Sambhaji deeply, the kingdom's dwindling revenues. In a private conversation with Pralhad Niraji, Sambhaji shared his concerns. The many battles fought over the years had drained the kingdom's resources. The wealth they had once acquired through looting Burhanpur had been spent, and the constant threat of Mughal invasions had disrupted agriculture. The peasants had been unable to cultivate their fields, leading to a sharp decline in trade and, subsequently, in revenue.

Sambhaji feared that the economic strain would erode his soldiers' morale, as they relied on their salaries to support their families. He worried about whether they would continue to fight with the same determination under such circumstances.

To address this, Sambhaji wrote two letters. One was addressed to Sikander, the Adilshahi ruler, and the other to Hassan, the Qutubshahi ruler. In both letters, he explained the situation and asked for their financial assistance. Sambhaji ended his letters with a plea for unity, writing, *'Aurangzeb will do everything it takes to defeat us. It is time for us to put aside our differences and stand united to protect the Deccan from the Mughal threat.'*

Meanwhile, in Aurangabad, Aurangzeb was constantly monitoring the progress of his troops. He sent a letter to the Portuguese, urging them to attack the Marathas from Goa. However, Tavora, bound by his peace treaty with the Marathas, did not respond.

Muazzam, stationed in South Konkan, had learned of the Maratha-Portuguese peace treaty. Sensing an opportunity, he wrote to Tavora, '*I have heard of your loss to the Marathas. While the peace treaty may have been a diplomatic win for you, your provinces are indirectly protected by the Mughals. It is because of our pressure on the Marathas that they agreed to make peace with you. You are indebted to us for this protection, and I expect you to pay us a monetary tribute.'*

Tavora was left in a dilemma. On one hand, he had Aurangzeb asking for military assistance, and on the other, Muazzam was demanding money for the protection he claimed to have provided. Conflicted and fearful of further Maratha retaliation, Tavora finally wrote back to Aurangzeb. He explained that the Portuguese could not assist due to their treaty with the Marathas and asked that Muazzam cease his demands for monetary tributes.

Back in Raigad, Sambhaji summoned Bahirji Naik, his chief spy. "Bahirji kaka," Sambhaji called, his voice filled with trust.

"Yes, Maharaj," Bahirji responded, ready to carry out whatever task the king required.

Sambhaji had made his decisions, and his plans were set into motion. In a private talk with Bahirji Naik, the plan of action was decided. The fate of the Deccan now rested on the shoulders of these brave warriors, as they prepared to face the might of the Mughal Empire.

16.

THE RAIN gods had not favoured Muazzam and his army. The torrential downpours drenched the Mughal forces, leaving them cold and miserable. Yet, what frustrated Muazzam even more than the weather was Tavora's refusal to pay the protection money he had demanded. His pride wounded, Muazzam seethed with anger. Instead of continuing his advance toward Raigad, he decided to vent his frustration by marching into Portuguese territories, burning down villages, and looting whatever meagre belongings the villagers had.

News of Muazzam's actions quickly reached Aurangzeb, who was far from pleased. The emperor mulled over the state of his empire and the disobedience of his sons.

"What wrong have I done?" Aurangzeb asked himself, his mind swirling with bitterness. "One son doesn't obey my orders, and the other disowned me to join the Marathas." He remembered the sacrifices he had made to seize the throne, the imprisonment of his own father, Shah Jahan, and the execution of his brother, Dara Shikoh. Perhaps his sins were finally catching up to him, he thought sombrely. But there was no time to dwell on regrets. Shaking off his concerns, Aurangzeb sent a stern message to Muazzam, ordering him to cease his plundering and rejoin Zulfikar's forces at Raigad immediately.

But Muazzam was not easily swayed. "It's time I stop being a puppet. I am the future of the Mughals, and I can decide what is right and what is wrong," he muttered under his breath, his resolve stiffening. Ignoring Aurangzeb's command, he continued looting Portuguese villages, exposing his entire army to the relentless rain and harsh conditions. The army's morale plummeted as many soldiers fell ill from the cold and starvation, with some even succumbing to death. Yet Muazzam remained indifferent, driven by his desire to teach the Portuguese a lesson.

In retaliation, the Portuguese closed off their ports, refusing to allow cargo ships from Surat to enter their provinces. This cut off vital supplies to Muazzam's forces, leaving them stranded and hungry. Desperate for food, Muazzam had no choice but to abandon his campaign against the Portuguese and march toward Raigad through the treacherous hilly terrain. The journey was brutal. The cargo ships carrying essential supplies were intercepted by Maratha forces, which launched a well-coordinated attack, destroying the shipments before they reached the Mughal camp.

The situation only worsened as Muazzam's army struggled to navigate the cliffs and slippery roads. The elephants, unaccustomed to the narrow mountain paths, slipped and tumbled into the valleys below, taking their mahouts with them. Starving and drenched, the infantrymen battled illness and exhaustion. The oxen, weakened by the lack of food, could no longer haul the heavy cannons through the mud. Hundreds of soldiers fell victim to fever, pneumonia, and hunger. Meanwhile, the Marathas capitalized on the Mughals' vulnerability, launching swift guerrilla attacks before disappearing into the dense forests, leaving Muazzam's forces disoriented and demoralized.

"These kafirs are everywhere. Where do they come from?" Muazzam asked, frustrated, turning to his general, Hassan Ali Khan. But Hassan, at a loss for words, could only remain silent. The situation was dire, and Muazzam knew it. "We are out of food, and the animals are starving too," a general reported, his face grim.

Irritated, Muazzam barked orders. "Send men to the local peasants. Loot their crops and grains. We need to survive."

Obeying his command, Mughal scouts fanned out across the countryside, invading nearby villages. But to their dismay, they found most of the homes abandoned. The peasants had fled, taking their supplies with them. Just when it seemed the search was in vain, the scouts stumbled upon a small peasant family who had not managed to escape in time. The soldiers ransacked their home, seizing whatever grains and food they could find. The terrified peasants wept and pleaded, "Please don't do this! This is our yearly income. We will starve without this."

But the Mughals showed no mercy. They took everything, leaving the peasants in tears as they marched back to camp with their loot.

For the first time in days, Muazzam's army sat down to a proper meal. The men devoured the meagre portions of lentils and grains they had stolen, while the leftovers were fed to the starving animals. Muazzam, used to rich meals of meat and beef, refrained from eating the not-so-overwhelming food and instead devoured the oxen's meat. At least they had something, he thought.

But the respite was short-lived. As the night wore on, disaster struck. One by one, the animals began to collapse, their bodies convulsing before they lay still. Men, too, fell ill, vomiting blood and writhing in agony. The camp was thrown into chaos as soldiers dropped to the ground, clutching their stomachs in pain. Thousands of Muazzam's men and animals succumbed to death before dawn broke.

Muazzam was beside himself with fury. The army's hakims inspected the dead and the ill, quickly concluding that the food grains and crops had been coated with and dipped in poison that even heating them could not neutralize the poison. Muazzam's rage knew no bounds. He immediately sent his scouts to track down the peasants responsible, determined to exact brutal revenge on those who had dared to defy him.

But the scouts returned empty-handed. The peasants had disappeared, vanishing into the mountains without a trace. Muazzam was left fuming, powerless to punish those who had inflicted such devastation on his army.

A few kilometres away, the very peasants Muazzam sought were making their way toward Raigad. Pride swelled in their hearts as they reflected on their success. Their leader, a man with a wicked smile, was especially pleased. "It's just the beginning," he said with quiet satisfaction.

"Definitely, Bahirji Kaka," one of the men replied, pride evident in his voice. They had done exactly what Sambhaji had instructed Bahirji Naik to do in secret, and the thought of their triumph filled them with joy.

17.

MUAZZAM, WHO had begun his ascent towards Raigad from South Konkan, was forced to turn back, his army devastated. The Maratha spies, led by the resourceful Bahirji Naik, had won Sambhaji a significant victory. The night they poisoned the Mughal food supply was the turning point that gave the Marathas a decisive edge. Sambhaji rewarded Bahirji and his men for their unmatched skill, praising them for saving countless Maratha lives and ensuring a crucial victory in the ongoing struggle against the Mughals.

Though the threat of Zulfikar Khan's forces descending from North Konkan still loomed, tension at Raigad began to ease in the following months. The mood in the Maratha court lightened further when a joyous event brought smiles to everyone's faces: Rajaram's second marriage proposal. Rajaram, Sambhaji's younger brother, was to wed Tarabai, the daughter of Sarnobat Mohite. The marriage was a significant union, not just politically, but also for the morale of the court and the people.

The wedding ceremony, though subdued due to the ever-present Mughal threat, was a moment of celebration. Tarabai, young and barely of age, was a striking presence who earned the admiration of many at the Maratha court. Sambhaji, in particular, was in awe of her maturity, even though she was less than half his age. Despite her youth and innocence, Tarabai spoke with a passion and conviction that belied her tender years. Her ambition was evident, as she boldly declared her desire to see the Mughal sultanate brought to its knees.

"You must be blessed to have such a daughter, Sarnobat," Sambhaji said, genuinely impressed by the young bride's fiery spirit.

The wedding celebration, though brief, was filled with hope and unity. But Sambhaji could not afford to linger long. The threats to his kingdom were still pressing, and he needed to leave for Panhala to strategize future defences and plans against the Mughals. As the preparations for his departure were underway, Yesubai, Sambhaji's wife, received a request for a private audience with her brother, Ganoji.

Yesubai was curious, though cautious, about what Ganoji had to say. She knew her brother well and suspected that his visit had more to do with personal gain than familial affection. Her instincts proved to be correct when Ganoji, after a hesitant start, boldly put forth his demand. He wanted the watandari rights of Dabhol, a region near Shringarpur that the family had once governed.

The landlords, who held hereditary rights to rule certain provinces, had long exploited the peasants by demanding exorbitant taxes and hoarding food grains. When Shivrai had founded Swaraj, he had abolished the watandari system, believing that there should be only one central authority to ensure justice and fairness. The watandars were instead given fixed salaries, stripping them of their power. Many, like Ganoji, had resented this, feeling entitled to their old privileges.

"Shivrai's daughter is my wife, and Sambhaji's sister is mine by marriage," Ganoji had protested in the past, believing this gave him the right to reclaim his family's lands. Yet Shivrai had refused to entertain the topic, which had caused a rift between the Ganoji's family and the Bhosales for years. Now, with Rajaram's marriage and Shivrai's death, Ganoji saw an opportunity to use his sister to regain what he believed was rightfully his.

"This is not going to happen, Dada," Yesubai said firmly, her voice calm but resolute.

"Sister, this is our right," Ganoji pleaded. "The Mughals are plundering the land. No crops have been cultivated in over a year due to the constant threat of invasion. Maharaj has positioned Kavi Kalash to protect the region, but he has too many responsibilities. He cannot give our province the attention it needs. Our people are suffering. If you help me reclaim the watandari, I can ensure their safety. I beg you, talk to Maharaj."

But Yesubai was unmoved. Rising from her seat, she questioned her brother's true intentions. Was Ganoji genuinely concerned for the welfare of the people, or was he simply after the power and wealth that came with the watandari rights? Her doubts deepened as Ganoji's desperation grew.

"This is not just about power, sister," Ganoji continued, his eyes glistening with tears. "I will protect the peasants. I will keep the Mughals at bay."

"I said no, Dada," Yesubai responded, her patience thinning.

Ganoji's frustration flared. "How can an outsider like Kavi Kalash rule our land? This is injustice!"

"Enough, Dada!" Yesubai snapped, raising her hand to silence him. "My husband is the Chhatrapati of this nation. He knows what is right and wrong. You accuse Kavi Kalash, but in doing so, you question the judgement of the king. I won't tolerate such disrespect."

The anger in her voice stunned Ganoji, who stood frozen in disbelief. His sister, once so kind and gentle, had turned him away. His eyes narrowed, filled with a mix of hurt and rage.

"You may leave, Dada," Yesubai said coldly, her words final.

Seething with humiliation, Ganoji stormed out of the room, leaving Yesubai deep in thought. She considered bringing up the issue with Sambhaji but quickly dismissed the idea. She knew her husband had far more pressing concerns to deal with. This was not the time to burden him with her brother's demands. Ganoji's fate, and the fate of Dabhol, would have to wait.

AZAM KHAN'S siege of the Adilshahi stronghold of Bijapur had ended in abject failure. Over the past year, despite his relentless efforts, he had neither instilled fear in the Adilshahi nor inflicted any significant damage upon them. Instead, the resilience of Bijapur had only seemed to strengthen as it withstood his attacks. The Adilshahi and Qutubshahi sultanates, once enemies of the Marathas, had found common cause and joined forces with Sambhaji in addressing their financial crisis. This unexpected alliance had aggravated Aurangzeb, who found the situation increasingly dire. Meanwhile, Muazzam had been busy looting the cities around Belgaum, and Zulfikar Khan was left isolated around Raigad, occasionally harassed by Maratha attacks. In response to the Mughal threat, Sarnobat Mohite shifted his focus to Wai, working tirelessly to protect the country from Mughal incursions.

In Bijapur, the political landscape had shifted significantly. The retirement of Sikander's wazir Masud, who had previously aided Sambhaji in reorganizing the Marathas and stabilizing the region after his brief association with Diler Khan, left a power vacuum. Masud's replacement, Sarza Khan, was a seasoned warrior with a reputation for valour and strategic acumen. Sarza Khan advocated for a robust response against the Mughals. Sikander, recognizing the gravity of the situation and the shift in strategic needs, decided to act against the Mughals. Despite the complex and often antagonistic relationship between the Marathas and the Adilshahi-Qutubshahi alliances since Shivrai's time, Sarza Khan understood that the Marathas, despite their enmity, were more reliable allies compared to the treacherous Mughal forces. Sikander, who felt indebted to the Marathas for their past assistance, was determined to repay that debt by resisting the Mughal advances.

The Qutubshahi leader Abul Hassan, residing in his fortified Golconda Fort in Hyderabad, shared similar concerns about the Mughals. Initially, he had attempted to appease Aurangzeb by fulfilling two significant demands: removing all Hindu ministers from his administration and paying a substantial tribute. However, these concessions did not yield the desired peace. Instead, the removal of Hindu ministers led the remaining Muslim officials to favour the Mughals, precisely what Aurangzeb had hoped for. Despite his physical limitations and inability to fight, Hassan continued to strategize from his impregnable fort. He appointed Sheikh Nizam to lead the military efforts against the Mughals while he himself remained in Golconda, overseeing the defence from a distance.

In Aurangabad, Aurangzeb's frustration with the stagnant siege led him to reinforce Azam Khan's efforts. He sent Bahadurshah Kokaltash along with additional troops to bolster the siege.

"They are coming from everywhere in huge numbers," Sikander exclaimed in panic, overwhelmed by the scale of the siege. The Mughal forces, numbering approximately one hundred thousand men and armed with around 250 cannons and 22,000 matchlocks, sought to starve Bijapur into submission by cutting off its food supply.

The Marathas, true to their guerrilla warfare prowess,

continued to harass the Mughal forces from the outside, disrupting their operations and supply lines. "The Marathas get on my nerves," Azam complained to Bahadurshah Kokaltash, who had recently suffered a significant defeat at Ramsej. The Mughal attempts to breach Bijapur's fortifications proved futile. Their cannons battered the fort, but the defences held firm. Attempts to scale the walls were thwarted by skilled Adilshahi archers and the formidable crocodiles in the moat surrounding the fort.

"This fort is invincible," Bahadurshah Kokaltash admitted, acknowledging their growing despair. The continuous Maratha attacks and the successful obstruction of food and ammunition supplies only worsened Azam Khan's situation. With mounting frustration and considerable resources already invested in the siege, Aurangzeb decided to take matters into his own hands. He marched with fresh reinforcements to Bijapur, joining forces with Azam Khan and Bahadurshah Kokaltash.

Aurangzeb wrote to Muazzam, requesting his assistance in the siege, but Muazzam, preoccupied with his own campaigns around Belgaum, ignored the call for aid. His focus remained on his ongoing battles, leaving Aurangzeb's forces to face the Adilshahi and Maratha coalition alone.

Meanwhile, Akbar, who had previously signed a treaty with the Portuguese, sought their assistance to reach Persia. He had hoped to enlist Persian support to build a force capable of overthrowing his father's rule. However, despite their promises, the Portuguese failed to provide him with a ship. Learning of Akbar's plight, Sambhaji extended his support. "I wish to go to Persia," Akbar confided in Sambhaji.

"What for?" Sambhaji inquired, intrigued by Akbar's request.

"I wish to build a force of my own," Akbar explained. "Only Emperor Shah Abbas can help me with an army strong enough to challenge Agra and end my father's rule."

Sambhaji saw merit in aiding Akbar's endeavour. Supporting him would not only help Akbar but also create another adversary for the Mughals. "When I am here, why do you need to reach out to the Portuguese? I am here to support you," Sambhaji assured him, offering Akbar a ship to take him to Persia. With renewed hope, Akbar boarded the ship, envisioning a future where he could challenge his father's dominion.

Back at the Golconda Fort, Aurangzeb realized the reasons behind their prolonged failure. The Marathas' strategic interference in cutting off food, gunpowder, and ammunition supplies to Solapur had exacerbated the situation. The formidable defences of Bijapur, its ten-foot deep moat and fifty-foot high, twenty-five-foot wide granite walls, had proven nearly impervious to the Mughal artillery. Understanding that conventional assaults would not succeed, Aurangzeb devised a new plan by constructing trenches and targeting the gates directly.

Motivating his troops with fervent promises of martyrdom and eternal reward of making way to heaven or Jannat, as he termed it, Aurangzeb urged them to attack with renewed vigour. "You shall be called martyrs and live an afterlife in heaven," he proclaimed to his soldiers, who were apprehensive about the impending battle.

The Mughals launched a brutal assault on Bijapur's gates, engaging in fierce combat with the Adilshahi defenders. The battle raged for eight gruelling days. Despite the Adilshahi's valiant defence, the gates eventually succumbed. Once the fortifications were breached, the Mughal forces poured into Bijapur, setting it ablaze.

As the Mughal forces advanced, Sarza Khan, loyal to Sikander, launched a desperate counterattack but was met with overwhelming force. Aurangzeb's sword found its mark, piercing Sarza Khan's chest. Sikander, fighting fiercely to protect his sister Shahr Banu from the Mughal onslaught, was eventually overwhelmed by hundreds of enemy soldiers. Severely injured, Sikander was shackled and dragged into the open, where Aurangzeb forced him to kneel before him, before subjecting him to public humiliation and torture.

The fall of Bijapur marked the end of the Adilshahi Sultanate, which had ruled parts of the Deccan for nearly two centuries. The once-mighty sultanate was now firmly under Mughal control. A shackled Sikander was imprisoned in the fort of Daulatabad, where he would spend his final months before dying in captivity.

18.

"PRINCE AKBAR has escaped to Persia," one of Aurangzeb's subordinates reported, his voice trembling slightly under the weight of his message.

Aurangzeb's face darkened with fury. "Who the hell helped the traitor?" he demanded, his voice a dangerous growl.

"Sambhaji," the man responded, his eyes cast downward, avoiding the wrath that seemed to radiate from the Mughal emperor.

"Kafirs!" Aurangzeb roared, his frustration evident as he pounded his fist on his throne. The triumph of capturing the Adilshahi Sultanate had been fleeting. Aurangzeb understood that with Akbar now on the loose, rallying support in Persia, the threat to his dominion had not diminished; it had merely shifted.

The next obstacle in Aurangzeb's path was the Qutubshahi Sultanate in Hyderabad. With over a hundred thousand infantrymen and cavalrymen, Aurangzeb, accompanied by his trusted commanders, Kilich Khan, Feroze Jung, and Anup Singh, moved toward the Golconda Fort, the bastion of Qutubshahi power.

The Marathas, ever the thorn in Aurangzeb's side, were not idle. They supported the Qutubshahi with their own network of scouts, who carried out relentless guerrilla attacks on the advancing Mughal forces. These attacks were aimed at disrupting Mughal supply lines, destroying provisions, and setting fire to the arms and ammunition. However, the sheer scale of the Mughal army meant that these efforts, while bothersome, were insufficient to halt the Mughal advance.

With Shivrai's death, Shaista Khan, who had been deeply scarred by his encounters with the Marathas, including a fierce attack that had left him mutilated, was now back in Aurangzeb's service. His return brought added experience and strategic acumen to the Mughal forces. Shaista Khan's presence doubled Aurangzeb's power, and with it, the Mughals tightened their siege around the Golconda Fort.

The Mughals faced an arduous task. Munnawar Khan was appointed to ensure the delivery of food and weapons to sustain the

Mughal siege, which stretched on for months. Despite the Marathas' best efforts to cut off supplies and provide some resistance, their actions were insufficient to bring the mighty Mughal army to a standstill.

Inside the fortress of Golconda, the Qutubshahi sultan, Hassan, had prioritized the protection of the Kollur mine, the only known diamond mine in the world at that time. The precious stones from this mine were crucial, for he knew that the day Aurangzeb would get his hands on them, it would provide the means to bribe and sway allegiances. Hassan's wazir, Muqarrab Khan, played a critical role in this defence. Hassan had immense trust in Muqarrab and had ordered him to use the fort's cannons to repel the Mughal assault.

In response, the Mughals, under the leadership of Feroze Jung, launched a relentless barrage of cannon fire. Feroze Jung was determined to break down the walls of the seemingly impregnable Golconda Fort. The fighting intensified, and the death toll among the Mughal soldiers mounted, making it increasingly difficult for them to press their assault. Despite these setbacks, Aurangzeb was resolute and sent another message to his son Muazzam, urging him to return to Raigad and aid in the siege. Yet, Muazzam remained unresponsive.

Around Raigad, Zulfikar Khan had begun a siege of his own, but the Marathas resisted fiercely. Their rebellion made it exceedingly difficult for Zulfikar's forces to hold their ground, compelling the Mughals to retreat. The Marathas proved to be an indomitable force, and Sambhaji, well aware that the Mughals would soon return, quickly sent a message to Muazzam.

'Let bygones be bygones, and let us together fight against your father's troops. In return, you shall achieve much more than you will by merely following your father's orders.'

Upon receiving the letter, Muazzam hesitated. The prospect of seeing his father fail in the Deccan and seizing the throne for himself was tempting. However, Muazzam was troubled by the possibility that Sambhaji might be playing another political game. Despite his reservations, Muazzam's desire to undermine Aurangzeb outweighed his doubts about Sambhaji's intentions. He resolved that if the opportunity arose, he would betray Sambhaji. But for now, making his father fail was his primary concern.

Without a response from Muazzam, Aurangzeb grew increasingly impatient. His spies had informed him of a probable alliance between Sambhaji and Muazzam. Irked, he dispatched his troops to locate and capture Muazzam, issuing orders to apprehend him on sight. Muazzam was taken into custody without resistance and brought before Aurangzeb, who punished him by imprisoning him, along with his son Moizuddin and his wives.

"One less traitor for me to handle," Aurangzeb muttered to himself, though his heart remained heavy with the thought of Akbar's continued freedom. "Even Akbar and his friends shall not be spared," he added, thinking of Sambhaji, who had aided Akbar and thwarted his plans. Aurangzeb summoned Sarza Khan, who had formerly served the Adilshahi but had aligned himself with the Mughals following their victory.

"I want to take down the Marathas," Aurangzeb declared as he sat on his throne in a tent situated near the Golconda Fort, the Mughal siege continuing unabated.

Sarza Khan, who had observed Shivrai and Sambhaji closely, looked at Aurangzeb with a measure of confidence and replied, "The Marathas are invincible."

"There is no word as invincible in the Mughal dictionary," Aurangzeb snapped, his temper flaring. "What I desire to achieve must be achieved. I want to put an end to the Maratha empire."

The intense anger in Aurangzeb's eyes caused Sarza Khan to falter momentarily. He explained, "There are four reasons that make the Marathas seem invincible: first, the Konkan ranges, where our army struggles against their guerrilla tactics; second, Chhatrapati Sambhaji, who is remarkably astute and valorous, unlike other leaders who remain distant from the battlefield; third, the Maratha spy network led by Bahirji Naik, which provides rapid and secret information to their soldiers; and fourth, their war general, Hambirrao Mohite, who excels at motivating his troops. Even with only a fraction of the manpower compared to the Mughals, these factors set the Marathas apart."

Aurangzeb, accustomed to hearing only his own voice, listened intently. He pondered Sarza Khan's insights as he devised his next strategy. His spies had informed him that the Maratha Sarnobat Hambirrao Mohite was stationed around Wai, a region considered less formidable compared to the Konkan.

"Sarza Khan," Aurangzeb said, "I want to take down Sarnobat Mohite at Wai. And who better than you, who knows the Maratha army inside and out, to undertake this mission?"

Sarza Khan bowed deeply before Aurangzeb, receiving the *pan*, a traditional token of authority, signifying his appointment to the task.

Next, Aurangzeb sent a message to Muqarrab Khan, the wazir within the Golconda Fort. Muqarrab had made up his mind. The deal Aurangzeb had offered was enticing, and Muqarrab knew that aligning with the Mughal emperor might be his best chance for survival and advancement.

THE BATTLE of Golconda raged on for eight long months. The fort, which had once been a bastion of resilience and strength under the Qutubshahi rule, was now the epicentre of a relentless siege. The fierce warriors of the Qutubshahi, led by their most valiant commanders, fought with unwavering resolve, their every action a testament to their indomitable spirit. Among them, Abdur Razzak, an esteemed and crucial commander of Hassan's forces, stood out. As the Mughal forces breached the fort's gates and began to pour in, Abdur Razzak decided to confront the invaders head-on.

The Mughal commander Kilich Khan Khwaja, mounted on his massive elephant, thundered through the fort's interior, crushing the Qutubshahi soldiers beneath the beast's relentless weight. The sight of Kilich Khan, a seasoned veteran and one of Aurangzeb's most trusted commanders, incited both fear and fury among the defenders. Abdur Razzak, determined to make a stand, leapt from the first floor of the fort, his sword gleaming with purpose. With a swift and decisive strike, he pierced Kilich Khan, ending the life of one of the Mughals' most formidable leaders.

The death of Kilich Khan sent a shockwave through the Mughal ranks, but the victory was bittersweet for Abdur Razzak. His heroic act came at a significant cost; he was soon trapped beneath the elephant's crushing weight. The loss of Kilich Khan was a grievous blow to Aurangzeb, akin to the loss of a family member. With their leader gone and the fort's defences crumbling, the Qutubshahi soldiers began to falter. As the Mughal forces advanced, the defenders, now leaderless, began surrendering their arms and retreating in disarray.

In the meantime, Hassan and his family had been escorted to a hidden sanctuary within the fort. The once-mighty stronghold of Golconda was now falling into the hands of the Mughals. As the Mughal troops pressed forward, they approached the Kollur diamond mine, a treasure trove of unparalleled value. Muqarrab Khan, Hassan's wazir, stood guard at the entrance to the mine, flanked by only two soldiers. When Aurangzeb arrived at the scene, a mocking smile curled on his lips upon seeing Muqarrab Khan's inadequate defence.

Before Aurangzeb could issue any commands, a sudden and swift attack cut down the two soldiers guarding the mine. The assailant was none other than Muqarrab Khan himself, who had betrayed his own men in a desperate act of allegiance to the Mughals. "Badshah, this way. Hassan is hiding this way," Muqarrab Khan said, pointing towards a concealed escape route. The Mughals, ever vigilant, quickly followed his lead, rushing through the hidden passage and capturing Hassan and his family within moments.

Hassan's fury was palpable as he glared at Muqarrab Khan, who remained impassive to the curses directed at him. Hassan was shackled and imprisoned in the dungeons of Daulatabad, where he joined Sikander, barely alive. The fall of Golconda marked a significant victory for the Mughals, who renamed the province Hyderabad Subah. With the acquisition of the Kollur diamond mine, the Mughals had secured immense wealth, further bolstering their power.

Aurangzeb, elated by the conquest, welcomed Muqarrab Khan with great honour. The emperor showered him with precious pearls and gold, elevating him to the rank of Mughal mansabdar. "I am proud that you have joined us in our battle against the kafirs," Aurangzeb proclaimed. Muqarrab Khan's face lit up with ecstatic pride as he responded, "Anything for you, Badshah."

Aurangzeb, with a glint of ambition in his eyes, continued, "Now that you are a Mughal mansabdar, I want you to demonstrate your valour against the Marathas. Eliminate Sambhaji and his family. If you succeed, I shall make you the chief of the Deccan." Muqarrab Khan's eyes sparkled with greed at the prospect of such power.

"I want Sambhaji dead, at any cost," Aurangzeb declared, his voice filled with resolve.

"It will be my honour to fulfil your wishes, Badshah," Muqarrab Khan vowed, bowing profoundly before the emperor. With his new mission clear, Muqarrab Khan assembled a formidable army and set his sights on Raigad, determined to capture Sambhaji.

Meanwhile, at Raigad, Sambhaji received distressing news from Kavi Kalash. The Portuguese and the British had rejected their proposal to assist the Marathas against the Mughal onslaught. This development left Sambhaji in a precarious situation. With Zulfikar Khan's forces besieging Raigad and the fall of both the Adilshahi and Qutubshahi, the Marathas were now isolated. The Mughal acquisition of the Kollur diamond mine had only increased their wealth and influence, potentially turning Maratha allies into adversaries.

The looming threat of betrayal from the watandars and fort commanders weighed heavily on Sambhaji. Faced with the prospect of internal treachery and the ever-strengthening Mughal siege, he knew he had to act decisively. "Yesu, I should leave," Sambhaji said, his voice tinged with urgency.

"Where Maharaj?" Yesu inquired, her concern for her husband masked by her composed demeanour. "Sarza Khan is approaching the provinces around Wai," Sambhaji explained. "From there, he could advance to Panhala and then onto Raigad, strengthening Zulfikar's position. I need to intercept him near Panhala before he reaches Raigad and fortifies Mughal strength."

Yesu's eyes filled with unspoken fear and worry. She had never seen her husband so troubled before. The gravity of the situation was evident, and though she was the queen and must remain strong, her heart ached at the thought of losing him. "Maharaj…" she began, but the inauspicious nature of stopping someone on their way prevented her from voicing her fears.

Sambhaji walked close to her, his eyes meeting hers. He could see tears in Yesubai's eyes.

"What's troubling you, Yesu?" he asked, sensing the discomfort.

"Everything is falling apart," Yesubai broke down, "The Adilshahi, the Qutubshahi and now, the enemy is starting at us."

Sambhaji could sense his wife's turmoil. He reassured her, "Don't worry, Yesu. We are Marathas. Only God can put an end to us. Nobody else. Our fight is for a good cause, unlike Aurangzeb and his men. The Gods are with us." To lighten Yesu's mood, he added, "Your Chhava is still alive, ready to battle any Aurangzeb who crosses our paths."

Sambhaji managed to bring a smile to Yesubai's face before she responded, "You have fought many battles till now, but I have never felt this way before. There is something wrong this time. I can sense it," Yesubai stopped, took a deep breath and added, "I fear something wrong. I fear for you."

"It's just mind games. I shall be back soon," replied Sambhaji, looking into her eyes. "Promise me, you shall stay strong. Together, we need to put an end to the Mughal dynasty. You are the queen. You have to not only look after our people and Rajaram, Tara, and Shahu but also lift arms against our enemies, if needed. The nation needs your guidance."

Yesu nodded, her emotions a tangled mix of fear and resolve.

Taking Yesu's leave, Sambhaji met his cousin Rajaram, who was now seventeen. "You are the prince of the Marathas. Now that you are of age, I trust you will lead our men if needed. But I hope such a situation never arises."

Rajaram nodded solemnly, accepting his brother's words. Sambhaji then took a moment to caress his son, Shambhu, tenderly.

Yesu returned with a thal for puja, lighting a diya and applying sandalwood paste on Sambhaji's head, while offering him sweets and praying fervently for his safe and victorious return.

With a heavy heart, Yesu bid her husband farewell. Sambhaji mounted his horse and set off towards Panhala with his ministers in tow. Yesu watched him disappear into the dense forest, her heart heavy with dread. She placed the diya thal before the temple, laying her head in supplication to the Almighty, pleading for her husband's safety and a triumphant return.

As she rose, her delicate mangalsutra snapped, its ebony beads scattering across the floor like fallen pearls.

"A LARGE troop of the Mughals are advancing!" a Maratha soldier shouted, his voice echoing in the quiet, moonless night. The Maratha troops had been camping near Wai, under the leadership of Sarnobat Mohite. The winter nights had been calm and serene until now. The soldier's urgent announcement jolted everyone awake, tearing them from their dreams of peaceful slumber.

Sarnobat Mohite, fully aware of the gravity of the situation, swiftly gathered his men. With the chilling wind biting through the camp, he rallied his troops with a commanding presence. "Brace yourselves!" he shouted, his voice resonating with authority. "We do not have the option of retreating to Raigad or Panhala. Raigad is under siege by Zulfikar Khan, and Panhala shall now face a Mughal invasion as well if the Mughals cross over Wai. Our only choice is to defend this camp with all our might and drive the Mughals back. Fight for the dream of an independent nation, even if death comes your way."

The Maratha troops, their spirits bolstered by the stirring words, stood tall with pride. They were prepared to face the Mughal forces head-on. The terrain of Wai, with its rugged hills and dense forests, provided them with a strategic advantage. The overgrown bushes and trees offered ample cover for ambushes. Ropes had been strung between trees, allowing the Marathas to manoeuvre swiftly from one position to another.

As the Mughal forces approached, they were unaware of the trap that awaited them. The soldiers, oblivious to the danger, stepped too close to the camp. Suddenly, the ground gave way, and a deep trench, dug meticulously by the Marathas, swallowed hundreds of Mughal soldiers and their horses.

'Har Har Mahadev!' The Marathas chanted as they filled the trench with oil and set it ablaze. The flames roared, consuming the trapped Mughal soldiers. Meanwhile, the Maratha warriors used their agility to slide across the ropes, launching surprise attacks on the Mughal soldiers from above. The Marathas had ropes tied across trees, which they lowered when needed to execute their enemy and swiftly disappeared into the dense forest, only to arise somewhere else. Those who remained hidden in the trees let loose a barrage of arrows, cutting down the enemy with precision.

Sarza Khan, caught off guard, struggled to make sense of the chaos. He was accustomed to conventional warfare, not this unpredictable and relentless assault. The Mughal soldiers were slaughtered, their bodies strewn across the battlefield. The Marathas, familiar with the terrain, used their mobility to their advantage, attacking from all directions.

Sarza Khan, filled with fear, scanned the battlefield from his horse. He soon identified the man orchestrating the Maratha defence, Sarnobat Hambirrao Mohite. Sarza Khan was struck by the Sarnobat's prowess and strategic brilliance. It was clear why Mohite held such a prestigious position among the Marathas. With his strong, muscular build and exceptional agility, Hambirrao Mohite cut through the Mughal ranks with a dandpatta, taking down groups of 20 soldiers at a time.

"Turn the direction of the cannon there!" Sarza Khan ordered urgently, his frustration palpable.

"But there are our men battling in the open," the gunman protested.

Sarza Khan, his patience worn thin, glared at the gunman and roared, "Do not question my orders!"

"Fire!" he commanded. The cannons unleashed a deadly volley, the balls exploding around Sarnobat Mohite. The Sarnobat was thrown from his feet by the blasts, his powerful presence momentarily subdued by the ferocity of the cannon fire. The Mughal soldiers were thrown away, too, each of them meeting their ultimate fate.

"Subhan Allah!" Sarza Khan exclaimed, raising his hands in triumph. "Few sacrifices are worth it when the prize is as significant as the chief of the army," he said, referring to both Sarnobat Mohite and the Mughal soldiers who had been injured or killed.

As the battle raged on, a Maratha soldier called out, "The Sarnobat is hit!" The soldiers rushed to assist Mohite, but he needed no support. Wounded and bleeding, the man was still unstoppable. He stood on his feet, grabbed a sword that lay on the ground and yanked it at the approaching Mughals.

"Attack the Mughals!" he commanded his soldiers, "Spare no one, leave no one, kill them all and bury them all."

Sarnobat Mohite cut through the Mughal soldiers. Not one or two but a double dozen of them. Sarza Khan was amazed to see the Sarnobat still standing on his feet, despite a cannonball having injured him minutes ago.

Sarnobat's eyes fell on Sarza Khan. With rage in his eyes, Sarnobat Mohite shouted, "Sarza Khan! I challenge you to get down from your elephant and fight against me." The Sarnobat's voice echoed through the forest. Sarza Khan was astounded. He feared the worst. Sarnobat Mohite grabbed a spear. Determined to charge towards Sarza Khan, the latter could sense chills running down his spine.

"Fire another cannonball!" Sarza Khan shouted, "Aim at him," he added.

"Quick, you fools," Sarza Khan turned impatient. The Sarnobat charged towards him, throwing the spear at him as another cannonball exploded just near the Sarnobat. The spear grazed through Sarza Khan's ear, injuring him. The Sarnobat fell on the ground, still staring at Sarza Khan. Fear was evident in Sarza Khan's eyes; he couldn't manage to meet the Sarnobat's eyes.

"Har Har Mahadev," the Sarnobat whispered as he breathed his last. His eyes still wide open, staring at Sarza Khan, haunted and terrified him.

"The Sarnobat is no more!" shouted one of the Maratha soldiers.

With Sarnobat Mohite's death, the morale of the Maratha troops plummeted. In a furious response, they charged at the remaining

Mughal forces, their anger turning into brutal vengeance. They slit throats, destroyed cannons, and left no Mughal soldier alive. Sarza Khan, witnessing the devastation and unable to rally his men effectively, had no choice but to retreat.

The victory at Wai was bittersweet for the Marathas. They had managed to thwart the Mughal invasion, but at the cost of their esteemed Sarnobat, a tremendous loss for their cause.

"Raje, the Sarnobat is no more. He breathed his last in Wai," a Maratha soldier wept before Sambhaji, sharing the news with the king on his way to Panhala.

"Jagdamb!" Sambhaji closed his eyes, his heart wrenching for his maternal uncle. Memories of the Sarnobat flashed in front of him. Not only had Hambirrao Mohite been the Sarnobat of the Marathas, but he had also been a tutor to Sambhaji and Rajaram, training them all through their childhood. The loss was personal to Sambhaji. Sambhaji hid his tears as he mourned his uncle's loss. Grieving, he stopped to light a diya at a temple and paid his last respects to Sarnobat Mohite. Realizing the threat looming around and the urgency for another leader to guide the Maratha troops, Sambhaji appointed Malhoji Ghorpade as the new Sarnobat.

Aurangzeb, too, received news of the battle and saw an opportunity. He sent reinforcements to bolster Zulfikar Khan's siege in Raigad and doubled Sarza Khan's forces. Sarza Khan, now reinforced, charged towards Panhala, gaining control of Panhala and its vicinity. With the Mughals now firmly established in the Konkan provinces too, Sambhaji was cut off from both Raigad and Panhala. Recognizing the dire circumstances, Sambhaji altered his course toward Sangameshwar in the Ratnagiri province. He dispatched a message to Kavi Kalash, instructing him to advance with his troops to Sangameshwar. It was a strategic retreat, seeking refuge, regrouping, and planning their next move against the Mughal forces.

Aurangzeb, ever shrewd, began exploiting the discontent among the Maratha watandars, turning them into allies through bribery. The death of Sarnobat Mohite had sown fear and uncertainty among the Maratha soldiers, further exacerbated by the financial strain that left them poorly compensated. The Mughal strategy was proving effective; they had managed to divide the Maratha nation and pit its factions against each other.

"Badshah, there is someone who wishes to see you," a minister announced, leading a mysterious figure into Aurangzeb's presence.

"I can help you capture Sambhaji," the man said boldly, his demeanour betraying no hint of fear.

Aurangzeb's interest was piqued. "How?" he inquired, his eyes narrowing with curiosity.

The man detailed his plan, and Aurangzeb's eyes sparkled with excitement. "I want you to give me…" the man began outlining his demands. Aurangzeb, eager to seize the opportunity, cut him off.

"Qabool hai!" Aurangzeb declared enthusiastically. "Everything is accepted." His jubilation was palpable. The prospect of capturing Sambhaji, and with it, achieving unrivalled dominance, was intoxicating. Aurangzeb yearned to be the Alamgir, the supreme ruler of the entire nation.

As the man prepared to leave, Aurangzeb called out to him. "But…" The man turned back, facing Aurangzeb's stern gaze. "If you fail," Aurangzeb warned coldly, "I shall personally behead you."

REACHING SANGAMESHWAR, Sambhaji immediately summoned his newly appointed Sarnobat, Malhoji Ghorpade, along with 25 of his trusted ministers. Kavi Kalash had also arrived with his forces, joining the Maratha king in the secret hideout. The journey to Sangameshwar had been a gruelling one for both Sambhaji and Kavi Kalash. Sangameshwar, a town in the Ratnagiri province was bound by the Sahyadiri mountain ranges to one side and the Arabian sea to the other. Sangama in Sanskrit meaning confluence signified the confluence of two rivers, Sonavi and Shastri. They had navigated secret routes, avoided detection, and travelled without any stops, pushing their endurance to the limit. Finally, they had reached their destination, a secluded hideout that was the last place the Mughals would think to search for them. Sambhaji, Kavi Kalash, Malhoji Ghorpade and the Maratha army now stationed in the houses of town, discussed the further plan of action.

Sambhaji's voice echoed as he addressed his ministers in one of the wadas, a Maharashtrian mansion or fortified residence served as both residential and administrative centre.

"The plan is clear," he declared, his eyes scanning the faces of his chief ministers, Sarnobat Malhoji, and Kavi Kalash. "Our strength has been divided into three regions. One, Raigad. two, Panhala and now three, Sangameshwar. It's only a matter of time before Raigad and Panhala shall completely fall into the hands of the Mughals. In such a situation, we have two options: one, to maintain a low profile, rebuild our army, and then strike the Mughals with full force. Second, to attack Raigad from the periphery before the Mughals at Panhala can reach Raigad." He paused, allowing the gravity of his words to sink in as his ministers nodded in agreement.

"Our revenues have crashed, and most of our ministers and soldiers have either turned martyrs or been bribed. The threat is looming large, and our position is precarious. We need to stay hidden here for a few days. In the first option, once the Mughals, after exhausting themselves in capturing Raigad and Panhala, give up on their invasions, and that's when we shall rebuild our forces and attack them. In the second option, we make an immediate move and attack the forces in Raigad before the Mughal forces attacking Panhala regroup with the Mughal forces at Raigad."

The room fell silent as Sambhaji's words settled in. While most ministers nodded in agreement, one of the soldiers couldn't hide his concerns. "Maharaj, what about our families? What about the safety of our men?" he asked, his voice trembling slightly.

Sambhaji knew the question was inevitable, and as a king, it was his duty to address such fears. "This will not take long," Sambhaji reassured them. "Akbar has reached Persia and will soon be attacking Agra with his forces. The Mughals will be compelled to return to Agra to fight their battles, much like we had to do when we signed the treaty with the Portuguese." Sambhaji's eyes sparkled with determination.

"We have two options to choose from, both equally perilous," stated Sambhaji.

"Which option do you find best suitable, Maharaj?" asked Kavi Kalash.

"Both," stated Sambhaji, had a look around and added, "Considering everything, Malhoji Ghorpade and I shall advance to Raigad before the Mughals at Panhala reach Raigad and save Raigad before it falls. Meanwhile, Kavi Kalash shall soon leave in disguise to meet the rulers in the south and seek their help. If we can ally with them, he shall lead another battle from the south."

"Raje, Zulfikar Khan has laid siege from all around. Reaching Raigad isn't possible at the moment. To reach Raigad, we shall have to cross the Sahyadri Ranges, and Zulfikar shall be waiting for us there. With their huge armies, we may not be able to sustain the assault," said Malhoji Ghorpade.

"Malhoji Kaka, we shall not cross over the Sahiyadri ranges. The Arabian sea lies to the west of where we are. We reach the Arabian sea, ally with the Portuguese through the treaty, cross over to the North-west of Raigad, and assault from there. Zufikar Khan shall be expecting us from the south of Raigad. The Maratha army inside Raigad shall fight the battle under the leadership of Maharani Yesubai and Rajaram, while we shall attack from the periphery, sandwiching the Mughals between two assaults. Meanwhile, Kavi Kalash shall expand our army in the south and regain provinces around Panhala. Once we accomplish this, we march onto Aurangabad and execute Aurangzeb."

Everybody in the room now could feel pumped up. Sambhaji had shown hope to the Marathas.

Kavi Kalash, who had remained silent until now, stepped forward, his voice calm and reassuring. "Owing to the geographical terrains, with no forts nearby, the Mughals shall least expect us to be here in Sangameshwar, which can act as our military base. This hideout was built for this very day, for our survival and resurgence."

The ministers were further reassured by Kavi Kalash's words; their earlier fears momentarily eased. They knew the days ahead would be challenging, but they placed their trust in their king's plan. As days turned into nights, the Marathas waited in their hidden refuge, preparing themselves for the attack.

Meanwhile, at Raigad, Yesubai was restless, feeling the weight of the looming danger. Zulfikar Khan had laid siege around Raigad, and the Mughals had begun bombarding the fort walls relentlessly. Yesubai could feel the capital slipping into Mughal hands, and the thought of being captured or killed did not frighten her as much as the uncertainty surrounding her husband's safety. She had not received any word from Sambhaji for a long time and knew only that he had last been seen travelling toward Panhala.

Over the next few days, Sambhaji tried to seek assistance from the Portuguese, writing letters to them. Francis De Tavora, who owed his life to Sambhaji, agreed to assist the Marathas by providing naval support from the Arabian sea. This had strengthened Sambhaji and his plans to attack the siege around Raigad and put an end to the Mughal onslaught once and for all. Sambhaji knew exactly that Muzzam had been captured and that Aurangzeb would be the lone warrior once he put an end to Zulfikar Khan's ambitions at Raigad. Everything was falling in place. Malhoji Ghorpade, along with his son, Santaji Ghorpade, had already begun strengthening the army and working with the blacksmiths to prepare for the major assault.

One day, as usual, busy with strategic planning, Sambhaji's train of thought was interrupted when Malhoji Ghorpade brought disheartening news.

He said, "Raje, Bahirji Naik is no more."

Sambhaji closed his eyes without a reaction. It had not been long since he had lost his uncle and ex-Sarnobat Hambirrao Mohite. With Bahirji Naik's death, Sambhaji could not bear yet another grievance.

Deep pain in his heart, but he didn't let it show on his face. He had a battle to fight. Gathering courage, he responded, "How did this happen?"

"Raje, the exact cause is unknown. People say the Mughals have killed him. A few others say that he died of a natural death."

Sambhaji did not want to react. He excused himself from the room, walked to the nearby temple, and tried to find his answers there. In his prayers, he questioned the Goddess.

'People around me are dying. The ones close to me are being killed. Common people are being looted and forced to convert to Islam. Alliances are being broken, Raigad is at stake. With no cultivation for the entire year, short of resources and income, watandars and soldiers are being easily bribed against Swaraj. In this crucial time, how do I save this nation?'

Sambhaji had many unanswered questions. Sambhaji was battling against emotions, an entire turmoil inside him.

Deep in his meditations, he awaited the answers from his Goddess. She had shown him the path on multiple occasions previously.

'How do I hold onto my men and not let them align with the Mughals?' his thoughts continued.

In his deep state of meditation, Sambhaji could see a picture he couldn't really make out. The Goddess had shown him his future and the last option he had, but Sambhaji couldn't decipher it.

The news reached Raigad too. Yesubai, standing amidst the chaos, muttered words of courage to herself, trying to muster the strength she needed for her people and her children.

Rajaram, who had just turned 17, could sense the turmoil Yesubai was going through. Meanwhile, Yesubai's son, Shahu, had little understanding of the unfolding crisis. They had been forbidden from playing in the fort premises due to the constant threat of cannon blasts raining down upon the walls.

"The Mughal strength has doubled. It looks difficult," Rajaram said, his voice tinged with worry as he stood beside Yesubai. Yesubai could only listen, her mind preoccupied with thoughts of the future. She feared for her children, for Rajaram's safety, and for the fate of the Maratha sultanate. She held onto hope, praying silently that Sambhaji would find a way out of this dire situation.

Meanwhile, the man who had once met Aurangzeb and promised to imprison Sambhaji was now standing before Muqarrab Khan.

"I have promised the Badshah," said the man.

"I hope you live up to the promise then," replied Muqarrab Khan.

"Why do you think I am here, then?" retorted the man. He looked at Muqarrab Khan and, with a sly smile, added, "Sambhaji is planning his attack on Raigad"

The piece of information raised multiple eyebrows.

"We should regroup with the forces at Raigad, then," stated Muqarrab Khan, only to be interrupted by the mysterious person again.

"No need. I shall show you the shortest route to Sangameshwar. That's where Sambhaji is," the man responded.

The Mughal commander could hardly contain his excitement. With the newfound support of this mysterious ally, Muqarrab felt invincible, far more confident than ever before. His ambition and determination to capture Sambhaji were now fuelled by the assurance that his plans would succeed. As his forces edged closer to their target, Muqarrab's mind raced with the prospect of a decisive victory that would secure his place in history.

Meanwhile, at Sangameshwar, Kavi Kalash, before leaving for the south, was immersed in deep prayer, performing sacred rituals in the hope of protecting the Maratha nation. His faith in the divine was unwavering, and he believed that the Almighty would guide them through this crisis. Inside the hideout, Sambhaji was engrossed in intense discussions with his ministers, strategizing their next moves. Soon after his prayer, Kavi Kalash joined him. Sambhaji Maharaj's childhood companion and adviser, Kavi Kalash, had shadowed the king wherever he went and was equally gearing up for a battle that could now put an end to the Mughals, once and for all. The Mughals were everywhere, but Sambhaji's plan of retaliation that he had discussed with his subordinates was going to shake the Mughals if executed well.

"We should leave now," said Sambhaji, determined to make a move. Sambhaji and Kavi Kalash, now to depart for their respective roles, looked at each other, unsure of what lay ahead, and hugged.

"May victory be ours," said Kavi Kalash, in a commanding voice.

Adjusting his imperial crown and sword, Sambhaji commanded the Sarnobat, "Malhoji, ready the palanquin and troops for departure."

"Ji Raje," responded Malhoji Ghorpade.

"I admire what transpires in your mind, Sambhaji," remarked Kavi Kalash.

With a smile, Sambhaji placed a reassuring hand on Kavi's shoulder, looked directly into his eyes with intensity, and said, "Delhi!" Pausing, he continued, "It won't be long before Aurangzeb and his Mughal Empire would crumble before the Marathas. The day will come when the foundations of Swaraj laid by my father shall be fulfilled. Once we finish Aurnagzeb and his tyrannical rule in the Deccan, we shall march onto Delhi."

"Are we ready?" asked Sambhaji, eager to set out on his mission. Not long ago, he had been thinking of his wife, Yesubai, who was battling for her existence at Raigad.

Suddenly, a commotion erupted. The loud and frantic voice of Sarnobat Malhoji Ghorpade pierced the room.

"Raje!" Malhoji burst into the chamber, panic evident in his eyes. "There is an ambush. Muqarrab Khan and the Mughals are here. Our hideout has been tracked!"

Sambhaji was stunned, struggling to comprehend how their secret refuge had been discovered. The hideout was known to only a select few; the betrayal was a bitter pill to swallow. Without hesitation, he grabbed his sword, his face set with determination. "Then let's fight them! We have no other choice," Sambhaji declared, ready to face the enemy head-on.

But Malhoji, recognizing the sheer magnitude of the Mughal forces, pleaded with his king. "No, Raje. They outnumber us greatly. We cannot withstand them. Your safety is of utmost importance for the future of our nation. You must leave, now!"

Sambhaji shook his head defiantly. "I cannot abandon you, Malhoji. We fight together, win together, and if fate allows, we die together."

Malhoji's eyes filled with tears, "Raje, you are our hope. Your survival means there is still a chance to defeat the Mughals. If we all perish here, who will save our people? Please, do not worry about me. Kaviji and you must escape to the south now. I will hold them off as long as I can."

Sambhaji was torn. He could feel the weight of his Sarnobat's words and the painful truth behind them. His thoughts flashed back to his father, Chhatrapati Shivaji Maharaj, who had once escaped from Panhala to Vishalgad under similar dire circumstances, protected by the valiant Baji Prabhu Deshpande. Today, Sambhaji found himself in the same predicament, with Malhoji standing as his shield.

Applying the sacred angara of Goddess Jagdamba, Sambhaji said, "Take care of yourself, Malhoji kaka. We need you. I want to see you on the other side."

"Of course, Maharaj! Let me teach these Mughals a lesson and savour a dawat with you by my side."

"My eyes will be searching for you, Malhoji kaka," said Sambhaji, his eyes welling with tears.

Malhoji called for his son, "Santaji, you will accompany Raje."

With a heavy heart, Sambhaji, Kavi Kalash, Santaji Ghorpade, and 25 of his loyal men began their escape. The attack on Raigad had now been temporarily halted. With the ambush, Sambhaji now knew he would have to ally with the southern rulers and then plan his future attacks. As they made their way through the dense forest, Malhoji and his troops stood as the last line of defence, shielding their king from the advancing Mughals. Malhoji glanced at Muqarrab Khan, who was seated on his mighty elephant, exuding arrogance and rage. Raising his dandpatta, Malhoji shouted defiantly, "Let's see what you're made of!"

He knew their chances of survival were slim, but the Marathas were prepared to embrace death rather than surrender. To them, protecting Sambhaji was a cause worth dying for.

Mashals in hand, the small unit led by Sambhaji darted through the dense jungles of Sangameshwar. Refusing the palanquin, which would have slowed their escape, Sambhaji decided to sprint through the wilderness. As he ran, the sounds of his men, led by Malhoji Ghorpade, chanting 'Har Har Mahadev,' echoed in his ears. Swords clashed, heads rolled, bones shattered, and blood stained the earth as Malhoji and his men fought fiercely.

"Hand over Sambhaji, and we will spare your lives!" Muqarrab

Khan bellowed from atop his elephant, offering them a chance at survival.

"Muqarrab Khan," Malhoji roared in response, "We are not traitorous serpents like you, who abandon their king for personal gain. You defected from the Adilshahi emperor Sikander, but we stand by our king! Sambhaji Maharaj is our God, and for our God, we shall happily lay down our lives a thousand times!"

The Mughal cockiness faltered as Malhoji's words echoed through the battlefield. Muqarrab Khan, angered and unyielding, gave the command, "Attack!"

"Har Har Mahadev!" Malhoji and his men shouted, charging at the Mughal forces with unrestrained ferocity. The Marathas fought relentlessly, disregarding their injuries and the overwhelming odds against them. From a distance, Sambhaji watched the battle rage, the clash of steel and the cries of the wounded filling the air. Malhoji, bloodied but unyielding, pressed forward, each strike fuelled by sheer determination. He knew his life was the price of his king's escape, and he embraced it without hesitation.

Killing hundreds of Mughals, Malhoji was suddenly struck by an arrow that pierced his chest. Ignoring the pain, Malhoji continued his onslaught. With one hand, he yanked the arrow from his chest, even as another struck him from behind. Wielding his dandpatta, Malhoji slashed through his enemies. Despite countless wounds, the warrior remained unstoppable.

Meanwhile, Sambhaji pressed on through the forest. Muqarrab Khan, perched atop his war elephant, spotted Sambhaji and his men slipping away.

"I want that man!" he roared, seated on his huge elephant.

The horsemen galloped in the direction of Sambhaji, the distance between them narrowing rapidly. Realizing the Mughals could reach him at any moment, Sambhaji decided to confront them. Turning towards the approaching troops, his sword rang out as he drew it from its scabbard. With Kavi Kalash by his side, Sambhaji and his men charged the horsemen.

"*Jai Parvati Pateh*!" The battle cries were relentless as Sambhaji and his men struck down the first wave of attackers. Soon, reinforcements arrived, but Sambhaji and his men fought them off with equal valour. The second wave met the same fate as the first.

Swiftly advancing, Sambhaji and his men continued to fight. At the other end, a gravely wounded Malhoji did his best to hold the Mughals at bay with his remaining men.

Sensing Sambhaji and his men escaping, Muqarrab dismounted from the elephant, mounted a horse, and spurred more soldiers into pursuit. Malhoji, reading his intent in an instant, charged forward to intercept, his battered body moving with unwavering resolve.

The Mughals swarmed around him, swords flashing, spears thrusting. Blows rained down from all sides, yet Malhoji fought like a tempest, his dandpatta slicing through flesh and steel alike.

"Malhoji, I admire your loyalty," Muqarrab said, "You are now the lone warrior left. I am giving you the last chance to drop your weapon and surrender to save your life."

"Muqarrab," Malhoji spoke with effort, breathless and bloodied, "Even if you chop me to pieces, my soul shall still fight for my Raje."

As even the fiercest warrior has his limits, Malhoji's time was near. Wounded beyond measure, his strength began to wane. With one final, defiant swing, he made his last stand before the relentless darkness overwhelmed him. As he fell, his sacrifice was written in blood, a testament to his courage, his loyalty, and his unshakeable duty to his king.

Charging at Malhoji, Muqarrab took him by surprise. His sword pierced through Malhoji multiple times as the Maratha Sarnobat retaliated in defence.

Laying on the ground, breathing his last, he cried for his king. With hazy vision, he could see Sambhaji at a distance. He muttered, "*Raje, akhri mujra swikarava* (King, accept my last bow)."

At a distance, Sambhaji's heart skipped a beat as if Malhoji's voice had reached him. He knew his Sarnobat had fallen, his instincts had told him.

"Jagdamb!" Sambhaji exclaimed, closing his eyes. The pain of losing his trusted Sarnobat hit him like a tidal wave, but there was no time to mourn.

With the Sarnobat out of the way, Muqarrab Khan embarked on a horse again. He and his cavalry started gaining on Sambhaji.

The air was thick with smoke and dust, the deafening roars of warriors drowning out the cries of the wounded at a distance where Malhoji Ghorpade had succumbed to the attack and the battlefield no longer just earth and stone… it was a graveyard of the fallen, their blood seeping into the soil. Sambhaji now knew escaping was no longer an option. Turning around again, he raised his sword and decided to face the enemy. Amidst the chaos, he stood tall, his presence alone a beacon of unyielding defiance.

The Mughals attacked in multiple waves, hoping to overpower the Marathas through sheer numbers. Positioning themselves in crescent formation, Sambhaji and Kavi Kalash defended themselves.

"Har Har Mahadev," they growled, slashing through the Mughal soldiers' necks, turning them to dust.

The Mughal horses galloped wildly, kicking up clouds of dust as they advanced like an unstoppable tide. At the centre of it all was Muqarrab Khan, his eyes locked onto Sambhaji with ruthless determination.

"Muqarrab!" Sambhaji growled, standing as a lone warrior as the horses galloped towards him and his men. Seeing the fierce Sambhaji, Muqarrab stopped. Sambhaji's eyes were red-hot with rage. Muqarrab let his cavalry charge towards Sambhaji, who stood at a distance.

Sambhaji dropped his shield and grabbed another sword, tightening his grip on both, feeling the weight of his legacy.

"Kavi!" Sambhaji shouted as he saw the cavalrymen charge towards him.

Kavi Kalash knew precisely what he had to do. Kavi Kalash bent down with his shield held high up as Sambhaji sprang towards the shield, stepped over it and jumped towards the cavalrymen. Giving him a higher altitude and better position for the attack, his swords slashed through the cavalrymen as he fell to the other side of the battlefield. Getting up, he swiftly dodged a cavalryman's attack and turned towards the other, pierced his sword, pulled him down, jumped onto the horse, gained control of it and galloped towards the other.

"Do whatever it takes, I want that man captured," Muqarrab ordered, left in disbelief, with the swift attack of Sambhaji.

"Hold the line!" Sambhaji commanded, his voice cutting through the battlefield like a blade as the horse now faced another Mughal attack.

The Marathas did not falter. They had been trained for this—warriors of the hills, sons of the soil. They knew that each moment they held their ground was another moment Swarajya survived.

The Mughals crashed into them like a wave against a rock, swords clashing, spears piercing, shields shattering. Sambhaji, like a storm, rode into the thick of battle, his blade a blur of death. Seeing Kavi Kalash surrounded by Mughal soldiers, Sambhaji rode his horse towards him, sprang from it, his sword kissing the Mughal necks, rescuing his old friend.

A Mughal soldier lunged at him. With a swift flick of his wrist, Sambhaji parried the attack and countered, his sword slicing through flesh and bone. Another came at him—this time, he raised his shield, bashing the attacker with such force that he collapsed to the ground, lifeless.

But the real test was yet to come.

"Ya Allah!" Muqarrab acknowledged Sambhahji's fighting skills. He had no choice but to take the attack himself now.

Through the battlefield, Muqarrab Khan and Sambhaji finally locked eyes. There was no hesitation, no turning back. Muqarrab Khan spurred his horse forward, his blade gleaming under the sun. He swung it downward, aiming straight for Sambhaji's head. Sambhaji reacted instantly, raising his sword to meet the strike. The clash of metal rang out like thunder, reverberating across the battlefield. Blow after blow, Muqarrab Khan attacked with brute force, but Sambhaji was swift, dodging, blocking, countering with the attack.

"Santaji!" Sambhaji called out urgently.

"Yes, Raje?" Santaji responded, ready to fight by his king's side.

"I want you to escape from here and make your way to Raigad," Sambhhaji commanded. "Regroup with our forces, protect the fort, and if anything happens to me, ensure Rajaram's safety. Establish a new kingdom under his leadership."

"But Maharaj, I can't leave you—" Santaji started to protest, but Sambhaji cut him off. "It is an order. You must avenge your father's death and secure the future of our people."

"No, Raje, I shall fight here," responded Santaji, "By your side."

Muqarrab charged again as Sambhaji responded with another blow, their swords clashing and every attack of Muqarrab going in vain.

"Santaji!" shouted Sambhaji, his eyes focused on Muqarrab's next move. "Even if the king dies, Swaraj shall prevail."

The words hit him hard. Santaji knew he had no choice but to obey his Chhatrapati's orders. "Ji Raje," Santaji wept as he said this. The Mughals charged towards Santaji and Sambhaji.

"Go, go, go!" shouted Sambhaji as he sprang in front of the Muqarrab and his forces with his shield, obstructing them from reaching Santaji.

"Jai Parvati Pateh!" Sambhaji's battle cry was loud as he single-handedly stopped a dozen Mughal soldiers. Piercing through the abdomens and slashing flesh and bone, Sambhaji covered Santaji as the latter disappeared into the dense forests. The next minute, he was sprinting toward Raigad.

Sambhaji knew what lay ahead, but he was not ready to surrender. As the Mughal soldiers perished, Muqarrab aimed at Sambhaji as the arrow pierced Sambhaji's back. Despite the arrow piercing, Sambhaji continued fighting, hardly bothered by it. Fuelled by rage, Sambhaji and his 25 men fought with unparalleled ferocity, proving themselves nearly invincible.

Muqarrab's attacks had gone in vain. The Chhatrapati of the Marathas was beyond control.

Agitated, Muqarrab Khan ordered his men, "Throw the barbed wires."

The Mughals followed their master's orders. The wires pierced through Sambhaji's battle gear. The Mughals tightened their grip as Sambhaji bled with the pierced wires. He held the wires and pulled them out of his body, roaring, fiercer than ever, staring with rage at the Mughal soldiers. Not even the wires could stop Sambhaji from retaliating.

"Muqarrab!" he roared, rechallenging him, "Your barbed wires cannot stop me and my Swaraj."

"Chain him down!" shouted Muqarrab, dreading Sambhaji's fierce eyes.

Muqarrab himself took charge, throwing a chain towards Sambhaji that wound around him. Another Mughal soldier threw another chain towards Sambhaji that held him from behind.

Sambhaji held the chains and pulled the Mughals to the ground, and with the other hand, used his sword to turn them into lifeless bodies.

By then, Muqarrab Khan had managed to chain Kavi Kalash and the others. But Sambhaji was still unstoppable. Although deeply injured, Sambhaji attempted to chain him, but he broke open the chains, raging at the Mughals. The roar echoed in the forests as Sambhaji stood as a lone warrior fighting the Mughals. The third attempt, and the Mughals, managed to chain Sambhaji but couldn't make him kneel. The soldiers pulled at the chains, but Sambhaji, with his immense strength, dragged them down instead.

What Muqarrab had been witnessing was no less than one of the greatest battles. The roar reverberated in his ears as he could see the lion's cub fighting against the Mughals. He wondered how aptly Diler Khan had named Sambhaji as Sher ka bacha – a Chhava!

"Muqarrab!" shouted Sambhaji, "Neither your men nor your techniques can stop me. Bring all that you have, and I will still chop your men to pieces."

Muqarrab was left astonished. He ordered his mahouts to pull the chains with the help of elephants. As the elephants applied their forces, Sambhaji could feel the pull. He roared in an attempt to set himself free. He remembered his Goddess.

'*Give me more strength,*' he worshipped. Holding the chains, Sambhaji overturned the elephants, making the mahouts fall to the ground, and the elephants crushed the Mughal soldiers beneath them.

Bleeding and exhausted, Sambhaji looked at Muqarrab and shouted, "What more have you got, Muqarrab?"

Exasperated, Muqarrab dismounted his horse and approached the bound Sambhaji.

"Better surrender, Sambhaji. You're captured. You have no other option," Muqarrab shouted.

"You may capture me, but you cannot stop the thousands of Marathas who will now rise with twice the strength to shake your empire," Sambhaji's voice echoed in the jungles.

The challenge caught Muqarrab off guard, but he laughed derisively and replied, "We will find a way to capture and crush anyone who dares to oppose us." He looked at Sambhaji and added, "Just like we did this time."

Fixing his gaze on Sambhaji, Muqarrab said, "Your own man helped us, Sambhaji!"

He snapped his hands as the man who had helped him with Sambhaji's location popped up.

Sambhaji stared intently at Muqarrab, desperate to uncover the traitor's identity. Moments later, a figure emerged from the ranks of the Mughal troops. As Sambhaji's eyes locked with those of the betrayer, a profound sense of defeat washed over him. The hundreds of chains, the multitude of soldiers, and even the mighty elephants that had failed to subdue the warrior now seemed to tighten their hold on him. The grip grew stronger with each passing second.

A tumult of emotions surged within Sambhaji—betrayal, anger, and deep sorrow. He closed his eyes in agony, memories flooding his mind: his wife, Yesubai, son Shahu and daughter Bhavani at Raigad, and the visage of his late father, Chhatrapati Shivaji Maharaj. It wasn't the myriad of wounds inflicted upon his body that caused him the greatest pain; it was the treachery of a trusted ally. For the first time in the last few hours of battle, Sambhaji could feel the Mughals overpowering him. He could sense a pain in his heart as the grip of the chains got tighter, before they could make Sambhaji fall upon his knees. Speechless, Sambhaji kept staring at the person who wouldn't make eye contact with him. Sambhaji felt cheated. That day, he had not lost the war against the Mughals but against his own family. The man who stood before him, his head bowed, was a relative.

19.

MUQARRAB KHAN, triumphant and determined to make a spectacle of his conquest, ensured that Sambhaji and his men were shackled tightly and tied to the horses as they were paraded through the villages. As they journeyed, Muqarrab made a point of flaunting his victory, threatening the villagers with dire consequences if they dared defy him. His arrogance knew no bounds as he displayed his captives, convinced that Sambhaji's capture marked the end of the Maratha empire. Some villagers watched in fear, but many brave souls chanted, "Chhatrapati Sambhaji Maharaj ki Jai!" The powerful slogans lifted the spirits of the wounded Sambhaji, giving him hope amid the pain and uncertainty. He hoped his men would rally and strike back against the Mughals, but his thoughts were clouded with concern for the future of the Maratha empire. He wondered whether this was truly the end or if the Marathas would rise again.

Back at Raigad, Yesubai received the devastating news that Sambhaji, Kavi Kalash, and the other Marathas had been captured. The ground seemed to shift beneath her feet, but she steeled herself, determined to remain strong in the face of this calamity. She attempted to send forces to rescue her husband, but the heavy siege laid by Zulfikar Khan around Raigad forced her troops to retreat. Santaji, having escaped through a secret route, arrived at Raigad and recounted the harrowing events at Sangameshwar. The atmosphere at the fort was tense, with every Maratha warrior and family member grappling with the enormity of the situation.

Meanwhile, Aurangzeb, having heard of Sambhaji's capture, had made his way to Bahadurgad, eager to confront the Maratha king who had long defied him finally. Thousands gathered at the foothills, anxious to witness the momentous event. Inside the court, Aurangzeb paced with anticipation, recalling the last time he had seen Sambhaji, when he was a mere child, accompanying his father Shivrai to Agra, only to escape the Mughal grasp later. Aurangzeb had made sure there would be no escape for Sambhaji this time. He had fortified the walls of Bahadurgad and taken security into his own hands, ensuring there would be no breach this time. The

Mughal emperor had longed for this moment, where he would finally bring the rebellious Maratha king to his knees.

As Sambhaji, chained and weary, was brought into the Mughal court, a heavy silence descended. The atmosphere was thick with tension as all eyes fixated on the Maratha king. Despite his wounds and the exhausting journey, Sambhaji held his head high, his gaze unwavering as he met Aurangzeb's eyes. A smug smile spread across Aurangzeb's face, believing that his greatest adversary had finally been subdued. This moment was, to him, the culmination of years of strife and warfare—a symbol of his supposed triumph over the Marathas.

Aurangzeb eagerly waited for Sambhaji to speak, expecting the Maratha king to beg for mercy. He had seen it before: powerful rulers who, when captured, would grovel and plead for their lives before him. Aurangzeb wanted nothing more than to see the proud Maratha king plead for his life.

"Sambha!" Aurangzeb called out, his voice echoing through the court. "What is your last wish before death?"

"To see you dead," Sambhaji replied, his voice calm. The court erupted in gasps, the boldness of his words sending a ripple of shock through the assembled crowd.

"Sambha!" Aurangzeb roared again, his anger bubbling over. He was unaccustomed to being spoken to with such disrespect, especially by a captive.

"What else can you do, Aurang?" Sambhaji taunted, unflinching. "You can tie me, shout at me, imprison me, or even kill me. There is nothing more you can do. I am ready for whatever comes my way."

Aurangzeb's frustration was evident. He had envisioned a broken and submissive Sambhaji, but instead, he faced a man who refused to cower.

"Sambha, you have been held captive. Your Swaraj has perished, the Maratha have perished. What you call your nation now is mine. You are defeated," Aurangzeb laughed devilishly, his voice boomed, aimed at reinforcing his authority.

Sambhaji chuckled darkly. "You defeated us? No! You captured me through treachery, using my people against me. You did not fight like a warrior! Neither you won nor I lost against you, but yes, I definitely lost against my own family. Had you not used him, I would have gifted you Muqarrab Khan's beheaded body." He paused, his fierce eyes locked onto Aurangzeb. "I am not the Maratha empire. We still have 220 forts, and in every one of them, there is another Sambha ready to rise against you. The Marathas are not defeated." Sambhaji stopped, stared at Aurangzeb and raised his voice in challenge, "You should now worry how you are going to fight and capture those 220 forts, for each of them has a Sambha thirsty for your blood."

The defiance in Sambhaji's voice echoed throughout the court, infuriating Aurangzeb. The emperor slammed his fist on the armrest of his gilded throne, his patience wearing thin. "How dare you speak to me like that? I am the Badshah!" shouted Aurangzeb

"A self-declared one. None of the Hindus consider you their king. The Agra throne you boast of was once owned by Raje Prithviraj Chauhan. It was never yours. Your ancestors probably never told you how they won it with treachery," chuckled Sambhaji.

Whispers ran throughout the court.

I will make your life a living hell," Aurangzeb threatened. "You will be tortured until you beg for death. I will strip you of everything."

Sambhaji met the threat with steely resolve. "I will never plead for my life, Aurang. Even in death, I will be immortalized in the hearts of my people, just as you immortalized Guru Tegh Bahadur."

"I will destroy any such memory," retaliated Aurangzeb.

"Only to ensure that somebody else rewrites it. I can see the future. The Maratha flags over Dilli and Agra," Sambhaji challenged Aurangzeb.

"Aurang!" Sambhaji stared at him, his voice commanding in the court filled with ministers and people out there to watch the verbal assault, "History shall remember you as a sinister for the crimes you have committed."

"It's you who is chained for now and you should worry about it," retaliated Aurangzeb.

"But my Maratha dynasty is free."

"Devoid of its king," barked Aurangzeb, "What happened to your Swaraj?"

"Swaraj is not a person, Aurang. It's an emotion that cannot be chained. My throne is safe. A new king is rising, Aurang! And this time, our eyes are on Agra. The day is not far when the Marathas shall dethrone you. Now that you have descended upon us in the Deccan, we shall make sure you never return to Agra."

Aurangzeb was stung by Sambhaji's unbroken spirit.

In a fit of rage, he ordered his guards, "Drag him from here, out of my eyesight."

"I shall still haunt you in your dreams. The day is not far when you shall yearn for your death and still death shall not be yours. You shall yearn to live and yet, life shall not be yours," Sambhaji laughed as Aurangzeb's men chained Sambhaji and his men to the dungeons, where not a single ray of sunlight would reach them. Though Aurangzeb had captured Sambhaji, he had not broken him yet. His victory felt hollow, as he realized that Sambhaji's spirit and defiance were beyond his grasp. Even in chains, Sambhaji's unyielding courage cast a long shadow over Aurangzeb's supposed triumph. The Mughal ruler could imprison the man, but not the indomitable spirit that had made Sambhaji a legend among his people.

ZULFIKAR KHAN and his men had tightened the siege around Raigad, determined to break the Maratha stronghold. His cannons roared relentlessly, pounding the fort's walls with a fury that echoed through the valley. Inside, the Marathas fought back valiantly, using whatever resources they had left, their resolve unwavering despite the overwhelming odds. For Yesubai, this battle was not just against the Mughals; it was also a fight against her own turmoil. She remembered Sambhaji's words, spoken with unshakeable conviction: if anything happened to him, she must ensure that the Maratha empire did not fall. Those words echoed in her mind, strengthening her resolve as she steeled herself against the dual battle that raged within and outside Raigad's walls.

Meanwhile, Muqarrab Khan had been rewarded handsomely for his role in capturing Sambhaji. Promoted to a Sapth Hazari mansabdar, he was showered with precious stones, gold, and silver by the Badshah, basking in his newfound glory and power. But as Muqarrab celebrated, Sambhaji's situation could not have been more different. Chained upright in a dark, dingy cell, Sambhaji was subjected to continuous torture. Denied sleep and sustenance, the jailers beat him with belts and rods, ensuring he was kept in constant agony. His flesh bore the marks of his defiance, yet his spirit remained unbroken. Spices were applied over his bleeding body but Sambhaji welcomed each of these pains without any signs of agony.

Mughal commanders had been entrusted with the task of overseeing Sambhaji, visiting him frequently, hoping to break the Maratha king's resolve. But despite the relentless pain inflicted upon him, Sambhaji never pleaded, never bent, and never surrendered.

"Sambhaji is determined and unbreakable," Qazi Mulla Sayyad Ulla confided in Aurangzeb, frustration evident in his voice. Disappointed by his inability to subdue Sambhaji, Aurangzeb decided to confront the Maratha king in person, hoping that his presence would finally crush Sambhaji's spirit. As Aurangzeb entered the cell, the jailor barked, "The Alamgir has arrived, bow before him!"

Sambhaji, however, refused to acknowledge the Badshah's presence, keeping his gaze defiantly fixed elsewhere.

Enraged, Sayyad Ulla struck Sambhaji across the chest and shouted again, "The Alamgir has arrived. Bow before him!"

Sambhaji simply laughed, the sound hoarse yet defiant. "Who Alamgir?" he mocked. "Alamgir means one who conquers the whole world, who is the ruler of everybody! How can you, Aurang, be the Alamgir when I still hold 220 forts? I am still the Chattrapati! And even if you manage to get rid of me, you still do not have my forts."

Sambhaji's words pierced Aurangzeb like a dagger. He had thought capturing Sambhaji would mean the end of Maratha resistance, yet the king's spirit remained unyielding. "I shall have them too," Aurangzeb shot back angrily. "You are no king. You are nobody now."

Sambhaji met Aurangzeb's furious glare with calm defiance. "That nobody made you leave your throne in Agra and come to the Deccan," he said, his voice steady. "Probably to never return."

"Sambha!" Aurangzeb roared, his patience snapping. *"You Kafir!"* His fury boiling over, Aurangzeb turned to Zulfikar and commanded, "He speaks too much. Get rid of his tongue!"

In an instant, a team of Mughal guards descended on Sambhaji. They held him down, forcing his mouth open as the red-hot tongs and knives were brought forward. The heat of the iron seared his tongue, and a wave of excruciating pain surged through him. Tears streamed from Sambhaji's eyes as the burning metal tore through his flesh, but he did not scream. Even as his tongue was ripped out, Sambhaji bore the agony in silence, his bloodied face a testament to his unbreakable will.

In that moment of searing pain, Sambhaji's inner voice spoke, *'Goddess Jagdamba, give me the strength I need to sustain all the pain.'*

'Abasaheb, I have many things to speak with you, but I have always felt short of words. With this tongue gone, I shall still be able to find words in this afterlife.'

Sambhaji refused to give Aurangzeb the satisfaction of hearing him cry out, but Aurangzeb was happy with Sambhaji's inability to speak.

"Subhanallah," Aurangzeb sneered, his voice dripping with malice as he watched the gruesome spectacle unfold. But despite the torture, Sambhaji still held his head high, his eyes blazing with defiance even as blood filled his mouth and dripped onto the cold stone floor. Aurangzeb stormed out of the cell. He said to Sayyad Ulla, "Intensify the torture, peel off his skin, beat him till he gives up, break his bones, do whatever it takes. Make his life a living hell so that he either pleads for death or begs for his life. If he doesn't give up, torture that Kavi Kalash in front of his eyes, so that he gives up."

Kavi Kalash, who was imprisoned in the same cell, witnessed the brutality firsthand. Sayyad Ulla walked up to Kavi Kalash and pulled him in front of Sambhaji.

Warning Sambhaji, Sayyad Ulla said, "If you don't apologize to the Alamgir, we shall torture him to death."

The Mughals beat Kavi Kalash, tortured him with nails and wires and even peeled off his skin, inflicting pain, but Kavi Kalash bore it all.

"Are you ready to give up?" shouted Sayyad Ulla at Sambhaji. Sambhaji lost his speech, now rolled his eyes, signifying his rejection.

"You might give up on your torture, but we won't," replied Kavi Kalash. This agitated the Mughals even more as they doubled the torture, applying chilly pastes all over Kavi Kalash's and Sambhaji's bodies.

"Raje, I am with you," assured Kavi Kalash, "We live together, we die together, but we shall never give up."

A Mughal soldier held Kavi Kalash's hand as the other pulled out his nails to inflict pain. To find strength, Kavi Kalash recited in Marathi:

Kshatriya Kulavantsi,
Dharila Abhang vratasi,
Milechchhanivari dharisi,
Talwari, Chandikechi
(You are a true Kshatriya, brave and bright
Bound by a vow of unwavering might.
Against these tyrants, your sword you raise,
Blessed by Goddess Chandrika's fiery blaze.)

The Mughals walked towards Sambhaji as they pulled out his hair. Sambhaji did not move an inch as Kavi Kalash gave him more strength with his words.

Kshatriya Kulabhushan,
Jagat naam nauhech dusara,
Swarajya rakhanya sathi,
Dharilisi he shastra hati
(You are the jewel of the Kshatriya clan,
A name unmatched since time began.
To guard Swarajya, brave and true,
This sword has always stood with you.)

20.

DAYS AND nights unfolded with a relentless passage of time, each merging into the next, as the weather shifted in its cyclical dance. Yet, despite the unceasing change in the world around him, Sambhaji's resolve remained unwavering. He continued to see himself as the rightful King of the Marathas, resolutely refusing to surrender before Aurangzeb. The imprisonment, torture, and the relentless psychological warfare waged against him had done little to alter his steadfast demeanour.

Inside his chambers, Aurangzeb grappled with growing distress. His efforts to break Sambhaji's spirit, to see him bow and submit, had met with failure at every turn. Aurangzeb, who had long harboured a deep-seated animosity towards Sambhaji, found himself reluctantly admiring the Maratha king's courage and fortitude. Despite the severe and ongoing torment inflicted upon him, Sambhaji remained undaunted. Aurangzeb had imprisoned his father, orchestrated the death of his own brother Dara Shikoh, and even held his son Muazzam captive. Yet, none of these individuals had displayed the unyielding bravery that Sambhaji did.

Aurangzeb sat in his opulent room, brooding over the situation. "Shivrai was blessed to have a son like Sambha," he muttered to himself as he sank into the plush cushions of his couch. His thoughts wandered to his own sons, who had consistently failed to impress him. Their lives had been marked by internal strife and ambition, often challenging him for the throne or engaging in conflict amongst themselves. Not one of them had shown the valour or fortitude that Sambhaji demonstrated.

The days of relentless questioning and torture had begun to take a toll on Aurangzeb's psyche. He found himself haunted by Sambhaji's words, which suggested that Aurangzeb had never truly achieved the grand title of Alamgir, the World Conqueror, that he had always regarded himself to be. The weight of these words seemed to sap his strength and resolve. He had lost weight and appeared increasingly gaunt. The realization that he was not the omnipotent ruler he had once believed himself to be gnawed at him.

Desperate for a resolution, Aurangzeb decided to extend an offer to Sambhaji. He approached the cell where the Maratha king was held, his face etched with a mix of determination and desperation. "I shall let you free if you agree to abide by my demands," Aurangzeb declared, his voice carrying a note of finality.

Sambhaji, lying shackled and bound, did not even bother to glance at Aurangzeb. His gaze remained fixed on the cold stone walls of his prison, a silent testament to his defiance.

Sayyad Ulla, who stood behind Aurangzeb, took a step forward and began reading the demands from a formal decree issued by the Badshah. "The Badshah puts forth three demands before you to set you free of all the tortures and live a life with dignity and freedom. One, you should surrender before him and give away all your forts to the Mughals. Two, you shall have to accept Islam as your religion and serve as a Mughal mansabdar. Three, you shall have to name all the Mughal commanders who have secretly aided you."

Sambhaji, his tongue having been gruesomely removed, could offer no verbal response. Instead, he fixed his gaze on Sayyad Ulla and Aurangzeb with unflinching resolve. Sayyad Ulla passed a blank piece of paper to Sambhaji, intending for him to write down his response. With deliberate calmness, Sambhaji took the paper and tore it to pieces, his action louder than words.

Kavi Kalash, who was shackled opposite Sambhaji, recited:

Maran swabhimanache,
Sharan kashas durjanache,
Karu de dhada vegale,
Pan dharma raho akhand.
(Death with honour is far more grand,
Why beg mercy from a cruel hand?
Let them sever my head,
But let dharma never shed.)

Aurangzeb's face contorted with fury at Kavi Kalash's words.

As the days passed, Aurangzeb continued his visits to Sambhaji's cell.

"Sambha, are you ready to accept Islam?" he would question him.

"Join the Mughal forces," he would add.

Each time, Sambhaji responded with a shake of his head or an averted gaze, irking Aurangzeb even more.

Aurangzeb's frustration mounted with each visit. He would shout at Sambhaji, demanding answers that never came. He would then retreat, filled with regret for having taken away Sambhaji's ability to speak, as he wanted Sambhaji to answer him. Sambhaji couldn't talk, but his loud growls could still reach Aurangzeb's ears as if a lion roaring into his ears.

"Aurang!" Kavi Kalash laughed, "You wanted us to beg for our lives, and now who is begging in the name of Islam?"

"Shut his mouth!" Aurangzeb shouted, "I don't want to hear him speak. His voice, his poetry, everything reverberates in my mind."

"Cut off his tongue as well," he ordered his men, acting like a maniac. "Make him as speechless as his friend," he shouted.

The Mughals held Kavi Kalash as the man kept reciting poems, unwavering in the face of Mughal torture. Moments, later, in agonizing pain, devoid of his speech, Kavi Kalash collapsed to the ground, his soul still alive and mind reciting poems of valour and patriotism.

"Sambha, I ask you once again," Aurangzeb was reluctant, "Do you accept Islam?"

Sambhaji stared at Aurangzeb, his eyes full of rage. Sambhaji shook his head.

Aurangzeb's mind was tormented by the fierce eyes of the Maratha king, which seemed to pierce through his very soul. The intensity of Sambhaji's gaze haunted Aurangzeb, invading his dreams and despite his speech taken away, his voice reverberating in his ears. He could almost hear Sambhaji's voice echoing the words, "My last wish is to see you dead."

Fearful of Sambhaji's unyielding stare, Aurangzeb issued a new order: "Gorge out his eyes. His gaze daunts me."

The soldiers held Sambhaji by his arms, as Sayyad Ulla appeared with the hot pair of tongs. His hands trembled but Sambhaji didn't. Instead, Sambhaji opened his eyes wide, welcoming the pain.

Sayyad Ulla gazed at Aurangzeb, questioning his decision. Aurangzeb was adamant.

As the hot tongs closed upon his eyes, Sambhaji remembered the early days of childhood, the small moments he had cherished with his Abasaheb, those games he had played in the gardens of the forts, how he had blinded himself with a piece of cloth and tried catching his Abasaheb.

'What is vision?' he thought.

'A visual perception of your own thoughts,' his mind answered.

'Even if they take away my vision, the thought is still mine,' his inner voice said.

The tongs pierced through his eyes, giving him agonizing pain. Sambhaji clenched his fists, devoid of nails. His soul wrenched but his tongue amiss, his voice did not find a way out.

'I have never seen you, Aausaheb. I shall now see you when I make my way to the afterlife,' his mind said.

'How desperately my eyes wished to see my mother but I have no memories of her. Now, after the soul departs, I shall be able to see her.'

Even as Sambhaji endured this new torment with the same stoic acceptance, Aurangzeb's unease grew. The relentless pain inflicted upon Sambhaji seemed to only solidify his resolve. Aurangzeb's own mental state deteriorated, as he began to fear the very existence of Sambhaji and the unusual attitude he displayed.

Despite his position of power, Aurangzeb found himself shaken by Sambhaji's fearless attitude. The tortures he had inflicted—pulling out nails, breaking bones, cutting ears, peeling skin, and amputating limbs—had failed to break Sambhaji's spirit. The Maratha king embraced each new pain with a stoic smile, never wavering in his commitment to his cause. Even as his ability to see and speak was taken from him, Sambhaji's thoughts remained firmly fixed on the concept of Swaraj.

He understood that his kingdom was crumbling, that some of his people were being bribed to join the enemy, and that internal divisions were threatening the Maratha cause. Yet he believed that his sacrifice was the key to saving his nation. In his days in prison, he could now recall what the Goddess's message to him was. It meant sacrifice – only a sacrifice could unite his men, against all bribes, all enemies, and all threats. Sambhaji was convinced that his death would serve as a rallying cry for his people, uniting them against the Mughal threat. The revelation of his torture would incite a profound outrage among the common people, shaking the very foundations of Mughal rule.

Sambhaji's refusal to kneel before Aurangzeb and to convert to Islam became a symbol of unwavering resolve and resistance. His stance would inspire future generations to stand firm against oppression, regardless of the cost.

As Aurangzeb's power waned, the once-feared ruler began to lose his glory. His subjects and those around him began to mock him, their respect eroded by his failure to convert Sambhaji to his religion. Sambhaji was leading the talk. If the king could rebel despite extreme torture, the people believed that even they could rebel against the jizya tax without fear of its consequences. People found strength. They no longer feared the Mughal threat. News of Sambhaji's unyielding resistance spread like wildfire, serving as a beacon of courage to villagers across the nation. The only way to put an end to their enemies is not to give up; they started learning from their very own king.

On March 21, 1689, at the banks of the Bhima River in Tulapur, Aurangzeb confronted Sambhaji one final time. "Are you willing to accept Islam? I shall forget everything, and together we shall rule the world. Team up with me and let us make a new beginning," his voice was tinged with desperation. Aurangzeb's voice fell on Sambhaji's and Kavi Kalash's deaf ears.

A profound silence fell over the scene. The Mughal soldiers, including Aurangzeb, waited for Sambhaji's response. Sambhaji shook his head.

Aurangzeb's frustration reached a boiling point. Never before had anybody been so fearless and refused any of Aurangzeb's demands. He no longer felt like the Badshah he was proud of. He said, "Had I one son like you, Sambha, I would have conquered the entire world." Turning towards Sayyad Ulla, he shouted in anger, "Behead them, put an end to this, once and forever!"

Under the bright daylight, the banks of the Bhima River bore witness to a sacrifice that would become legendary. The swords of the executioners gleamed in the sunlight, just about to descend upon the two of them.

Kavi Kalash's inner voice recited the poem as Sambhaji's mind recalled it:

Navhata ha janma jinyasathi,
Swarajya Nirmanyasathi,
Hoil deh raakhecha,
Pan dharma jail nasht nhawe.
(This life was not for mere existence,
But to forge Swarajya with unwavering persistence.
Though my mortal form may crumble to ash,
Dharma endures – no power can dash.)

'We live together, we die together,' Kavi Kalash's words echoed inside Sambhaji's mind. He knew his mortal end was near, only to make him immortal forever.

His mind raced:

Yesu, I turn away from you, my journey now begun,
Rajaram, the empire's future now rests with you alone;
For Swarajya's honour, our spirit shall never break,
Shahu, soon you'll know the legacy we undertake.
Abasaheb, I march to you with a flame that won't tire,
Aausheb, with you beside me now, destiny lifts me higher.

The shining swords descended upon Sambhaji and Kavi Kalash

Aurangzeb, consumed by frustration and rage, shouted incoherently. He pretended to be satisfied with the revenge he had sought, but deep down, he knew that he had achieved little. The act of violence did nothing to quell the inner turmoil he felt.

Even after Sambhaji and Kavi Kalash had breathed their last, Aurangzeb did not find peace. Victory did not loom near him.

"Chop them to pieces and let them drift down the river," he ordered, hoping it would give him satisfaction, but it didn't.

Returning to his quarters, still unhappy and unsatisfied, Aurangzeb wondered what finality was. Why was he still not content with his revenge?

Aurangzeb decided to pen his emotions. He vowed to inscribe his feelings around his coffin when he would meet his own end.

EPILOGUE

The dismembered body parts of Sambhaji and Kavi Kalash were carried by the river's current, a grim procession of mutilation that spoke volumes about the cruelty of their end. Aurangzeb, in his vindictive fury, had issued a stark warning across the nation, forbidding anyone from performing last rites or cremating the bodies of Sambhaji and Kavi Kalash. To Aurangzeb, they were infidels, deserving of such dishonourable treatment. His decree was an attempt to erase their legacy and ensure their memory was sullied beyond redemption.

Yet, the brutality of the act did not have the intended effect. The people who witnessed this travesty were outraged, and even some of the Mughal soldiers who had once followed Aurangzeb with blind loyalty began to question their leader's morality. There was no valour or glory in killing Sambhaji; instead, it was seen as a heinous crime that tainted Aurangzeb's rule. Despite his conquest extending from the Narmada River to the Tungabhadra, Aurangzeb struggled to win the hearts and minds of his men. His scribe was summoned to draft a narrative where Sambhaji was portrayed as a traitor and a kafir who had slaughtered Muslims in the name of religion. But even this attempt at revisionist history failed to blind the people to the truth.

Amidst the chaos, Govind Mahar, a renowned wrestler, came across the floating body parts of Sambhaji and Kavi Kalash. Defying Aurangzeb's orders, he plunged into the river, retrieving the dismembered pieces with a determined resolve. With remarkable courage and compassion, Govind Mahar painstakingly stitched the body parts together, his eyes moist and hands trembling with the sight of cruelty. News of Sambhaji's heroic act spread rapidly, and thousands gathered to perform the last rites. The death of their king had united people from all walks of life. Even those who had been bribed to align with the Mughals returned to their original loyalties. Thousands of people shed tears as the pyre was lit. Aurangzeb was about to face the fierce backlash of his own deeds.

At Raigad, Zulfikar Khan and his forces had managed to breach the fort's defences. The once impregnable walls of Raigad had fallen. Yesubai, whose heart ached with grief and rage for Sambhaji, was determined to seek revenge. The Mughals had overrun the region, and Aurangzeb's ambition seemed to have no bounds. Just as Zulfikar's army poured into Raigad, Yesubai summoned Santaji Ghorpade and Rajaram.

"Take him along and establish an empire that even Aurangzeb cannot shatter," Yesubai instructed Santaji, her hand resting gently on Rajaram's cheek.

With the fate of the Maratha empire hanging in the balance, Santaji Ghorpade and Rajaram made their escape through hidden passages. They mounted their horses and rode swiftly toward Ginjee Fort, their secret stronghold. Tarabai, Rajaram's wife, joined them on this perilous journey. Meanwhile, Yesubai, along with her son Shahu, were captured by the Mughals. They were to be imprisoned in the same dungeons where Sambhaji had once been held. As she descended the fort's steps, Yesubai cast a final, sorrowful glance back at Raigad. The sight of the Mughal flags waving triumphantly was disheartening, but she steeled herself with the vision of a saffron flag flying high over Raigad once more. She knew this was merely the beginning of the end for the Mughals; a new Chhatrapati was rising, one whose flame would set the entire Mughal Sultanate ablaze.

In the Mughal cantonments, Aurangzeb remembered his vow to bathe in Sambha's blood in the Deccan and to wear the crown only after his death. It had been a while since Sambhaji's death. Although still discontent, he was hoping to find his victory by reclaiming the crown he once flamboyantly displayed. He called his soldier with the crown and wore it, hopeful of a renewed spirit. Just as he wore his crown, a Mughal commander came up with some news.

"Badshah," he said, to grab his attention.

"What is it?" Aurangzeb was irked with the disturbance in his joy.

"The Marathas have named their new Chhatrapati."

"Ya Allah…" Aurangzeb cried, removing his crown and throwing it away in agony.

At Ginjee, Santaji Ghorpade and Rajaram began their strategic planning. They were joined by Dhanaji Jadhav, another esteemed Maratha warrior from Sindkhed, a town located in the Buldhana district of Maharashtra. The atmosphere was charged with righteous indignation.

"Aurangzeb has crossed all bounds of tyranny. No Mughal emperor before him has dared to defile the codes of war with such barbarity—humiliating a king, a warrior, in chains. This injustice will not go unanswered. We swear upon the blood of our ancestors—our vengeance shall carve a lesson so fierce that the Mughals and their descendants will tremble at the very name of the Marathas!" Santaji declared, his voice resonating with fervour as he addressed his troops.

The Maratha kingdom, once weakened by financial crises and the loss of key leaders like Hambirrao Mohite, Bahirji Naik, and Malhoji Ghorpade, was now receiving recruits. The youngsters, fuelled by a burning desire for vengeance, joined the army with little regard for their own lives or financial compensation. Neither money nor bribes could buy these young recruits now.

Santaji continued, "Blessed by Goddess Jagdamba, Shivrai, and Sambhu Raje, we shall be undeterred by the consequences. We shall fear no one. We will avenge the deaths of our loved ones. Aurangzeb may have journeyed all the way to the Deccan, abandoning his throne in Agra to wage war against us, but like our Raje had vowed, he shall never return to that throne. He shall never be emperor again!"

A surge of pride and determination swept through the soldiers. Their thirst for justice and retribution was evident.

"Are we ready?" Santaji Ghorpade's voice rang out, charged with anticipation.

"Yes!" came the thunderous response from the Maratha army, their unity and resolve unwavering.

"Chhatrapati Sambhaji Maharaj ki…" Santaji began the battle cry, raising his sword high.

"Jai…" the soldiers echoed in unison, the morale high and spirits unwavering.

Flags were raised high, and swords gleamed in the sunlight as the Marathas prepared to embark on their mission.

"Har Har Mahadev!" the war cry resounded, as thousands of horses galloped toward the Mughal cantonments.

"Aurangzeb, we are coming for you!" said Santaji to himself, his horse galloping towards Aurangzeb's camp.

Years Later

Aurangzeb hid away in Bhingar, a remote area in Ahmednagar, consumed by fear of the relentless Maratha invasions. Santaji Ghorpade and Dhanaji Jadhav had created chaos around him, haunting him with a sense of finality. The once-mighty emperor had lost significant weight and was plagued by various illnesses, leaving him incapable of standing or walking unaided. His own sons were locked in a bitter struggle for the throne, and true to Sambhaji's prophetic words, Aurangzeb was unable to return to Agra to reclaim his imperial seat. Facing a dire financial crisis, he was left with only three hundred rupees for his personal needs. The isolation was complete; no one came to visit him as he grappled with the encroaching grip of death.

Clad in tattered clothes, Aurangzeb lay on his bed, awaiting the inevitable. Yet, even death seemed reluctant to embrace him, prolonging his misery. He pleaded for his death, just as he had wanted Sambhaji to, but even death did not fall into his fate. His life had become a tableau of suffering and poverty. Years earlier, after Sambhaji's death, Santaji Ghorpade and Dhanaji Jadhav had launched a fierce assault on his camp, resulting in the slaughter of two thousand soldiers. Aurangzeb had been presumed dead in that attack but had managed to escape in secrecy. Since that harrowing escape, Santaji and Dhanaji had been his constant fear, ever looming as he remained perpetually on guard.

As Aurangzeb lay there, he began to reflect on the choices and actions that had led him to this desolate state. He was haunted by the memories of how he had punished his own father, Shah Jahan, and how he had killed his own brother, Dara Shikoh. He had ensured that Shah Jahan was deprived of food and water, and given only a small, broken vessel with very little water, which he could either use for drinking or for the latrine. He had then beheaded his brother and gifted his mother his head wrapped in a silk cloth. The most grievous of his crimes, however, was the killing of Sambhaji. He was now reaping the bitter harvest of his own transgressions. In a moment of profound introspection, he penned his final words, capturing his remorse and acceptance of his fate:

I do not know who I am, where I shall go, or what will become of this wretched soul burdened with sins. It is time for me to bid farewell to this world. I have been a failed father, and I do not wish for my sons to continue their strife. Allah has been in my heart, yet my obscured vision failed to perceive His light. I have not understood Allah's will. There is no hope left for me in the future. I am consumed by fever, dying moment by moment. In my quest for God through religion, I failed to recognize that Shiva and Sambha were His true sons. I came into this world empty-handed, and I depart with nothing but a load of sins. If only I had one son like Sambha, I would have conquered the entire world. With the last 300 rupees I possess, I wish to give them to those in need. For the crimes I have committed, bury this lost and sinful man with his head uncovered. For every sinner who is buried bare-headed before God is destined to receive mercy. Cover my coffin only with a simple white cloth and no offerings, for I do not deserve any.

On the 3rd of March, 1707, Aurangzeb took his final breath, having lost everything he once held dear. The Marathas had harried him throughout his reign under the leadership of Rajaram, Santaji, and Dhanaji—a saga of rebellion, an unheard tale of resurgence. The fire in the eyes of the Marathas and the blazing hearts had all charged upon the Mughals. But that's a story that needs to be told, separately!

Decades later, Aurangabad was renamed Chhatrapati Sambhaji Nagar.

ABOUT THE AUTHOR

Aditya Nighhot, hailing from Pune, is a national bestselling author of five books, a doctor specializing in MD Radiology, a screenwriter, an entrepreneur, a motivational speaker, and a social media influencer. His literary journey has garnered both critical acclaim and commercial success, with his books consistently ranking among the top 50 bestsellers on Amazon for months. To date, Aditya has sold over 1,00,000 copies of his works, which have been translated into Hindi and are soon-to-be published in Sinhalese, German, French, and other international languages.

Aditya's popular books, *Tagged for Life – Will You Be My Wife?* and *Unhooked & Unbooked*, were declared the #1 and #3 most loved books of the year by ANI, respectively. He has been honoured with the 'Best Romance Book of the Year – Readers' Choice Award.' Mid-Day, one of India's leading media outlets, has compared his success to that of legendary author Amitav Ghosh, and *The Global Asian Times* in Toronto, Canada, featured him with the headline, "Love Not Worth Dying For Proves Doctor and Author Aditya Nighhot." Known for pushing creative boundaries, Aditya is one of the few Indian authors to explore the realm of chatbot fiction on the Readify app. His book *Unhooked & Unbooked* achieved record-breaking media attention, with over 200 mentions in a single day.

Academically, Aditya stood forty-seventh in the All India BVP Medical Examination and completed his medical education from one of India's top medical colleges. A member of the Screenwriters Association, he has also honed his screenwriting skills at the Ramesh Sippy Academy and is currently working on several scripts.

As the co-founder of Dreamboat Publishing, Marketing, and Distribution, Aditya has helped over a hundred authors achieve bestseller status within months of release. Dreamboat is a one-stop destination for authors, now expanding to promote not only writers but also actors, models, influencers, entrepreneurs, and startups. The company is committed to nurturing young talent and transforming ideas into successful stories.

Aditya is highly active on social media, where he enjoys interacting with his readers and followers. Connect with him through the following platforms:

- **Instagram**: @adityanighhot
- **Facebook Profile**: www.facebook.com/authoradityanighhot
- **Facebook Page**: www.facebook.com/adityanighhot
- **WhatsApp**: +91-9623068037

For speaking engagements, guest appearances, or collaborations, visit his website or contact his team via email:

- **Website**: www.adityanighhot.com
- **Emails**:
  contact@adityanighhot.com
  aadi9626@gmail.com
  manager@adityanighhot.com

REFERENCES

Books:

1. Sawant, S. (1989). *Chhava*. Pune: Continental Prakashan.
2. Patil, V. (1999). *Sambhaji*. Pune: Mehta Publishing House.
3. Sarkar, J. (1920). *Shivaji and His Times*. London: Longmans, Green, and Co.
4. Purandare, B. M. (2002). *Swarajya Rakshak Sambhaji*. Pune: Purandare Prakashan.
5. Savarkar, V. D. (1927). *The Life and Times of Sambhaji*. Pune: Savarkar Prakashan.
6. Kulkarni, U. (2011). *Solstice at Panipat: 14 January 1761*. Mumbai: Mula-Mutha Publishers.
7. Apte, B. (1974). *A History of the Maratha Navy and Merchantships*. Pune: State Board for Literature and Culture.
8. Pagadi, S. (1993). *Sambhaji Maharaj*. Mumbai: Maharashtra Rajya Sahitya Sanskriti Mandal.
9. Bhaskaran, M. D. (2020). *Life and Death of Sambhaji*. New Delhi: Penguin Random House India.

Research Papers and Articles:

1. Deshpande, A. (2010). *Sambhaji: The Forgotten Maratha King. Indian Historical Review, 37*(2), 154-172.
2. Kulkarni, R. (2015). *The Political and Military Achievements of Sambhaji Maharaj*. Paper presented at the National Seminar on Maratha History, Pune University.
3. Naik, S. (2012). *Sambhaji Maharaj and the Maratha Navy: A Historical Analysis. Journal of Indian Naval Studies, 4*(1), 45-61.
4. Joshi, M. (2016). *Sambhaji Maharaj's Conflict with the Mughal Empire. Journal of Medieval Indian History, 29*(3), 201-219.
5. Sharma, V. (2018). *Cultural and Religious Policies under Sambhaji Maharaj. South Asian Historical Research Journal, 11*(4), 88-104.
6. Shinde, P. (2019). *Sambhaji Maharaj's Defence Strategies and Fort Architecture. Fort Heritage Studies, 5*(2), 33-49.
7. Rao, N. (2020). *Sambhaji's Diplomacy with European Powers: A Study of Foreign Relations. Colonial Encounters Journal, 12*(1), 92-110.
8. Bhave, S. (2017). *The Last Stand of Sambhaji: An Analysis of His Final Battle. Military History Quarterly, 8*(3), 77-91.

Dissertations and Theses:

1. Kamat, R. (2014). *The Administration and Governance of Sambhaji Maharaj*. Ph.D. Dissertation, University of Mumbai.
2. Mahajan, D. (2016). *Naval Warfare under the Marathas with Special Reference to Sambhaji Maharaj*. M.Phil. Thesis, Savitribai Phule Pune University.